CAREERS IN ORGANIZATIONS

Goodyear Series in Management and Organizations

Lyman W. Porter, Editor

Published:

Hall: *Careers In Organizations*
Lawler/Rhode: *Information and Control in Organizations*
Schneider: *Staffing Organizations*

Forthcoming:

Beer: *Organizational Development*
Braunstein/Stone: *Research Methods in Organizational Behavior*
Campbell/Motowidlo: *Leadership: Theory, Research, and Practice*
Dachler: *Motivation In Organizations*
Duncan: *Organizations and Their Environment*
Lewicki: *Conflicts In Organizations*
Schollhammer: *Comparative Business Management*
Steers: *Organizational Effectiveness: A Behavioral View*
Tosi: *Organization and Management Theory*

CAREERS IN ORGANIZATIONS

DOUGLAS T. HALL

**Department of Organizational Behavior
Graduate School of Management
Northwestern University**

**Goodyear Publishing Company, Inc.
Santa Monica, California 90401**

Library of Congress Cataloging in Publication Data

Hall, Douglas T
    Careers in organizations.

    (The Goodyear series in management and organizations)
    Includes bibliographical references and index.
    1. Success.   2. Organization.   3. Prediction of
occupational success.   I. Title.
HF5386.H234   658.4   75-13446
ISBN 0-87620-156-7
ISBN 0-87620-157-5 pbk.

GOODYEAR SERIES IN MANAGEMENT AND ORGANIZATIONS

Current printing (last digit):
10 9 8 7 6 5

Y-1567-0 (Case)
Y-1575-3 (Paper)

Printed in the United States of America

To Fran

CONTENTS

FOREWORD

The Goodyear Series in Management and Organizations embodies concise and lively treatments of specific topics within the broad area indicated by the Series title. These books are for supplemental reading in basic management, organizational behavior, or personnel courses in which the instructor highlights particular topics in the larger course. However, the books, either alone or in combination, can also form the nucleus for specialized courses that follow introductory courses.

Each book stresses the *key issues* relevant to the given topic. Thus, each author, or set of authors, has made a particular effort to "highlight figure from ground"—that is, to keep the major issues in the foreground and the small explanatory details in the background. These books are, by design, relatively brief treatments of their topic areas, so the authors have had to be carefully *selective* in what they have chosen to retain and to omit. Because the authors were chosen for their expertise and their judgment, the Series provides valuable summary treatments of the subject areas.

In focusing on the major issues, the Series' authors present a balanced content coverage. They have also aimed at breadth by the unified presentation of different types of material: major conceptual or theoretical approaches, interesting and critical empirical findings, and applications to "real life" management and organizational problems. Each author deals with this body of material, but the combination varies according to the subject matter. Thus, each book is distinctive in the particular way in which a topic is addressed.

A final word is in order about the audience for this Series: Although the primary audience is the student, each book in the series concerns a topic of importance to the practicing manager. Managers and supervisors can rely on these books as authoritative summaries of the basic knowledge in each area covered by the Series.

The topics included in the Series to date have been chosen on the basis of their importance and relevance for those interested in management and organizations. As new appropriate topics emerge on the scene, additional books will be added. This is a dynamic Series both in content and direction.

Lyman W. Porter
Series Editor

PREFACE

This book is about our lives. Or, to be more precise, it is about those aspects of our lives that are associated with work. This volume will examine how we choose our occupations, the stages we go through as our work careers unfold, factors that make us successful or unsuccessful, how organizations can help our careers develop more effectively, and current problems organizations face in the management of our careers.

The focus here will be upon organizations as career systems, or settings in which most careers develop. We will examine ways organizations influence people and vice versa (although there is less evidence of vice versa).

We will not restrict our attention to any particular occupation, except in Chapter 4, where we will study managers for illustrative purposes. The general concepts of career development and organizational influences apply equally well to nurses, engineers, teachers, doctors, lawyers, mechanics, social workers, and many others.

This book is intended for students interested in organizations and their effects upon people. Courses in management, organizational psychology, personnel, vocational psychology, guidance, sociology of the professions, and administration would lie within the scope of our discussions here. No prior knowledge of behavioral science is assumed, although it probably would be helpful in providing the reader with a conceptual framework.

It should go without saying that this book and the issue of work careers is equally applicable to women and men. The book will use both masculine and feminine pronouns and adjectives. When only one sex is referred to, it is used in the generic sense.

We realize not everyone reads the preface so we have placed the plan for this book at the end of Chapter 1.

The editor of this Series, Lyman W. Porter, has been most helpful in the planning, writing, and revising of the manuscript. The comments of Ben Schneider, Clay Hamner, Allen Schuh, and John Henricks on an early draft were extremely helpful. Three typists—Leona Burns at York University and Marie Dumeney and Doris Singer at Michigan State—have done the bulk of the typing, far more competently and cheerfully than I deserve. Most of the writing of this book was done when I was at Michigan State University. The facilities and support of the Department of Management were extremely valuable conditions for this effort. In particular my gratitude goes to the department chairman, Richard Gonzalez.

This book is dedicated to Dr. Francine S. Hall, college professor, mother, and wife, among other subidentities in her repertoire. Together we are learning by experience a great deal about the management of careers and dual-career families.

Douglas T. Hall

CAREERS IN ORGANIZATIONS

THE STUDY OF CAREER DEVELOPMENT

Why should we study career development? And how? We might as well start with the tough question first. Why should the reader, a student and future practitioner of business, education, law, social work, medicine, or some other profession, need to learn about career development in organizational settings? Certainly there is little material about careers in most graduate and professional school curricula. Isn't the career a private matter, of concern only to the individual employee himself, not to his supervisor or organization? Isn't career development the domain of counseling psychologists, personnel or guidance specialists, rather than the line manager?

Obviously, the position taken in this book is that career processes are of great interest both to the individual and to the management of an organization. To support such a stand, we should consider exactly what the term *career* means and why it is relevant to professionals and organizations.

WHAT IS A CAREER?

The term *career* suffers from surplus meaning. If *career* were used in a free association test it would undoubtedly elicit an impressive range of meanings and feelings. *Career* conjures visions of Potter-style gamesmanship, the "organization man," the Wall Street jungle, and of government civil servants, slowly but steadily working their way upward, grade by grade. In both the popular and the behavioral science literature, there are four distinct meanings in which *career* is used.

1

1. *Career as advancement.* Most of the free-association examples given above entail the notion of vertical mobility—moving upward in an organization's hierarchy, as in Vance Packard's *The Pyramid Climbers.* By this definition *career* represents the sequence of promotions and other upward moves (e.g., lateral transfers to more responsible positions or moves to "better" organizations or locations) in a work-related hierarchy during the course of a person's work life. It is not necessary that the person remain in one single occupation in order to "advance." For example, the university president who becomes a cabinet member in the federal government is generally considered to have moved upward in the overall status hierarchy of the world of work. This concept of *directionality* ("up is good, down is bad"), then, is a pervasive theme in our thinking about careers.

2. *Career as profession.* A less common way of viewing careers is that certain occupations represent careers, while others do not. This is related to the career-as-advancement theme, since "career" occupations are generally those in which some clear pattern of systematic advancement (a "career ladder") is evident. For example, in the legal profession, there is a clear advancement ladder from law student to clerk (preferably for a Supreme Court judge) to associate (preferably for a major New York firm) to partner (again preferably for a major New York firm). Within the group of partners, there are varying degrees of status (and share of the firm's income) based upon influence and performance. Politics and government service are available as additional career moves for the lawyer. Doctors, professors, businessmen, teachers, and clergymen, as well as other professional people, also have a generally understood path of career movement. This means that their members periodically pass through what sociologists call "regularized status passages"—regular movements from one status to another. For example, in the management career one frequent path is the following: undergraduate science or engineering major, student in MBA program, management trainee, staff specialist, supervisor, and then manager and executive at various levels. (The concept of career stages will be discussed in more detail in Chapter 3.)

   By way of contrast, jobs that do not generally lead to advancement or to a long-term series of related positions are often viewed as not constituting a career. According to this idea, keypunch operators, secretaries, and parking lot attendants are not considered to "have" careers. (As we will see later, people in these occupations do in fact have careers, by the definition to be used in this book.)

   These first two meanings of *career* are likely to be found in popular writings. The next two are more representative of behavioral science writings on the subject.

3. *Career as a lifelong sequence of jobs.* By this definition the person's career is his particular job history—the series of positions held, regardless of occupation or level, during tne course of his work life. According to this definition, all people who work—all people with work histories—have careers. No value judgment is made about the type of occupation or the direction of movement. Career here is a more neutral, less value-laden term than it is under our first two definitions. Everett Hughes, one of the foremost scholars in the sociological research on occupations and careers, refers to the person's sequence of jobs as his *objective career* and the particular experiences he has in those jobs as his *subjective career.*

4. *Career as a lifelong sequence of role-related experiences.* By this definition, *career* represents the way the person experiences the sequence

of jobs and activities that constitute his work history. This is the subjective career, as defined by Hughes—the changing aspirations, satisfactions, self-conceptions, and other attitudes of the person toward his work and life. To understand fully the course of a person's work life, both the subjective and the objective careers must be considered together as two facets of the same process. Goffman describes this dual approach to careers as follows:

> One value of the concept of career is its two-sidedness. One side is linked to internal matters held dearly and closely, such as image of self and felt identity; the other side concerns official position, jural relations, and style of life, and is part of a publicly accessible institutional complex. The concept of career, then, allows one to move back and forth between the personal and the public, between the self and its significant society, without having to rely overly for data upon what the person says he thinks he imagines himself to be.*

Using this career-as-life-process view, it is even possible to consider careers independent of work; the term could refer to the history of a person in any particular role or status, not just in a work role. Thus, it is possible to refer to the career of the housewife (Lopata, 1966), the marihuana user (Becker, 1963), the mental patient (Goffman, 1961), and the dying person (Glaser and Strauss, 1968). Goffman described the concept of career as follows:

> Traditionally the term *career* has been reserved for those who expect to enjoy the rises laid out within a respectable profession. The term is coming to be used, however, in a broadened sense to refer to any social strand of any person's course through life. The perspective of natural history is taken: unique outcomes are neglected in favor of such changes over time as are basic and common to the members of a social category, although occurring independently to each of them. Such a career is not a thing that can be brilliant or disappointing; it can be no more a success than a failure.*

A WORKING DEFINITION OF CAREER

Let us now consider what the working definition of *career* will be within this book. We will start with a few assumptions:

1. *Career per se does not imply success or failure,* "fast" advancement or "slow" advancement. Our focus will be on understanding what happens during the process of the career, rather than evaluating how successful the person is in managing it. Therefore, the career-as-advancement approach will not be employed here.
2. *Career success or failure is best assessed by the person whose career is being considered, rather than by other interested parties,* such as researchers, employers, spouses, or friends. This important assumption is made for two reasons, one pragmatic and one normative. First, because

---

*From Erving Goffman, "The Moral Career of the Mental Patient," in Erving Goffman, ed., *Asylums* (New York: Anchor Books, 1961), p. 127.

there are no absolute criteria for evaluating a career (the most likely criterion, advancement, has just been eliminated in point 1 above), the evaluation can best be performed by the person in relation to his own particular criteria. Second, consistent with an ethic of self-direction or internal control, it would be inappropriate for one person to evaluate another person's career. It seems that one element at the core of recent social movements—civil rights; women's liberation; national liberation; job redesign; reform of laws regarding sex, birth control, and drugs; etc.—is an increasing recognition of the person's right and responsibility to make his or her own life choices. One effect of these social changes has been to make people examine their own careers more closely and consider what their own career interests and goals are, rather than those someone else (such as parents, employers, family, or friends) may have for them. Therefore, external criteria of career success seem inconsistent with the emerging ethic of personal choice as a key element in career development.

3. *The career is made up of both behaviors and attitudes;* i.e., things the person *does* and *feels.* Thus, one aspect of a career (the subjective career) consists of the changes in values, attitudes, and motivation that occur as he grows older. Another aspect (the objective career) is made up of the observable choices one makes and the activities one engages in, such as the acceptance or rejection of a particular job offer. Thus, both the subjective and the objective facets must be considered in obtaining a full understanding of a person's career.

4. *The career is a process, a sequence of work-related experiences.* Any work, paid or unpaid, pursued over an extended period of time, can constitute a career. Thus, the career-as-profession concept will not be accepted here. (Indeed, it is not accepted in most behavioral science writings on the subject.) This also means that the career-as-life concept is not endorsed here; much as the career-as-profession and the career-as-advancement views are too restrictive, the career-as-life idea is too broad. Our focus is on work and organizational settings. The work need not necessarily be a formal, paid job—it could be volunteer work, homemaking, political work, school work, as well as job work. This puts our orientation, then, somewhere between the career-as-sequence-of-jobs approach (definition 3) and the career-as-life-experiences view (definition 4).

Putting all these assumptions together, the following working definition of career emerges:

The career is the individually perceived sequence of attitudes and behaviors associated with work-related experiences and activities over the span of the person's life.

By saying "sequence . . . over the span of the person's life," we see career as a lifelong process, but restricted to work-related activities. By saying "attitudes and behaviors," we include both the subjective and the objective aspects of the career. We assume nothing about what sequence represents "up" or "down" for a particular person, and nothing about the type of work in which **4** the person is engaged.

WHY ARE CAREERS IMPORTANT?

Career as Life

Now that we have a working definition of career, we can return to the original question: Why are careers important? The most important reason is that the career represents the person's entire *life* in the work setting. And work, for most people, is a primary factor in determining the overall quality of life (Burke, Goodale, Hall, and Joyner, 1972; Rosow, 1974). Work provides a setting for satisfying practically the whole range of human needs—physiological, safety, social, ego, and self-actualization (using Maslow's typology); achievement, affiliation, and power (using McClelland's trilogy); as well as other needs such as aggression and altruism, autonomy and applause. In a study by Morse and Weiss, respondents indicated that they would continue to work (perhaps after a good holiday!) even if they inherited a huge fortune (Morse and Weiss, 1955). And it has been found that people near retirement often fantasize about dying very soon after they stop working (Sofer, 1970). Indeed, there is some evidence that mortality rates do rise immediately following retirement. Therefore, it is important to study careers because work plays a key role in a person's life.

Equality through Careers

A second consideration is that work is being seen increasingly as a fundamental area in which to achieve social equality and personal liberation. Civil and women's rights activists are seeking equality in job hiring and promotion practices. There is also evidence of increased pressure on organizations to eliminate job conditions that threaten the physical or emotional well-being of the employee (Porter, Lawler, and Hackman, 1975). Indeed, in recent years job quality (not just employment per se) has been used in political campaigns as a means of fighting social inequality, and it may become an even more important issue in the future.Therefore, because the career is so important to the person, and because the work career is being recognized as a primary target in the politics of social change, organizations will be forced to give more attention to the nature of the career experiences they provide for their employees.

Career Mobility

Another reason for the present emphasis on the importance of careers is the increased mobility that is resulting from the thrust toward personal liberation in our society. As Jennings (1971) **5** points out very clearly, it is no longer necessarily seen as undesirable to have changed jobs frequently; rather than suggesting personal instability, it represents varied experience and personal drive.

Taking advantage of better job opportunities and looking for a better match between job characteristics and personal interests and needs can cause frequent job changes. This is also a hedge against obsolescence; the person who specializes by staying in one job or organization too long may have difficulty finding and adapting to other work if technological, economic, or company policy changes force him out of his present job. Thus, with our present social norms favoring freedom of choice and "doing your own thing," employees—from storeroom clerks to company presidents—are far more likely today to change jobs and careers if they are not fulfilled or otherwise satisfied at present.

Related to this tendency toward greater career mobility is the growing reluctance to sacrifice personal and family gratifications for the sake of one's career. This may be reflected in more frequent refusals of job transfers, even with promotions and pay raises; more weight given to location and physical environment in selecting a job; and the challenging of work norms regarding work hours, personal appearance, and job involvement. More dramatically, this increased sense of career-related freedom is seen in the decisions of bright, high-performing youth not to go to college or to pursue conventional careers; the decisions of women to seek both families and careers; the decisions of homosexuals to stop concealing their personal lifestyles; and the decisions of many established professionals and executives to leave their present occupations and take up quite different lines of work, often requiring years of additional education. All these moves toward greater personal choice represent a significant change in the norms and internal environment of the organization. Increasingly, organizations and administrators will not be permitted the "luxury" of overlooking the impact of their actions upon the personal life and careers of their employees (Hirschman, 1970).

These three considerations represent external pressures that may force managers to become more concerned about employee careers. The picture is not entirely one of threat, however. There are three other factors which represent inducements or rewards to the administrator who takes careers into account in his decision making and problem solving.

The Employee's Prime Concern

The administrator's prime responsibility is to manage his subordinates. However, one of the subordinate's prime concerns is to manage his career. He tends to see job and organizational situations in relation to the way they will affect him personally, not just in relation to what is best for the company. Therefore, the manager who can understand career interests and career dynamics will be more effective in managing people.

Change

A related factor is that much of the administrator's work involves managing change, if only a change in the work procedures of employees. However, any change in the job or in the organization implies a perceived change in the career of the employee; it will be seen as either an aid or a threat (generally the latter) to his or her best interests at work. Again, by being sensitive to the career interests and aspirations of his subordinates, the manager will be able to bring about change more effectively.

The Administrator's Own Career

Finally, and certainly not of least importance, any administrator needs to understand careers in order to manage his own career more effectively. Most people do not consider such vital issues as how to make well-informed career choices, how to cope with conflicts between work and personal life, and how to arrive at career goals. One study indicates that people adopt a rather passive stance, letting important career decisions be initiated by others rather than by themselves on the basis of their own interests and goals (Roe and Baruch, 1967). Many people fail to use outside knowledge and resources to determine their career goals. In fact, professionals and administrators probably make higher-quality decisions about managing their subordinates and their capital assets than they do about managing their own careers. This lack of career awareness can be very damaging. For example, when a fledgling professional leaves graduate or professional school, he or she will probably suffer what is termed *reality shock* in the first permanent job assignment. The formal knowledge and skills acquired in business school are often seen as irrelevant to the low challenge and high personal resistance encountered in the first job. Yet schools do little to prepare students by telling them what lies ahead or by helping them acquire interpersonal skills in overcoming resistance to change. Professional education does a far better job of preparing students for the work they will do than for the lives they will lead. Understanding of career processes can be a great aid to the individual's self-awareness and self-control.

SUMMARY

In this chapter we have discussed the different meanings which the term *career* has in both everyday usage and in social science writings. We have investigated career as advancement, as profession, as lifelong sequence of jobs, and as lifelong sequence of work-related experiences. After reviewing these different interpretations, we arrived at a working definition to be used in this book: Career is the individually perceived sequence of attitudes and behaviors associated with work-related experiences and activities over the span of the person's life.

Next we considered the "so what" question: Why are careers important and worthy of another book? Issues such as careers and quality of life, careers as a vehicle for social change, career mobility, and people's general lack of career awareness were examined as responses to this question.

PLAN FOR THIS BOOK

Now that we have some common understanding of the term *career,* we can go on to see how people's careers are influenced by (and sometimes influence) organizations.

In Chapter 2 we will consider the process of career choice. For many people, this comes mainly at the beginning of their work lives. However, today it often occurs at various points in one's career, particularly in mid-career. In Chapter 3 we will examine the general stages people pass through during the course of their working lives in organizations. Although a person's specific experiences will depend greatly, of course, on the particular occupation and type of organization he or she enters, current studies suggest that there are certain rather general phases that seem to occur in fairly regular order. Chapter 3, then, will give us a broad overview of the person's total life/career experience. Chapter 4 will examine what happens after a career choice has been made—in particular, how the individual level of performance can be predicted. Performance will be viewed as one of four important dimensions of career effectiveness.

Chapter 5 will discuss factors related to three other dimensions of career effectiveness—identity, attitudes, and adaptability. Again we will examine possible predictability of these dimensions, although there has been far more research on performance.

In Chapters 6 and 7 we will turn from research to the practical issues involved in applying theory to actuality in career and organizational effectiveness. Chapter 6 will present some ideas for changing organizational policies and procedures that bear on individual careers. The goal here is to make organizations more flexible internally, in contrast to the recent tendency to stress external flexibility of the organization as related to its environment. From the point of view of the person, this internal flexibility would represent an individualizing or humanizing of the organization. Chapter 7 will be an "organizational survival kit," showing how individuals can manage their own careers more successfully.

The final chapter (Chapter 8) is our "crystal ball." Here we will discuss some of the current and not-so-obvious problems of organizational careers that will become more pressing in the future.

Discussion Questions

1. What is your definition of the term *career*?
2. How does the concept of career as a lifelong sequence of work experience compare with the models of man (implicit or explicit) found in most organizational approaches to human behavior?
3. Why do you think the concept of career is more important in the 1970s than it was in the 1960s?
4. What are some of the implications for organizations of measuring career success from the individual's perspective rather than that of the organization?

2

CAREER CHOICE

Here I am 58 years old, and I still don't know what I want to do when I grow up.

Peter Drucker (1968),
quoting a friend.

Many writers believe that career choice is a single event or a terminal process, usually occurring in adolescence or the early twenties. In reality, a career choice is not just the choice of an occupation (which could occur or recur at any point in one's adolescent or adult life), but any choice affecting one's career. In this chapter, we will discuss two important types of career choices—the choice of an occupation and the choice of an organization in which to work.

There is probably more theory and research dealing with the choice of an occupation than with any other single issue in the field of career development. Occupational choice theories fall into two general categories:

1. *Matching theories* (or models, in some cases) which describe what kinds of people enter what kinds of occupations, based upon some measure of compatibility between the person and the chosen occupation
2. *Process theories* (or models) which describe the manner in which people gradually arrive at a choice of an occupation

In this chapter we will begin by examining these two types of theories as means of answering two important questions: (1) How are individuals matched with careers? (2) How is the career choice made? Next we will get more specific and examine how individuals choose to enter particular organizations. Then, based upon the theory and research literature, we will consider ways in which career choice can be facilitated. Finally, we will consider the important issues that arise in the study of career choice.

MATCHING PEOPLE AND OCCUPATIONS

As Super (1957) has pointed out, career choice and development is basically a *synthesizing process,* a process of achieving compatibility between the person and the chosen occupation. Because such a large proportion of a person's life revolves around work, it is not surprising that people try to choose work that will best enable them to fulfill their interests, meet their needs, and express themselves. Maslow (1968) found evidence of this connection between career and personal needs, interests, and identity in a study that indicated that people who were highly self-actualized were also likely to be highly identified with their career work. When Maslow asked the people in his study what they would be if they were not in their respective vocations, many hesitated and had difficulty in answering. Others responded with comments such as, "I can't say. If I weren't a (doctor, scientist, etc.), I just wouldn't be me. I would be someone else."

How can a person be compatible with a particular occupation? Recent research indicates that there are four general personal characteristics which tend to be considered in relation to job compatibility: (1) interests, (2) self-identity, (3) personality (e.g., needs, personal orientation, values), and (4) social background (e.g., socioeconomic status). Studies in these areas have attempted to determine the degree to which these attributes are possessed by most people in various occupations, and the degree to which they are required for effective performance in various occupations or are perceived by the person to be associated with various occupations. Then, by various means (e.g., profiles, peak scores), the researchers identify the occupations that best fit the characteristics of the people being studied. Generally, tests and questionnaires are employed, and the researchers tend to be differential psychologists. In the following sections we will examine each of these four approaches to the study of career selection in more detail.

Interests

According to Super and Bohn (1970, p. 83), "with the exception of intelligence, more is known about interests than about any other single personality variable." Probably one of the most familiar instruments that measure interests is the Strong Vocational Interest Blank (SVIB), developed by Edward K. Strong, Jr. (1943). Most of Strong's work involved experimentally identifying relationships **11** between occupations and interest patterns. He defined an interest as a response of liking related to a particular object; an aversion is a response of disliking. Operationally, Strong measured an interest by asking the respondent to indicate liking (L), indifference (I), or disliking (D) for a particular activity, occupation, or other object (e.g., factory manager, farmer, florist).

Strong defined "vocational interest" as the sum total of many interests that bear in any way upon an occupational career. He computed interest scores from each person's responses to the items in the SVIB. Strong's basic assumption was that certain occupations involve work activities which best enable a person to pursue a particular range of interests. He reasoned that people in a given occupation, such as management, would hold certain interests similar to other members of that occupation and different from people in other occupations. To test this idea, he examined the likes and dislikes of people in a particular occupation, contrasting them with the likes and dislikes of people in other occupations and also with people in general. He looked for interest areas that discriminated between the particular occupational group and the general population. In this way he was able to obtain scoring weights for each individual occupational scale. A person's interest blank score on each occupational scale was a measure of how much his interest profile was similar to that of members of that occupation.

Self-Identity

One of the major theories and programs of research focusing on the impact of self-identity upon career choice has been created by Donald Super (1957). Super, whose research began in the late 1930s, sees the career as a synthesis of the person's self-concept and the external realities of the work environment. Self-concept is a general term describing a person's image of himself—his abilities, interests, needs values, past history, aspirations, and so forth. This synthesis develops gradually as the person becomes aware of (1) his self-concept, (2) the opportunities and requirements in particular occupations, and (3) his experiences in implementing his self-concept by working in particular occupations. Development in the career consists of passing through a sequence of stages brought about by the interaction between self-concept and occupation. Each of these stages is described in a chapter of Super's book, *The Psychology of Careers:*

- —Adolescence as Exploration: Developing a Self-Concept
- —The Transition from School to Work: Reality Testing
- —The Floundering or Trial Process: Attempting to Implement a Self-Concept
- —The Period of Establishment: The Self-Concept Modified and Implemented
- —The Maintenance Stage: Preserving or Being Nagged by a Self-Concept
- —The Years of Decline: Adjustment of a New Self.

Personality

Personal orientation. A major theory relating personal orientation to career selection has been put forth by John Holland (1966). Holland starts with the straightforward assumption that there is an interaction between personality and environment, such that people gravitate toward environments congruent with their personal orientations. He proposed six personality types and six matching occupational environments:

1. *Realistic.* Involves aggressive behavior, physical activities requiring skill, strength, and coordination. (Examples: forestry, farming, architecture.)
2. *Investigative.* Involves cognitive (thinking, organizing, understanding) rather than affective (feeling, acting, or interpersonal and emotional) activities. (Examples: biology, mathematics, oceanography.)
3. *Social.* Involves interpersonal rather than intellectual or physical activities. (Examples: clinical psychology, foreign service, social work.)
4. *Conventional.* Involves structural, rule-regulated activities and subordination of personal needs to an organization or person of power and status. (Examples: accounting, finance.)
5. *Enterprising.* Involves verbal activities to influence others, to attain power and status. (Examples: management, law, public relations.)
6. *Artistic.* Involves self-expression, artistic creation, expression of emotions, and individualistic activities. (Examples: art, music education.)

Various occupations were assigned to these six types of occupational environments, largely on an intuitive basis. The individual's personal orientation is assessed with an instrument devised by Holland called the Vocational Preference Inventory (VPI). (A newer version, the Self-Directed Search—SDS—is discussed on p. 182. Holland, 1973.) The VPI contains a list of 160 occupational titles; the respondent indicates which he likes and which he dislikes. The assumption here is that people reveal or project their own personal orientation in giving their perceptions of those occupational titles. The responses are then scored in terms of the six classifications described above, plus certain other, nonvocational scales.

The central hypothesis in Holland's theory is that the person's VPI score or profile will be a good predictor of his present career aspiration or later career choice. For example, enterprising people will tend to choose careers in enterprising environments, such as management. This hypothesis has been generally well-supported in empirical studies.

Research based upon Holland's theory has also been used to study the stability of vocational choice. His theory would predict that a college student majoring in a field congruent with his personal orientation would be more likely to remain (or persist) in that major than would a person whose orientation did not match his major. This hypothesis, too, has received a degree of support from empirical studies, although the nature of the personal orientation alone and the college environment alone also strongly influ- **13**

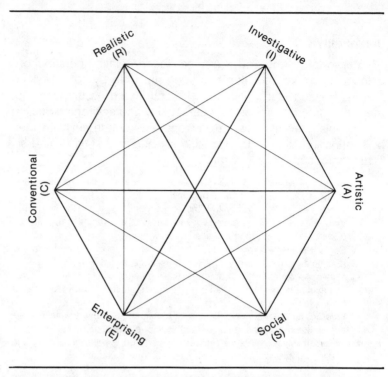

FIGURE 2-1
Holland's
Hexagonal Model
of the
Relationships
Among the
Occupational
Personality Types

From John L. Holland, *Making Vocational Choices: A Theory of Careers* (Englewood Cliffs, N.J.: Prentice-Hall, 1973), p. 23. Used by permission. (This model originally appeared in J.L. Holland et al., "An Empirical Occupational Classification Derived from a Theory of Personality and Intended for Practice and Research." ACT Research Report No. 29. Iowa City: The American College Testing Program, 1969.)

ence stability or change. For example, social people change fields more often than others, while intellectuals change less, independent of major field. Furthermore, students in colleges with social environments are more likely to switch majors than people in non-social colleges.

Based upon factor analysis* of VPI scores, Holland has derived a hexagonal model for describing the relationships between different personal orientations, as shown in Figure 2-1. According to Holland's data, the closer two fields or orientations are in this figure, the more compatible they are. Thus, adjacent categories (social–enterprising, realistic–investigative) are quite similar, while those diagonally opposite (investigative–enterprising or artistic–conventional) are highly dissimilar. People whose scores fall roughly in the order shown in the hexagon are quite internally consistent, while those with high scores in diagonal categories would probably have internal conflicts about their choices.

---

*Factor analysis is a statistical method of identifying groups of variables which are highly correlated with each other and weakly correlated with variables in other groups.

Like the research in self-concepts and vocational maturity, investigations of Holland's personality and occupational environment categories have not generally been extended to samples of employed people. Holland's typology could be employed usefully in the study of organizational climates, and the VPI would seem to have good potential as a predictor of organizational choice in addition to occupational choice. For example, people's images of an organization could be assessed with the VPI, and we could predict that social individuals would enter social organizations, conventional people would enter conventional organizations, and so on. Furthermore, turnover (and floundering) would be lower for those whose self-images provide the best fit with the climate of the organization. Such an analysis would also be helpful in providing better understanding of why people who are floundering are having difficulty settling into any one organization or career.

A promising instrument for career guidance is Holland's Self-Directed Search, a self-administered, self-scored guide to career selection. The respondent answers questions about personal preferences and then is given instructions about how to score his responses and compute his own profile. He is told the meaning of the various categories and is then directed to a range of occupations that are compatible with his own particular orientation. Although this is quite a new instrument, research has been conducted which shows that the SDS increases the number of occupations to be considered, increases respondents' satisfaction and certainty about vocational plans, and is rated by respondents as moderately positive in effectiveness (Zener and Schnuelle, 1972).

As an illustration, let us consider what Holland's theory tells us about the type of person who is oriented toward management. The would-be manager is most probably an enterprising person, verbally skilled, who uses this skill to influence and dominate rather than to help and support others, and who aspires to power and status. From Holland's hexagonal model, we may infer that the next most likely management candidates would be either social (affiliative) or conventional (rule-oriented conforming) types. These three possibilities fit well with the two dimensions of leadership identified in the Ohio State Leadership studies: consideration (supportive, helpful leader behavior), and initiating structure (task direction, clarifying, instructing, planning, etc.). The enterprising type is high on both dimensions (using social skills to influence and structure the activities of others). The conventional person would be high on structure and low on consideration; the social type would show the opposite pattern, as illustrated in Figure 2-2. If people who are high on both dimensions are in fact more effective leaders, it would make sense that that the person who rates **15**

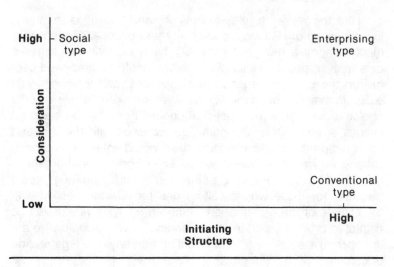

High ⊢ Social
         type

Enterprising
type

Consideration

Conventional
type

Low

High

Initiating
Structure

FIGURE 2-2
Hypothesized
Relationship
Between
Leadership Style
and Personal
Orientation

high on both (enterprising) would be the most likely of the three types to become a successful manager.

Holland's instruments, VPI and SDS, have been criticized because women tend to receive high scores on the social or artistic scales, while few receive high scores on the realistic scale. However, when the instrument was revised by a female graduate student to remove possible sex bias, the results were unchanged. Furthermore, the instrument predicts occupational aspirations equally well for men and women. Holland's position is that all people are subject to strong cultural socializing influences (such as sex, race, and class) that determine one's personal orientation (or type on the SDS). Personal orientation, in turn, affects occupational choice. Therefore, sex affects career choice through sex role socialization and its effects on personal orientation; this seems to be a real social influence, not an artifact of the measuring instrument (Gottfredson and Holland, 1975; Holland, personal correspondence, June 27, 1975).

Needs. In addition to personal interests, self-concept, and personal orientation, human needs also have a strong bearing on vocational behavior. It seems reasonable to assume that there is a tendency for people to choose careers that will enable them to satisfy their most important needs through their work. Such a theory has been proposed by Anne Roe (1957).

The need approach to career choice is based on the assumption that human needs are developed and ordered in a Maslow-style hierarchy, ranging from the lower-order physiological needs through safety, affection, ego concerns, and self-actualization. There is also an assumption of prepotency, meaning that higher needs (e.g., ego needs) would not become important until the needs lower in the hierarchy (physiological, safety, and social affection) had been generally satisfied.

16

Roe argues that needs satisfied after a very long delay will become unconscious motivators of behavior, and lower-order needs, if rarely satisfied, will become dominant motivators, blocking the emergence of the higher-order needs. She maintains that a major influence on need strength is a person's childhood experiences.

The affiliative (social) needs during childhood are important in Roe's theory. Persons whose parents were attentive to them (either loving, overprotective, or overdemanding) tend to develop an orientation toward people, which they try to express and satisfy through their work. People who had less attentive parents (casual, neglecting, or rejecting) tend not to be people-oriented in their vocational preferences. After determining the basis of the personal needs and orientation a person develops, Roe predicts the kind of occupation that might be chosen. A schematic presentation of Roe's theory is shown in Figure 2-3. The formulation of this model was preceded by research on scientists in various fields, in which physical and biological scientists reported more distance and less contact with their parents than social scientists.

Subsequent research has not provided especially strong support for the theory, perhaps partly because of the problems of obtaining retrospective measures of childhood experiences. Furthermore, most of the difficulties which this writer and others have encountered in testing Maslow's need hierarchy are also present in testing Roe's model. There is also little in the way of practical implications for managers, counselors, or personnel specialists in Roe's model (although it does have much to say to parents). Part of the problem is Roe's stress on childhood experience and her chain of reasoning: childhood experiences influence personal orientation, which in turn influences career choice. Even if this causal chain is valid, childhood experience should show a weaker relationship to career choice than does personal orientation, because its effects are less direct. If childhood experience influences career decisions through its impact on personal orientation, why not just use personal orientation itself as a predictor? Furthermore, personal orientation is already pretty well-established by the time the person is being studied. Therefore, there would seem to be greater payoff, both in research and practical terms, in focusing on personal orientation as a more direct predictor, as Holland has done with considerable success, than on the less direct influence of childhood experiences.

Social Background

To this point we have been concentrating mainly upon characteristics of the individual as possible determinants of career choice. We know, though, that a variety of forces in the environ-

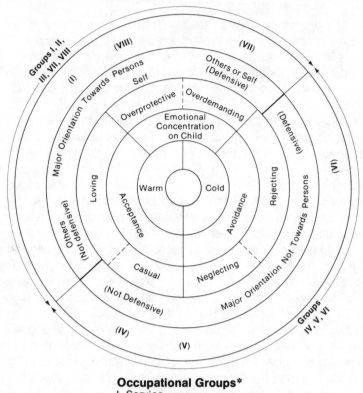

Occupational Groups*
I. Service
II. Business Contact
III. Organizations
IV. Technology
V. Outdoor
VI. Science
VII. General Cultural
VIII. Arts and Entertainment

FIGURE 2–3
Schematic Model
of Roe's Theory

*Note: The positions of occupational groups I and IV through VII are entered in parentheses by Dr. Roe, to indicate the tentative nature of their placement. Groups II and III are not shown in the outer ring of the model, because any exact location for them is even more difficult to determine. However, in Roe's article (1957), she does indicate that many or most people in groups II and III would have major orientation toward persons.

In Anne Roe, "Early Determinants of Vocational Choice," *Journal of Counseling Psychology*, 4 (1957), 216. Copyright 1957 by the American Psychological Association. Reprinted by permission.

ment are also extremely potent in channeling people into various vocational paths. During the Sputnik era and the famous "missile gap" scare of the late 1950s and early 1960s, an impressive array of resources—money, school and university staff, training personnel, etc. was marshaled to produce more engineers and scientists. Also, public attitudes toward science and technology became more positive; engineers and scientists, especially those in NASA and other space-related organizations, were the new national heroes. Starting salaries and job opportunities in science and engineering shot up. Many more young people chose to enter occupations in this area.

Then in the late 1960s as the NASA budget was reduced and the Southeast Asia war and the space program were wound down, jobs in science and engineering began to dry up, there were still many young people being turned out of universities, and there was a surplus of talent. In the early 1970s schools were less geared to science, engineering recruiting dropped off, public attitudes were more critical, and fewer young people thought about careers in science and engineering. Then, in the mid-70s, engineers were in great demand again as technology was needed to solve energy, pollution, transportation, and cost-reduction problems. Therefore, we see that factors such as historical trends, the job market, opportunities, training, and public attitudes, as well as self-concept, personal orientation, and interests, can influence a person's career choices.

In his book, *The Psychology of Careers,* Super reaches far beyond the limitations of psychology to identify some of these environmental influences on career choice and development: the family, disabilities, chance, and economic factors. Under economic factors he includes supply and demand for manpower in various occupations, business cycles, technological change, taste and style, acts of God, depletion of natural resources, public policy, unionization, management policies, and socioeconomic status.

One of the first attempts to integrate the various personal and social effects upon career choice was presented in a model developed by Blau and his associates. This model is shown in Figure 2-4. The authors describe the determinants of occupational choice as follows:

> Eight factors, four pertaining to occupations and four characterizing individuals, determine occupational entry. First, the demand for new members in an occupation is indicated by the number of vacancies that exist at any one time, which can be more easily ascertained, of course, for the employed than for the self-employed. The size of the occupational group, its tendency to expand, and its turnover rate will influence the demand for new members. The second factor, functional requirements, refers to the technical qualifications needed for optimum performance of occupational tasks. The third one, nonfunctional requirements, refers to those criteria affecting selection that are not relevant to actual performance, such as veteran status, good looks, or the "proper" religion. Fourth, rewards include not only income, prestige, and power, but also opportunities for advancement, congenial fellow workers, emotional gratifications, and indeed, all employment conditions that are defined as desirable.
>
> Turning now from the attributes of occupations to those of potential workers, a fifth factor that influences occupational entry is the information people have about an occupation—their knowledge about the requirements for entry, the rewards offered, and the opportunities for employment and advancement. Two characteristics of individuals are complementary to the two types of occupational requirements, namely, their technical skills to perform various occupational duties and their other social characteristics that influence hiring decisions such as a Harvard accent or skin color. Finally,

19

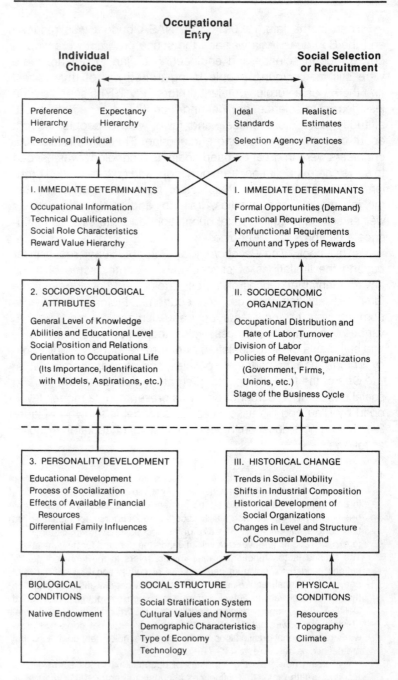

Occupational Entry

Individual Choice ↔ **Social Selection or Recruitment**

Preference Hierarchy Expectancy Hierarchy Perceiving Individual	Ideal Standards Realistic Estimates Selection Agency Practices
I. IMMEDIATE DETERMINANTS Occupational Information Technical Qualifications Social Role Characteristics Reward Value Hierarchy	I. IMMEDIATE DETERMINANTS Formal Opportunities (Demand) Functional Requirements Nonfunctional Requirements Amount and Types of Rewards
2. SOCIOPSYCHOLOGICAL ATTRIBUTES General Level of Knowledge Abilities and Educational Level Social Position and Relations Orientation to Occupational Life (Its Importance, Identification with Models, Aspirations, etc.)	II. SOCIOECONOMIC ORGANIZATION Occupational Distribution and Rate of Labor Turnover Division of Labor Policies of Relevant Organizations (Government, Firms, Unions, etc.) Stage of the Business Cycle
3. PERSONALITY DEVELOPMENT Educational Development Process of Socialization Effects of Available Financial Resources Differential Family Influences	III. HISTORICAL CHANGE Trends in Social Mobility Shifts in Industrial Composition Historical Development of Social Organizations Changes in Level and Structure of Consumer Demand

BIOLOGICAL CONDITIONS Native Endowment	SOCIAL STRUCTURE Social Stratification System Cultural Values and Norms Demographic Characteristics Type of Economy Technology	PHYSICAL CONDITIONS Resources Topography Climate

FIGURE 2–4
The Blau et al.
Model of
Occupational
Choice

From Peter M. Blau, John W. Gustad, Richard Jesson, Herbert S. Parnes, and Richard Wilcox, "Occupational Choices: A Conceptual Framework," *Industrial and Labor Relations Review, 9* (July 1956), 534. Used with permission.

people's value orientations determine the relative significance of different kinds of rewards and thus the attractive force exerted by them.

To be sure, many other characteristics of individuals influence their careers—their level of knowledge, ability, and education, their social position and relationships, and their orientation toward occupational life, to cite only the most general ones. It may be hypothesized, however, that the effects of all other factors can be traced through the immediate determinants of occupational entry. In other words, unless a social experience or attribute affects the information individuals have about occupations, their technical or social qualifications for entry, or their evaluation of occupations, it is not expected to influence their careers. Similarly, whereas many aspects of the socioeconomic organization must be examined to explain the four charac-teristics of occupations outlined in Box I, it is these four (plus the four directly relevant characteristics of individuals) that directly account for occupational entry, according to the hypothesis advanced here (Blau et al., 1956, pp. 536–37).*

In sum, then, Blau, a sociologist, and his colleagues see oc-cupational choice as being influenced by the social structure in two ways: (1) the social experiences of the person influence his personality development (needs, self-concept, orientation, inter-ests, values), which in turn orients him toward particular fields; and (2) the social and economic conditions of occupational oppor-tunity influence (restrict or aid) the attainment of the person's aspirations and choices. The authors also point out that career choice is not made once and for all at one dramatic point ("the crossroads") in life, but that such a choice is made and revised repeatedly throughout the course of the person's working life. These decisions are interrelated, such that earlier choices general-ly restrict the range of future possibilities and thus influence later choices. Finally, Blau and his associates point out that career choice is actually two separate choices: the choice of an occupa-tion by the individual and the selection of that individual for the occupation (i.e., personnel selection and recruitment).

Usually the social science disciplines treat these choices sep-arately, with individual career choice being handled by counselors and guidance experts, usually in high school and college, and organizational selection/recruitment handled by personnel and industrial psychologists within these work organizations. And given the lack of contact between professionals (academics and practitioners alike) in these two fields, it is not surprising that our national manpower planning is so poorly integrated. As Blau et al. conclude,

To be sure, it is legitimate scientific procedure to treat the actions of selectors as given conditions in the investigation of occupational choice, and it is equally legitimate to treat the actions of choosers as given conditions

---

*Taken with permission from the *Industrial and Labor Relations Review*, Vol. 9, No. 4 (July 1956), pp. 536–37.

in the investigation of occupational selection, but only the combination of both procedures makes it possible to explain why people end up in different occupations (Ibid., p. 543).*

Since the work of Blau and his associates, two separate streams of research on determinants of occupational entry have emerged in the sociological literature. One, represented by Blau, Duncan, and others, has focused on the effects of social structure (socioeconomic status, parents, education, and occupation) as the main predictors. The other, represented by researchers at the University of Wisconsin (Sewell, Haller, Portes, and others) has examined the social psychological influences (e.g., expectations of parents, teachers, and peers) which develop as a result of the influences of the social structure (Box 2 in the Blau et al. model).

Both streams of research have demonstrated the impressive impact of social background (socioeconomic status, parent's educational and occupational level) upon the educational and occupational aspirations and attainments of the individual. For example, in one recent study, there was high correlation between the occupational level of fathers and the aspired occupational levels of a group of tenth-grade high school students (Goodale and Hall, 1976). Generally, the impact of parental background and attitudes is stronger than the influence of peers, teachers, and other significant people in the person's social environment.

It should be stressed that social background influences the *level* of the aspired occupation. Social background could be measured either by the occupational level or the educational attainments of the parents. A scale of occupational levels could be measured as follows:

1. High-level professional, executive, and managerial
2. Professional
   Managerial (middle-level)
3. Semiprofessional
   Supervisory (low-level managerial)
4. Skilled worker
5. Semiskilled worker
6. Unskilled worker

Educational attainment would be measured by the years of formal education of the father and/or mother. The occupational level or educational attainments of a person's parents would probably influence strongly the *level* of occupation or education which the person would attain. On the other hand, the parents' background would not predict well the particular occupation or *field* in which the person would choose to work (e.g., chemistry, construction, law, etc.).

---

*This point is further elaborated by Porter, Lawler, and Hackman (1975), in their discussion
of ''Individuals and Organizations Attracting and Selecting Each Other,'' pp. 131–60.

This high correlation between parents' and children's attainments raises important issues about the equality of educational and occupational opportunity available in our society. The data available to date indicate that a person born to parents with little formal education and doing unskilled work is most likely to wind up in an occupation at or perhaps just above that level (Goodale and Hall, 1976). It appears that this is due in large part to the expectations parents hold for their children and to the "significant others" (teachers, friends) the person meets in his everyday surroundings. These social psychological factors may place more limits on the person's opportunities than any lack of opportunities in the educational system and in the job market. Further discussions of these "macro" societal influences are found in Glaser (1968) and Slocum (1966).

PROCESS THEORIES OF CAREER CHOICE

So far, we have considered various factors in the person and in the social environment which influence the choice of occupations. Although these factors tell us *what* influences choice, they give us a rather static view of choice; they don't say much about the dynamics of *how* and *why* career choices are made, reconsidered, and revised as the person gains insight, information, experience, and maturity. Therefore, to round out our analysis of choice, let us now turn to the *process* by which career decisions are made.

Stages in Career Decision Making

Making choices. According to Ginzberg and associates, the process by which people work on the task of career selection takes place in three stages (Ginzberg et al., 1951). The first is a *fantasy* stage, covering the childhood years up to around age 11. During this time the child imagines various things he would like to be when he becomes an adult—a fireman, doctor, policeman, etc. Here the person is not really making a choice or even a preference—only beginning to imagine what it will be like to be "grown up."

Next, between the approximate ages of 11 and 16, the person begins to do some career planning, making *tentative* choices, or stating preferences for particular occupations. This tentative career planning is first based upon the person's *interests*. Then later, the young person begins to think more about his *capabilities* and how that would direct or limit him to particular occupations. Later, the person's *values* become more crystallized and begin to influence career preferences. Thus, the increasing maturity and development (i.e., identity resolution) of the person manifests itself in the way he or she works on career planning tasks.

23

The third stage is one of *realistic* choices, which are more likely to be implemented by the person than are fantasy choices or tentative choices. Starting around age 17, the person has to make specific career decisions, such as whether or not to attend college, what to major in, what kind of job or training to seek if he does not attend college, and so forth. There are three sub-stages in the realistic stage: an *exploratory* period, in which one examines several possible career options; a *crystallization* sub-stage in which preferences become more sharply focused; and a *specification* period, in which the person chooses a particular occupation.

The realistic choice period may continue for many years, long into adulthood, as the person may go through several cycles of exploring-crystallizing-specifying in an attempt to find a career that fits his needs, interests, and abilities. This "floundering" process can last into the thirties, for people with advanced education. The realistic choice process is also re-activated in many cases for men around their forties, in what has come to be known as the "mid-life crisis."

This brings us to repeat the generalization that is stated frequently throughout this book: the process of career choice takes place at several different times throughout a person's career. Career choice is not a "one-shot" selection of an occupation in the early twenties. We will expand upon this idea later in this chapter.

Once the person has made a choice regarding his or her career, the next task will be to implement or carry out that decision. However, there is one intervening stage, between the selection of an alternative and its implementation, when the person clarifies the choice and dissipates some of the earlier doubts he had about the decision (Tiedeman and O'Hara, 1963). This could also be called a period of *dissonance reduction,* as the term is used in social psychology, in which the person attempts to reduce his internal conflicts over (a) the attractive aspects of the unchosen alternatives and (b) the fact that he did not choose them. This process is more likely to be in evidence if the original alternatives were quite similar in attractiveness. For example, assume a student is undecided about whether to take an exciting job in marketing research with General Motors or go to graduate school for a Ph.D. in marketing. Assume that he eventually chooses the GM job, after much soul-searching. During the period between the time of choice and the time he starts working, he will probably be doing a lot of "cognitive work," building up in his mind all the positive features of the marketing research job and all the negative aspects of the graduate program he rejected. This process of dissonance reduction following job choice has been found in research on MBA students (Vroom, 1966).

If one examines the choice process very closely, as Soelberg (1966) did in another study of graduating MBA students, it appears that the person has subconsciously made a choice and is performing the clarification tasks even *before* he is consciously aware of having made it. Soelberg found through intensive interviews at various points in the decision process that the perceived attractiveness of the job eventually chosen became noticeably higher than that of the other job offers weeks before the person consciously decided he was going to accept the offer. It appears that people often make a decision "deep down inside" before they admit to themselves and others that they have done so. What appears to be the process of deciding is then often rather one of clarifying and reducing the dissonance between the preferred alternative and all others.

An important implication of this finding is that once a person knows what his available choices may be, even though he says he is undecided, if he is asked which way he is leaning, or what seems most attractive right now, his answer will very likely be his eventual choice. A question that is often useful in counseling students or helping anyone with an important decision is, "If you had to make a decision right now, what would it be?" Very often the person himself is surprised to hear his own answer to this question, since he hadn't been consciously aware that he had a preference.

Choice implementation. Once a career decision has been made, the next series of tasks involve the execution or implementation of that decision (Tiedeman and O'Hara, 1963). When the decision involves a choice of vocation, implementation means beginning the actual work or the training and education necessary to enter that field of work.

As we will see in Schein's discussion of career stages in Chapter 3, the first stage in the person's career experiences within a particular organization is that of his socialization into the organization. Here his task is to enter and be trained to become a fully functioning member. He learns what is and is not appropriate behavior according to the rules and norms of that organization. The power/influence relationship is tilted in favor of the organization, as represented by the person's boss and other supervisors, peers, and often even subordinates (e.g., the seasoned sergeant who has "trained" scores of green lieutenants).

After the person becomes more established in the organization, he or she may then exert efforts toward *innovation* or change. At this point the new employee has been accepted and is secure and competent enough to attempt to alter the work environment in some way. According to Schein, the person's likelihood of innovating increases as he accumulates seniority, while his rate of socialization decreases with time.

25

If the organization is satisfied with the person's socialization and if the person is satisfied with his ability to influence the organization, the person reaches a state of *integration* with the organization. A satisfactory "psychological contract" (Schein, 1970) has been achieved under which each party understands and honors the expectations of the other. This state of integration is by no means stable and permanent, since it is affected by changes in the person or in the work environment, as Tiedeman and O'Hara indicate:

> [In integration] this new part of the self-system [the work identity] becomes a working member of the whole self-system. In integration, individual and group both strive to keep the resulting organization of collaborative activity. . . . The individual is satisfied, at least temporarily, when integration occurs. The group considers him successful. Of course, the person is likely to have an image of himself as successful in these circumstances too. Integration is not unalterable; it is merely a condition of dynamic equilibrium. A new member joining the social system, new striving of existing members of that system, or a quickening of the strivings of the person himself may disturb the status quo at any time (Tiedeman and O'Hara, 1963).

In summary, this process of career choosing may be seen graphically in the model in Figure 2-5, adapted from Tiedeman and O'Hara (1963). The two general periods of anticipating/deciding and implementation are seen in the upper and lower parts of the model, respectively. The time dimension indicates that the normal course of personal development takes the individual toward a state of integration with the work environment. The double arrows indicate that these stages are not irreversible and often blend into each other. As new information or conditions arise (e.g., lack of job opportunities just as the person is about to graduate and enter the job market), the person may move to an earlier stage in the choice process.

Vocational Maturity

Because we are talking about careers in terms of development over time, we must consider what development means. When is a person at a more or less "developed" stage in relation to his career, compared to someone else? A central concept is *vocational or career maturity*, which is defined as *the person's readiness to cope effectively with the developmental tasks of one's life stage, in relation to other people in the same life stage* (Super and Bohn, 1970). Therefore, career maturity is a relative (rather than absolute) concept in two senses: it involves (1) behaviors related to a particular life stage and (2) an assessment of coping in relation to the person's peers. In this sense, then, we cannot say a person becomes more vocationally mature as he advances in years. Each life stage brings a new set of demands, and the

26

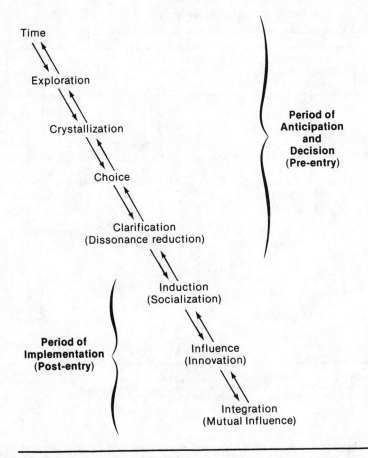

Time

Exploration

Crystallization

Choice

Clarification
(Dissonance reduction)

Period of
Anticipation
and
Decision
(Pre-entry)

Induction
(Socialization)

Period of
Implementation
(Post-entry)

Influence
(Innovation)

Integration
(Mutual Influence)

FIGURE 2–5
Stages in Career
Decision Making

Adapted from David V. Tiedeman and Robert P. O'Hara, *Career Development: Choice and Adjustment* (New York: College Entrance Examination Board, 1963), p. 40.

person must "re-establish" his vocational maturity in dealing with them in each stage.

One implication of this is that what constitutes mature behavior at one stage may be considered as less mature at a different stage. For example, examining various career options is appropriate behavior in the exploratory stage, but it might be seen as less mature during the establishment, maintenance, or decline stages. Similarly, attempting to achieve occupational success is considered mature behavior in the establishment stage, yet it may be seen as premature for adolescents. In this sense, then, career maturity is worked for but never finally and permanently attained. It is worked for, attained for a period of time, then challenged, worked for again, obtained again, and so forth, in a series of developmental cycles. To assess a person's career maturity, then, we should examine the process by which he is dealing with career issues, not the outcomes of his career work, such as satisfaction or success.

27

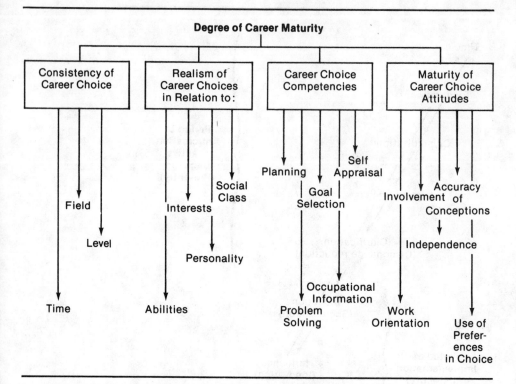

Degree of Career Maturity

Consistency of Career Choice
- Field
- Level
- Time

Realism of Career Choices in Relation to:
- Interests
- Social Class
- Personality
- Abilities

Career Choice Competencies
- Planning
- Self Appraisal
- Goal Selection
- Occupational Information
- Problem Solving

Maturity of Career Choice Attitudes
- Involvement
- Accuracy of Conceptions
- Independence
- Work Orientation
- Use of Preferences in Choice

FIGURE 2–6
A Model of Career Maturity in Adolescence

From John O. Crites, *Theory and Research Handbook, Career Maturity Inventory*, p. 6. Copyright © 1973 by McGraw-Hill, Inc. Reproduced by permission of the publisher, CTB/McGraw-Hill, Del Monte Research Park, Monterey, CA 93940. All rights reserved. Published in the U.S.A.

Most of the work of measuring career maturity has been conducted with adolescents, although there has been more interest recently in adult maturity.* Crites (1973b) has developed a model of career maturity in adolescence, in which maturity is defined in terms of four factors: (1) *consistency* of career choices, (2) *realism* of career choices, (3) *competencies* in career choice tasks, and (4) *maturity of career choice attitudes*. This model is shown in Figure 2-6. Published instruments have been developed by Crites to assess career attitudes and career choice competencies, although his work focuses upon the process of choosing an occupation, which makes it difficult to use these instruments for adults. However, the variables comprising career maturity, as shown in the model in Figure 2-6, seem promising as a basis for assessing the maturity of career behaviors in later life stages.

One promising development here is the Adult Vocational Maturity Inventory, which has been found to be related to occupational success (Sheppard, 1971). Given the problems of employ-

---

*Donald E. Super's Career Pattern Study is conducting a twenty-year follow-up of subjects now in their mid-30s. See also Sheppard (1971).

ees who continue floundering well into their careers and who persist in fields for which they are not well-suited, a good measure of adult vocational maturity would be of immense value in the selection, placement, and career development of personnel.

Psychological "Success" as a Facilitator of Career Decisions

If career maturity is a person's effectiveness in coping with the developmental demands of a particular life stage, what then influences this coping effectiveness? In other words, what facilitates the movement of a person through one stage and into the next?*

To answer this question, let us first assume that people generally strive to increase or maintain their sense of self-esteem. As we have seen earlier, one important factor in career choice is self-identity; one important means of achieving a high level of self-esteem is through the development of a *competent self-identity,* or an identity containing a sense of personal competence (White, 1959). As one comes to see oneself as a person who can effectively act upon his environment, he values himself more as a total person and thus experiences increased self-esteem.

The person's identity is made up of several *subidentities,* which represent the various aspects of the person which are engaged when he is behaving in different social roles. Each social role performed (e.g., worker, mother) presents the social stimuli in the form of behavioral expectations; the corresponding subidentity represents the individual's perceptions of himself as he behaves in response to these role stimuli. The *career subidentity* may be defined as that aspect of the person's identity which is engaged in working in a given career area, and the *career role* is the expectations people hold for individuals in that career. The degree of congruence between the career expectations (role) and one's own perception of his career (subidentity) is defined as *career adjustment.* High career adjustment means that there is little or no conflict between the person's career subidentity and his career role. *Career satisfaction* is the extent to which the person values this career adjustment. *Career involvement* may be considered as the importance of the career subidentity relative to other subidentities, the extent to which the person is psychologically identified with the career role. Sample subidentities of two hypothetical people, with high and low career involvement, are shown in Figure 2–7.

Occupational selection is the process of choosing a career role in which a high or satisfactory degree of adjustment and satisfaction can be attained. This selection process is not simply a matter of selecting a career role; it is also one of choosing

---

*This section is based on the author's work on career identity development. See Hall (1971a).   **29**

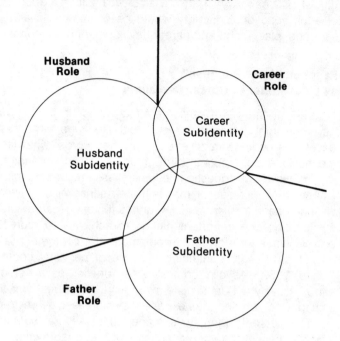

Low Career–Involved Person

Husband
Role

Career
Role

Career
Subidentity

Husband
Subidentity

Father
Subidentity

Father
Role

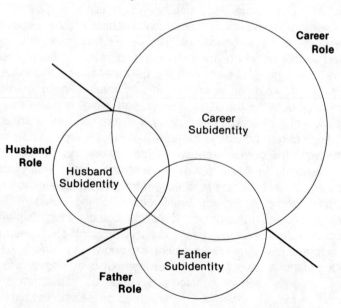

High Career–Involved Person

Career
Role

Career
Subidentity

Husband
Role

Husband
Subidentity

Father
Subidentity

Father
Role

FIGURE 2–7
Sample
Subidentities of Two
Hypothetical
People, One with
Low Career
Involvement and
One with High
Career Involvement

aspects of one's self (skills, interests, etc.) which will be developed through one's career work. Indeed, one reason occupational choice is so difficult is that it means deciding *who I will be* as well as deciding what I will do. Thus, in terms of the present model, occupational choice could also be called *subidentity selection.*

As the person acquires more competencies and characteristics relevant to his career role, his career subidentity grows. This subidentity extension in the context of the career role is called *career growth.* Specifically, career growth can consist of increases in the individual's knowledge, ability, or motivation related to his career role. Career growth involves personal development, the actual *creation of new aspects of the self,* in the career area. Thus, the career setting can be highly conducive to self-actualization or self-fulfillment. As the career subidentity expands, proportionately more of the total identity is invested in the career role; i.e., the person becomes more ego-involved in his career.

This *career involvement* is a measure of the strength of one's motivation to work in a chosen career role. Commitment to the entire career field or role is to be distinguished from commitment to the job (i.e., job involvement) or to one's organization (i.e., organizational identification). These three forms of commitment are often correlated, but they are theoretically distinct and may often have different causes and consequences.

Choice, growth, and involvement can form a spiraling cycle in which each variable feeds back and reinforces the others. As the person sees himself becoming more (or less) competent and successful in an area he has chosen, his satisfaction will increase (or decrease) his involvement in that area, and he will then choose to do more (or less) work in that area, and so on. The term *career development* can be used to describe this spiraling combination of career choice, subidentity growth, and commitment.

A person will experience career subidentity growth when he experiences *psychological success* in a career-relevant task. Psychological success is defined as the person's *feelings* of success, as opposed to external measures of success. A sense of psychological success is likely to be achieved under the following conditions:

1. When the person sets a challenging goal for himself (i.e., one representing a high level of aspiration)
2. When the person determines his own means of attaining the goal
3. When the goal is important to his self-concept (i.e., he values the task)
4. When he actually attains the goal (Lewin, 1936).

This sense of personal success will lead, in turn, to an increase in self-esteem.

The basic personality process of developing a competent identity through a perceived personal satisfaction with one's development in career may be illustrated as follows:

31

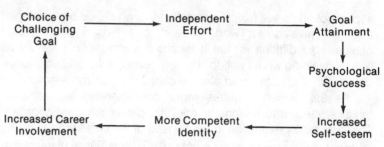

The need for self-identity as a competent person leads the individual to seek situations in which his self-esteem will be enhanced and to avoid situations in which it will be reduced. Indeed, a person's orientation toward a particular task situation is a function of his present level of self-esteem. If it is high, he will probably be most concerned with seeking success and further developing his competence (i.e., his perceived ability to act effectively upon his environment). If his self-esteem is low, on the other hand, he may be more oriented toward avoiding failure and protecting his sense of competence. This idea is supported by Lewin's theory that the person most likely to set a new, higher level of aspiration following a successfully attained goal is the one with a history of previous success. The person accustomed to failure tends to "quit while he is ahead" (Lewin, 1936).

Now let us apply this general personality predisposition toward increasing one's self-esteem and competence to the process of occupational selection. Our first proposition comes directly from what we have just said about the determinants of psychological success:

> Proposition I: In an attempt to experience psychological success in the career, the person will tend to select career roles congruent with present or potential subidentities which are (a) potentially or presently competent, and (b) highly valued.

Self-esteem is an important factor in determining how successful the person will be in obtaining a good match between subidentity and career role. The more the person searches for information about alternatives, the more effective his choice will be. However, examining oneself critically and objectively requires being receptive to "self-data." Since this kind of examination runs the risk of negative discoveries about oneself, the higher one's self-esteem, the lower the likelihood that the person will be threatened by these new insights. Thus, the greater one's level of self-esteem, the more self-aware he will be and the more likely he will be to make a good career selection.

> Proposition II: The higher the individual's level of self-esteem, the more extensive his search will be for information about (1) available career roles, and (2) the value he attaches to the relevant subidentities, and (3) his present or potential competence in these areas.

Proposition III: The more the individual searches for information about available career roles, personal values, and competencies, the more aware he is likely to be of these entities.

Proposition IV: The more aware the person is of his subidentities and available career roles, the closer the match will be between the selected career subidentity and role.

Proposition V: (Derived from II–IV) The higher the individual's level of self-esteem, the closer the congruence will be between the selected career subidentity and career role.

Support for Proposition V is found in the work of Korman (1967), who found that self-esteem was a moderator of the relationship between vocational choice and self-perceived abilities. Other possible moderators of this relationship might be awareness of choice or degree of internal versus external control.

The individual's level of self-esteem can also affect the degree of risk an individual is willing to take in choosing an occupation— i.e., the level at which the career subidentity–role match occurs. It seems reasonable that people with high self-esteem are more likely to take risks in areas important to them than are those with low self-esteem. Thus, we are led to two additional propositions:

Proposition VI: The higher the individual's self-esteem, the greater the likelihood that he would risk committing himself to a career role providing challenge to a highly valued subidentity.

Proposition VII: The higher the individual's self-esteem, the higher will be the difficulty level at which the role–subidentity match occurs.

Proposition VII is supported by Korman's (1967) thesis that the ability level of a chosen occupation was higher for people with high self-esteem than for those with low self-esteem. Similarly, it has been found by Burnstein (1963) that the following outcomes were associated with fear of failure (which could presumably be an inverse function of self-esteem): "(a) the prestige of aspired-to occupations decreased, (b) willingness to settle for less satisfying and less prestigeful occupations increased, and (c) the person became more likely to perceive that occupations with extremely low probabilities of attainment were within his reach."

In contrast to other views of occupational choice, these propositions explain choice in terms of a process of psychological success. Like other theories, the present model is based upon person-career fit, but it attempts to show how the discovery of a good fit and the degree of fit are affected by psychological success.

Career Choices of Women

Because we have been discussing the process of career choice in terms of such basic personality concepts as identity, self-esteem, and involvement, it would be tempting simply to argue that these are unrelated to sex and that therefore everything said to this point applies equally well to men and women. However, **33** a rapidly growing literature on women's careers is telling us that many of our theoretical concepts about careers are in fact concepts about *male* careers.

It is well known that women have tended to choose different occupations from men and that they have encountered barriers to entry and advancement in "male occupations." In the area of employment, the options open to women have been restricted, both by lower aspirations than men (Epstein and Bronzaft, 1974) and by occupational restrictions (O'Leary, 1974).

In another sense, however, the career choices available to women, particularly married women, have been wider than those open to men in the past, because women have had more freedom not to be employed, or to be employed part-time, as alternatives to full-time employment. With the coming of greater equality for women, these alternatives to full-time employment are now becoming open to men as well, ironically enough. For example, we now see male "housespouses," who spend full time taking care of the home and the children.

Choice and satisfaction. When we examine the process by which women make career choices, however, it seems that the findings are often contrary to expectations. For example, one study of married women made the rather obvious prediction that satisfaction would be related to the extent to which women actually did the kind of career work they would ideally prefer to do. The possible types of career work studied were full-time employment, part-time employment, volunteer work, and being a full-time housewife. This prediction was supported in the case of housekeeping and volunteer activities, but not for employment either part-time or full-time. In other words, this straightforward prediction was supported in reference to the stereotyped female activities, but *not* in the case of occupational activities (Hall and Gordon, 1973). These results were interpreted as suggesting that

> the career choices of the work-oriented married woman are more difficult to implement successfully than are the choices of home-oriented women. Home-related tasks and volunteer activities are part of the traditionally accepted roles of wife and mother. The woman who by her own choice prefers to do these activities will find external role support, acceptance, admiration, and intrinsic satisfaction for doing them. Since employment is outside the traditional home roles, the woman preferring to work may encounter increased role conflicts, time pressure, prejudice, and discrimination when she seeks employment. These problems may offset the satisfaction which a work-oriented woman would otherwise receive by doing what she prefers to do (Hall and Gordon, 1973, p. 47).

Choice and success. Another study of women with surprising findings was conducted by Horner. In a review of research by herself and other investigators, she found evidence in women

of a *motive to avoid success* (M–s), "a disposition to become anxious about achieving success because they expect negative consequences (such as social rejection and/or feelings of being unfeminine) as a result of succeeding" (Horner, 1972, p. 159). In contrast, the studies found that men have quite positive attitudes toward success. In Horner's research women were classified as being high or low in their need to avoid success. They were then tested on a number of achievement tasks under both a noncompetitive condition and in competition with men. The majority of the women high in the motive to avoid success performed worse in competition with men than they had without competition. On the other hand, the majority of those women low in M-s performed better under mixed-sex competition, as did the majority of all the men.

Horner concludes as follows:

> In light of the high and, if anything, increasing incidence of the motive to avoid success found among women in our studies, the predominant message seems to be that most highly competent and otherwise achievement-motivated young women, when faced with a conflict between their feminine image and expressing their competencies or developing their abilities and interests, adjust their behaviors to their internalized sex-role stereotypes. We have seen that even within our basically achievement-oriented society the anticipation of success, especially in interpersonal competitive situations, can be regarded as a mixed blessing if not an outright threat. Among women, the anticipation of success especially against a male competitor poses a threat to the sense of femininity and self-esteem and serves as a potential basis for becoming socially rejected. ...In order to feel or appear more feminine, women, especially those high in fear of success, disguise their abilities and withdraw from the mainstream of thought, activism, and achievement in our society. This does not occur, however, without a high price paid by the individual in negative emotional and interpersonal consequences and by the society in loss of valuable human and economic resources (1972, p. 173).

Later research has shown that this phenomenon may be restricted to traditionally male-dominated fields (Tresmer, 1974). Fear of success may be less evident among older, married women, for whom there may be less conflict between affiliation and achievement (Tomlinson-Keasey, 1974).

It would appear, then, that the psychological success model of career choice and development would be less valid for women than for men, or, to be precise, less valid for women with a need to avoid success. When faced with the opportunity for success in a mixed-sex situation (e.g., in school or in a mixed-sex occupation), women may tend to behave like people with low self-esteem and attempt to avoid situations in which opportunities for psychological success are present (autonomy, challenging tasks, etc.). Once in such a success-relevant situation, they might, according to Horner's data, be likely to fail, if it is a mixed-sex environment.

If they do happen to succeed, the effect on their future involvement may depend upon the reinforcement they receive. If they **35** experience the traditional male resentment, they might avoid future task activities in that area. But if they feel rewarded by men for their success frequently enough, the success cycle will become increasingly applicable to their behavior. Indeed, one operational measure of women's *psychological* liberation would be the extent to which self-esteem for women becomes linked to (i.e., correlated with) career achievement and success.

HOW PEOPLE CHOOSE ORGANIZATIONS

So far in our discussion the type of career choice or decision we have considered in most detail has been the choice of an occupation. Career choices can deal with decisions among many different types of alternatives—occupations, job assignments, transfers, promotions, competing job offers, education, approaches to job performance, etc. Aside from the choice of an occupation or field of work, probably the most important career choice most people make involves deciding what organization to work for.

Far less research has been conducted on organizational choice than on occupational choice. However, the theories of person-environment fit that have guided occupational choice research are equally applicable to predicting what organizations people will join. For example, the Holland scheme of personal orientation and occupational stereotype could also be extended to include organizational stereotypes. We would predict that realistic-type people would tend to enter realistic organizations, enterprising people would enter active, enterprising organizations, and so forth. Furthermore, turnover would be expected to be lower among people with a good person-organization fit than for those who have less of a match. The degree of fit would probably be less strongly related to performance, however, than to satisfaction, attitudes, and satisfaction-related outcomes (such as turnover).

Person-Climate Fit

Similarly, people may choose organizations on the basis of the fit between their needs and the climate of the organization. People with high needs for achievement may choose aggressive, achievement-oriented organizations. Power-oriented people may choose influential, prestigious, power-oriented organizations. Affiliative people may choose warm, friendly, supportive organizations. We know that people whose needs fit with the climate of an organization are rewarded more and are more satisfied than those who fit in less well (Downey et al., 1975) so it is natural to reason that fit would also be a factor in one's choice of an organization. Therefore, because the relevant theory and measurement technol-

36

ogy are available and fairly well-developed, the prediction of organizational choice is a promising untapped area for researchers. This is illustrated by a study which used Super's theory to predict and find a fit between people's self-concepts and their descriptions of their most preferred organizations (Tom, 1971). Another instrument that could be adapted to the analysis of organizational choice is Holland's (1973) Self-Directed Search.

Expectations

One important study of organizational choice is that by Soelberg (1966), referred to earlier. Soelberg found that by asking people to rate the attractiveness of various organizational "choice candidates" over a period of time, it is possible to see the gap between the ultimately chosen organization and the others before the person is aware of having made a choice.

Using expectancy theory, Vroom (1966) predicted that MBA students would tend to choose organizations which they saw as most instrumental in helping them attain their work goals. This hypothesis was supported. Vroom also found that the gap between chosen and unchosen organizations in his expectancy-instrumentality index (a measure of the degree to which the organization is seen as aiding one's goal attainment) increased after the person made a decision. (Vroom did not obtain ratings as frequently as Soelberg, so we don't know if this gap increased just before the actual choice was made.) This finding is consistent with dissonance theory.

In an interesting follow-up to this study, Vroom and Deci (1971) went back to the MBA students after they had graduated and had been working for several months. They were again asked to rate the organization they chose and the others they had considered. Vroom and Deci found that at this point the gap between the chosen and unchosen organizations decreased after the person had started work. Given the "reality shock" of actual work experience in the chosen organization, which provides more accurate information than one gets in the recruiting process, the organization didn't look as rosy as it had just after the decision to join. This finding also raises doubts about the permanence of attitude change through dissonance reduction.

Reality Shock

Our final point about organizations concerns this issue of "reality shock" versus realistic information as the person enters the organization. From many studies examining lawyers, teachers, doctors, priests, and managers, we know that young people leaving an educational system (college, business school, prison, law school, seminary, etc.) and entering a work organization tend to experi- **37** ence unmet expectations, surprise, disillusionment, anxiety, and other feelings of not being fully prepared for the day-to-day activities and problems of the work environment. This is what we mean by reality shock (Hall and Schneider, 1973). Therefore, anything that would reduce this reality shock would ease adjustment and help performance during the early work career.

One factor which undoubtedly contributes to reality shock is the one-sided (positive) view recruiters paint of their own organizations. Indeed, some students "psych out" recruiters by seeing what features of the organization the recruiter stresses most strongly. This point, they say, is often one the company feels most defensive about and reflects an area of greatest weakness.

However, several studies have shown that when companies attempt to communicate *realistic expectations* to recruits, stressing both positive and negative features of the organization, the result is lower turnover among the people who are hired (Wanous, 1973, 1975). Furthermore, the company's success in recruiting does not seem to be hurt by more honest information, either. It is not clear whether these realistic job previews result in a different type of person accepting the offer or if the company gets the same type person with more reasonable expectations. Either way, the result is a better fit between person and organization at the time of entry.

Recapitulation: Explaining Occupational Choice

Although we have reviewed several different theories of occupational choice, the process boils down to one simple operation: the attempt by the person to obtain a good fit between himself and his career work. Much of the disagreement among the career theorists concerns what personal characteristics the person is attempting to match with the work environment—needs, personal orientation, values, or identity. In view of the strong support for Holland's model, it appears that personal orientation may be one of the most salient personal characteristics in occupational selection. Another possibility, however, is that Holland has simply developed more valid and reliable measures, which could account for the successful predictions from his theory.

The process models of occupational choice suggest that the person is able to increase the person-career fit as time goes by. However, except for the promising but still fuzzy concept of vocational maturity, we don't know what exactly happens over time that improves this career adjustment. The Tiedeman and O'Hara model, with its focus on basic decision-making processes, appears to be our most promising lead, but there has been little additional

38 research since its publication in 1963. More research on adult careers and on the contrast between adult and adolescent career decision making would shed more light on how this process changes over time.

HOW TO FACILITATE CAREER CHOICE

In most academic fields it is easier to conduct research on a process than it is to help people do it better. The process of choice in the career is no exception. However, there is a sizable body of literature on the practice of career counseling (see, for example, the *Journal of Counseling Psychology* and the *Journal of Vocational Behavior*) which links the practitioner to the researcher to a considerable degree. This section will examine some ways in which the theory and research on careers might be applied to aid individuals in their career choice activities.

Provide Information Through Experience

The most important input to any decision or choice is obviously information. Because the career is a synthesis of the person's identity and the occupational role, the person needs information on three elements: the occupations or options available, his own self-identity, and self-in-occupation. Self-in-occupation refers to the fit between the person and various career options, how he would feel and perform in various occupational roles. Because the interaction between person and occupation may provide more information than could be inferred from knowledge of either element alone, it is useful for the person to obtain data on himself in various work situations. These could be part-time jobs, summer jobs, trial jobs, laboratory occupational simulations, computer-aided simulations, role playing, career games, and so forth. The important feature of information about self-in-occupation is that it is generated from *experience* and *direct observation*.

Information about occupations is probably obtained superficially and haphazardly by most people. This may be partly because of the sheer number of occupations in existence and partly because people feel they already know as much as they need to know about most lines of work. Note, however, that these are contradictory statements. In fact, most people spend less time gathering and consciously analyzing data on possible occupations to enter than they do on the cars they buy. Useful aids to gathering occupational information are Holland's Self-Directed Search and computer-assisted search programs, such as one being developed at the Educational Testing Service (Katz, 1973; *Behavior Today*, April 14, 1975, p. 444.). In the ETS program, the person diagnoses his own career-related values with the aid of an on-line interactive **39** computer, which then directs him to appropriate occupations. It then will describe the job activities, education and training required, salary levels, market demand, promotion prospects, and other salient information on any occupation for which the person requests more data. By changing various personal value criteria, the person can increase or decrease the number of possible occupations that would be satisfactory.

Information on the person's self-identity can be uncovered through self-examination, counseling, therapy, discussions with friends, teachers, bosses, and various kinds of life-planning exercises. In the latter, the person takes and usually self-scores various tests and questionnaires (such as the Thematic Apperception Test or the Allport Vernon Lindzey Study of Values) which measure work-related needs, values, and interests. Following the scoring, he discusses the results with his advisor or other group members, considers their validity, and discusses what they add to his self-conceptions. He would also obtain feedback on his behavior and apparent needs, values, and interests. Another wrinkle, originally used by Herb Shepard, is for the person to: (1) write ten answers to the question, Who am I?, (2) write an obituary as it would appear tomorrow, if the person died today, and (3) write an epitaph. These data would also be discussed with the advisor or group.

Another way of finding out about oneself is to write an obituary as you would like it to look in ten years (i.e., what do you want to accomplish over the next ten years?). Another activity is to develop a list of career goals, being as specific as possible about: (1) how the goal is defined, (2) what criteria would be used to measure goal attainment, (3) resources and people that would help in attaining the goal, (4) obstacles that would have to be overcome and how, etc.* Most managers, when asked how much time they spend on their own career planning, are surprised to realize how little they do. Usually they spend far more time managing their subordinates' careers than their own. The active role managers play in directing the affairs of the organization and their passivity in managing their own lives is incongruous. Bolles' (1975) book, *What Color Is Your Parachute?*, is an excellent general manual for career planning. More information on better self-management of careers is found in Chapter 7.

Stimulate Task Success

Most research on underachievers in educational and occupational settings has found that an unfavorable self-concept and low expectancies of success are important correlates of failure. There-

*More complete descriptions of career planning are found in Kolb et al. (1974); Golembiewski (1972); Fordyce and Weil (1971); and Hall, Bowen, Lewicki, and Hall (1975).

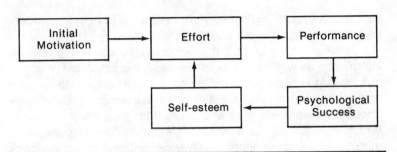

FIGURE 2–8
A Simplified Model
of Psychological
Success

fore, one major strategy in remedial educational and occupational programs has been to try to increase the self-esteem and involvement of the student or employee. This strategy is based upon the same assumptions as the psychological success model described earlier. An oversimplified version of this cyclic model is shown in Figure 2-8. If the success process is indeed cyclic, intervention at any point could theoretically get the cycle "operating." Given all we have learned about the difficulty of changing a person's self-concept (even long therapy has unclear effects), it would appear that there would be much greater payoff in attempting to improve work performance and increase the person's perception of his success directly. Then experiences of success would indirectly enhance the person's self-concept. We know we can increase a person's chances for task or job success through putting him on a difficult but not impossible job, which he values, which involves personal autonomy but with opportunities for coaching and support from boss and co-workers. By carefully selecting jobs or tasks that would constitute good success opportunities for a given person, a manager, teacher, counselor, or other helping agent could probably do more to aid career choice and development than would months or years of counseling, therapy, or other forms of direct self-concept development.

Deal with Needs in Different Career Stages

In helping a person through the process of career development, it is important to *diagnose* what career stage the person is in and then to choose the form of assistance on the basis of the needs of that stage. At the fantasy stage, children can use information about a wide range of possible vocations. The goal here is to keep the child "loose," free to think of a full range of occupations. For example, girls should be encouraged to fantasize about traditionally "male" careers—manager, doctor, politician, athlete, salesperson, etc. During the exploratory stage, a person should be given more in-depth information about specific occupations: data on educational aptitude, and skill requirements, job activities, ad- **41** vancement opportunities, etc. Here the task is to help the student crystallize thoughts about particular careers.

In the selection phase, the person could again use specific information as well as trial experiences, either simulated or actual trial jobs. After becoming established in an occupation, the person should be encouraged to examine his satisfaction and perform- ance with his present work and to see if his personal job fit could be better elsewhere. Job mobility should not be discouraged at this point. During the period of advancement, one needs feedback and advice on performance, as well as cues on the criteria for evaluation and one's potential. In the maintenance stage, the per- son needs stimulation to stay "current" in his field and encour- agement to help develop younger colleagues. In the decline period the person should be helped to gradually reduce his work commit- ments and to develop non-work pursuits in which he can invest his self-esteem and sense of meaning. In contrast to basing inter- ventions upon the needs of different career stages, most organiza- tions offer the same career development activities to all employees, independent of age or needs in general.

Use Variety of Career Guidance Agents

Because we have been arguing that career development is largely facilitated through task experiences and success at work, anyone who influences the person at work is likely to be a career guidance agent. The co-worker who offers help on the job, the boss who talks over a possible promotion or transfer, and the subordinate whose performance gives feedback on one's managerial skills are all offering inputs to career decisions and occupational self-image. Managers in particular can be more effective as career develop- ment resources by being more conscious of the long-term impact of their actions on the work attitudes and performance of their subordinates. Because of the manager's tremendous impact on the careers of his subordinates, supervisors should be trained in career planning and counseling.

Integrate Learning and Work

In a recent undergraduate class the author asked the students to identify characteristics of effective settings for learning, either in college or work organizations. Some students insisted that *either* the university or a work organization be specified, because the conditions for learning are not the same in school and at work. Furthermore, some argued that learning is simply not rele- vant at work. On the other hand, people who work full-time and take graduate courses part-time (at night, usually) generally see a close integration of learning and work, and of course work and

42   job work. When students go straight through an MBA program

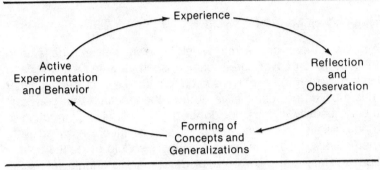

FIGURE 2-9
The Kolb, Rubin,
McIntyre Model of
Learning

From D. Kolb, "On Management and the Learning Process," in David Kolb, Irwin Rubin, and James McIntyre, *Organizational Psychology: A Book of Readings,* 2nd ed. (Englewood Cliffs, N.J.: Prentice-Hall, 1974), p. 28. Reprinted by permission of Prentice-Hall, Inc., Englewood Cliffs, N.J.

after their undergraduate degrees, they often experience "reality shock" in their first jobs. They also often have trouble appreciating the content of their MBA courses. In contrast, students who have worked several years and then return for a full-time or part-time MBA usually see the MBA program as much more relevant for their needs, and they experience little reality shock following graduation. The same benefits are usually reported by students in good "co-op" programs, in which they alternate terms of full-time work and terms of full-time study.

One can view the process of learning and development as shown in Figure 2-9. After an important experience, we often reflect upon it and then form some sort of concept or generalization about it (e.g., "workers are lazy," or "workers can be motivated by interesting tasks"). Then we behave on the basis of our generalizations, which leads again to various experiences. For learning to be fully integrated (i.e., really a "part" of a person), it should be based upon all four of these stages. However, many students seem to learn mainly through reflective observation and abstract conceptualizing, because this is the "scientific method" taught in school. Managers and other practicing professionals, on the other hand, learn often through experimentation and experience. The most effective learning and personal development, however, is that which *integrates* all four processes shown above. By lengthening the time span of formal education (e.g., by having people work for several years before the completion of college) and integrating educational and occupational experiences (e.g., co-op programs, part-time degree programs), one attains a better integration of experience, observation, conceptualizing, and experimentation.

OVERVIEW: ISSUES REGARDING CAREER CHOICE

In examining the literature on career choice, two issues arise repeatedly: the need for theory and the apparent dichotomy between choice and work. Let us consider each of these briefly in turn.

Need for Theory

Although there are some widely known research-generating theories which cover career choice, such as Super's (1957) and Holland's (1966), much research on choice has been neither theory-based nor cumulative. And of the research that does test theory, usually it goes no further than confirming or refuting it; there is little *development and revision* of theory as a result of the findings. Ideally, in research, theory should guide the collection of data, and the results of data analysis should refine the theory, yielding cycles of theory → data → theory → data, etc. Or, with an inductive approach, the cycles could be data → theory → data, etc. However, theory and data on careers seem to coexist quite happily, both conflicting with and unaffected by each other.

Perhaps part of the reason for this problem is that career researchers are usually in educational or personnel settings, where they have access to large numbers of students or employees, test scores, and computation services. This could lead to an understandable bias toward large-sample empirical, statistically elegant analyses. Perhaps if the journals banned empirical data for one year, the field might show a spurt of growth!

More small theories of how people perform various career processes are needed: what leads to career search, how a person becomes committed to an area of work, how one chooses an organization or decides to quit, how one moves successfully from one career stage to the next, how women's careers are different from men's, what organizational factors affect the career development of minority people and women, etc. We have just barely scratched the surface of important career issues to be studied.

In the organizational/industrial literature, we need to apply what we know about jobs and roles to lives and careers. We know, for example, that participation in decision making on the job usually results in greater acceptance of decisions, more satisfaction, and improved performance. However, do these favorable results continue over time, or do they fade eventually? What happens to the person's career aspirations? Does he come to consider participation in decision making as a minimum feature of the job? Does this increase his aspiration to higher-level jobs with even better opportunities for freedom and participation? How are workers at different career stages affected by participation? Does the "advancing" person respond more favorably than the "maintainer" or the "decliner"? We need to add a long-term lifetime perspective to our research on the impact of the job upon the person.

Ironically, it may be those areas in which the applied problems are the most pressing that the best theory may emerge. (Generally,

44

we think of theory and applied problems as antithetical.) For example, the problems of mid-career change and of women in organizations are both areas where considerable theory is being generated to help explain and clarify the issues. In the mid-career area we have psychoanalytic, sociological, theological, psychological, and philosophical writing, as well as fiction and poetry. Regarding women's careers, there is work on female socialization, biological factors, anthropology, role theory, the economics and politics of financial resource allocation, etc. It would not be surprising to discover in a few years that we have better theory about women's careers than we do about men's, despite the fact that most of the career research thus far has had a male bias. This is consistent with the earlier point that more mini-theories on specific career problems (e.g., Korman's work on occupational choice, or Vroom's on organizational choice) would greatly advance the state of the field.

Dichotomy between Career Selection and Work

In general, the literature on the selection of a vocation (counseling psychology) and the literature on work experiences in a vocation (industrial/organizational psychology and sociology) have been quite separate. The research has been reported in different journals, investigators have been in separate university departments; and in different types of organizations (schools versus companies) research has focused on different settings (school versus work), and the subjects have been in different career stages (adolescents versus adults). Therefore, given this discontinuity in the literature, it is difficult for students scholars, or managers to think of career choice and development as a continuing process. The theories and models of counseling psychology fail to use the most appropriate criteria—occupational satisfaction and performance, which are in the "domain" of organizational research. On the other hand, organizational studies do not give enough attention to the process by which young people enter careers and to the impact of good or bad person–career fit upon job behavior and attitudes.

An example of the problems caused by this dichotomy is the fate of organizational choice as a process to be studied. This is a highly important problem, one faced by most people more often than the choice of an occupation. In fact, for many people, organizational choice precedes occupational choice (A. Shuh, personal communication, 1975). However, it "falls in the cracks" between the interests of schools and the interests of employing organizations, with the result that it is a vastly underresearched topic.

As education expands into the adult years and becomes more integrated with occupational experiences, these two research **45** fields will probably become correspondingly more integrated as well. As organizational behavior becomes a more accepted area of psychological study and as organizational researchers become more interested in careers, these developments too should help bring the two areas together.

SUMMARY

Here we have dealt with career choice—including both the ideal and the actual. We have discussed some of the changes that need to be made in the extent of involvement on the part of the (1) individuals trying to make a career choice; (2) those in the management level of organizations; and (3) those concerned with developing research and deriving theories about career choice. In this chapter we have stressed individual differences in the way people make career choices. In the following chapter we will consider the opposite phenomenon: shared experiences. We will move beyond the stage of choice and consider what common experiences most people have as they move through various stages in their careers.

Discussion Questions

1. What is the difference between the content and process theories of career choice?
2. Which theory of career choice fits with your own career choice? Which theory has received the most research support?
3. What is vocational maturity? How can organizations increase the vocational maturity of employees?
4. Describe the experiences of an acquaintance that illustrate the Tiedeman and O'Hara model of career choice.
5. Try to arrange an interview with an employed person. Ask about the factors that influenced his choice of career. After the interview, determine which theory of career choice best explains that person's experiences and evaluate the correspondence between the person and the career. Does this correspondence relate to the person's career satisfaction?
6. What are your major subidentities? What conflicts among subidentities do you experience? How do you deal with them?
7. Think of occasions when you experienced psychological success. What were the conditions that led to this feeling?
8. Do you believe that women are motivated to avoid success?

CAREER STAGES

3

Once I was listening to a group of children trying to deal with a member who was being quite obstinate about not permitting anyone else to play with his toys. As the hostility level was increasing, peace was restored by a wise old 10-year-old who said, "He's not usually like this; it's just a phrase he's going through."

If she was a bit off in her jargon, our young neighborhood sage was correct in her understanding of human development. People do go through phases and stages when they experience changes in their mood, needs, aspirations, values, skills, motivations, and other important human characteristics. We have all heard comments like, "He's a new man since he started working," and "She isn't the same person I married twenty years ago." People do change over the course of their lives and work careers, and in some fairly predictable ways. In this chapter we will examine some of these stages.

LIFE STAGES

We may see a person's life cycle as a series of stages characterized by changing patterns of developmental tasks, career concerns, activities, values, and needs, which emerge as he ages and passes through various age ranges (Hall and Schneider, 1973; Hall and Nougaim, 1968; Kroll et al., 1970). But we should remember, as Cain observes,

> In spite of the observed ambiguity of age status and of the abundance of descriptive data on the subject, supplied by historians, anthropologists, demographers, researchers in social welfare, and others, sociologists have yet **47**

to devote more than passing attention to these data and to their implications for the total social structure (1964, p. 272).

(This is as applicable to psychologists as well as sociologists.)

Unlike the life stages of childhood and youth, which are well-defined by age and institutional role transitions (e.g., the start of grade school, high school graduation, driving age, university graduation, legal age, marriage, etc.) the important changes in the adult years are harder to delineate (Mills, 1970). Marriage and parenthood are often the last institutionalized status passages experienced until retirement; thus a person tends to pace his own life cycle in terms of the life cycle of his children and the total family unit. In fact, a person's social behavior is probably related more to his stage in the family life cycle than to his age (Lansing and Kish, 1957). Cain has said, "To be the father of a teen-age daughter elicits certain behavior patterns, whether the father be 30 or 70 years of age" (1964, p. 289).

The person's stage in his or her work career is another factor that can strongly affect (and is likewise affected by) social behavior and attitudes; this variable may not be closely tied to age either. A lawyer or manager who is on the first permanent job following professional training (law school or business school) will probably be concerned about advancement and establishing a reputation among colleagues, whether he or she is 25 or 45. (However, the 45-year-old who *started* a career in that occupation at 25 will probably have quite a different set of concerns, which we will describe later.)*

Erikson's Theory of Life Stages

From clinical psychology, part of Erik Erikson's theory of the eight stages of the life cycle can be logically applied to the study of working careers. (The first four of these stages—oral, anal, genital, and latency—describe childhood and therefore are not relevant here.) Erikson believes that each stage is characterized by a particular *developmental task* which the person must work through before advancing fully into the following stage.

In the first stage of youth, *adolescence,* the central developmental task is achieving a sense of ego identity:

The growing and developing youths, faced with this physiological revolution within them, and with tangible adult tasks ahead of them are now primarily concerned with what they appear to be in the eyes of others as compared with what they feel they are, and with the question of how to connect the

---

*A good collection of cases that illustrate and apply some of the development concepts in this chapter can be found in Lorsch and Barnes (1972).

roles and skills cultivated earlier with the occupational prototypes of the day (Erikson, 1963, p. 261).*

The main danger at this stage is role confusion, the opposite of a clear identity. Although the person may experience confusion about his sexual identity, "in most instances, however, it is the inability to settle on an occupational identity which disturbs young people" (Ibid., p. 262). It is a time of searching for values and role models and testing various possible identities, a time of thinking about one's own ideology and purpose in life.

The next stage is *young adulthood,* during which the developmental task is to develop intimacy and involvements. This includes, but is not limited to, interpersonal intimacy; it entails learning how to let oneself become ego-involved with another person, group, organization, or cause.

> Thus, the young adult, emerging from the search for and the insistence on identity, is eager and willing to fuse his identity with that of others. He is ready for intimacy, that is, the capacity to commit himself to concrete affiliations and partnerships and to develop the ethical strength to abide by such commitments, even though they may call for significant sacrifices and compromises (Ibid., p. 263).*

The danger at this stage is that the person may be so afraid of losing or compromising his new-found sense of identity and autonomy that he shuns involvements and develops a deep sense of isolation and self-absorption. To describe these issues further, Erikson referred to Freud's famous reply when asked what he thought a normal person should be able to do well: *"Lieben und arbeiten"* (love and work).

> It pays to ponder on this simple formula; it gets deeper as you think about it. For . . . when he [Freud] said love *and* work, he meant a general work-productiveness which would not preoccupy the individual to the extent that he loses his right or capacity to be a genital and a loving being (Ibid., p. 265).*

One of the behaviors that occurs in this stage as a sign of intimacy is finding and committing oneself to a mate. Also, close, lifelong friendships are established with those with whom one interacts intensively during young adulthood—college chums, roommates, army buddies, co-workers, etc. This is also a time when young people test out their occupational identities and go to work, creating involvements in and commitments to work organizations, bosses, and co-workers.

The seventh stage described by Erikson is *adulthood,* during

---

*Reprinted from *Childhood and Society,* 2nd ed.; by Erik H. Erikson. By permission of W.W. Norton & Company, Inc., and The Hogarth Press. © 1950, 1963 by W.W. Norton & Company, Inc.

which the person deals with issues concerned with the generation of that which is of lasting value to other people—his contributions to following generations, and thus in a sense his antidote to mortality.

> Generativity, then, is primarily the concern in establishing and guiding the next generation, although there are individuals who, through misfortune or because of special and genuine gifts in other directions, do not apply this drive to their own offspring. And, indeed, the concept of generativity is meant to include such more popular synonyms as *productivity* and *creativity,* which, however, cannot replace it (Ibid., p. 267).*

In the work setting, generativity may be achieved through such things as building organizations; developing creative theories, discoveries, or products that will endure; coaching and sponsoring the development of younger colleagues; and teaching and guiding students. Generativity is really an outgrowth of the preceding stages (as is the case for any other stage): once the person has developed a sense of identity and has committed it to a cause, person, or organization, the next stage is to accomplish or produce something as a result of that commitment. The opposite of generativity is what Erikson calls *stagnation,* which means standing still, producing nothing. Stagnation also carries the connotation of decay, not just the absence of growth.

The eighth and final stage of development is *maturity,* during which the fully developed person acquires a sense of *ego integrity* (versus despair). This is the feeling that the person is satisfied with his life, with his choices and actions. He sees it as meaningful, and is willing to leave it as it is.

> [Ego integrity] is the ego's accrued assurance of its proclivity for order and meaning. It is a post-narcissistic love of the human ego—not of the self—as an experience which conveys some world order and spiritual sense, no matter how dearly paid for. It is the acceptance of one's one and only life cycle as something that had to be and that, by necessity, permitted of no substitutions. . . . In such final consolidation, death loses its sting.
>
> The lack or loss of this accrued ego integration is signified by fear of death: the one and only life cycle is not accepted as the ultimate of life. Despair expresses the feeling that the time is now short, too short for the attempt to start another life and to try out alternate roads to integrity (Ibid., pp. 268–69).*

One characteristic of a cycle is that it has no beginning or end, in a sense; the completion of one cycle feeds into the beginning of the next.† Erikson ends his discussion of the eight stages by showing strikingly the connection between the end and the beginning of life:

---

*Reprinted from *Childhood and Society,* 2nd ed., by Erik H. Erikson. By permission of W.W. Norton & Company, Inc., and the Hogarth Press. © 1950, 1963 by W.W. Norton & Company, Inc.

†These views on the process of development are similar to Maslow's notions about the prepotency of Motives in the hierarchy of needs. See Abraham A. Maslow, *Motivation and Personality* (New York: Harper, 1954).

Webster's Dictionary is kind enough to help us complete this outline in a circular fashion. Trust (the first of our ego values) is here defined as "the assured reliance on another's integrity," the last of our values. I suspect that Webster had business in mind rather than babies, credit rather than faith. But, the formulation stands. And, it seems possible to further paraphrase the relation of adult integrity and infantile trust by saying that healthy children will not fear life if their elders have integrity enough not to fear death (Ibid., p. 269).*

A person must achieve a satisfactory resolution of the issues in one stage before he can deal competently with the issues at the next stage. Thus, it is possible for a person's development to become arrested, in a sense, at any given stage. If a person were "hung up" at the identity level, for example, he may remain plagued with doubts about his career choice, shifting from job to job and perhaps career to career, long after his contemporaries, who had settled on a career and an employer, were advancing within their firms. According to this theory, a person cannot achieve a full, deep commitment (intimacy) to an organization, person, or cause until his identity is pretty well-defined; similarly, he cannot attain higher-stage experience such as creative production (generativity) or ego fulfillment (integrity).

The work of Erikson is based upon his clinical, anthropological, and historical observations, and has not really been tested with experimental and statistical methods. However, the theory has received considerable support from clinicians and has a great deal of face validity. It has been extremely useful in understanding specific developmental problems, such as identity confusion and mid-life career crises. For example, it has been found that students who had made well-adjusted vocational choices and had developed mature career attitudes (as measured by Crites' Maturity Inventory, discussed in Chapter 2), had also been most successful in moving through the first six stages identified by Erikson (Munley, 1975).

There may be sex differences in the course of the life stages. One study (Douvan and Adelson, 1966) found that adolescent girls often achieve a sense of identity only after they have established a sense of intimacy (generally heterosexual) in their relationships. Thus, the intimacy stage may precede the identity stage for girls†; adolescent boys, on the other hand, are seen by these researchers to be able to achieve intimacy after they had attained a sense of identity, which fits with Erikson's model (Douvan and Adelson, 1966).

*Reprinted from *Childhood and Society*, 2nd ed., by Erik H. Erikson. By permission of W.W. Norton & Company, Inc., and the Hogarth Press. © 1950, 1963 by W.W. Norton & Company, Inc.
†The women's movement seems to agree implicitly that this reversal of stages occurs; however, women's activists see this as an unnatural pattern of development, a distortion caused by the socialization of females toward certain stereotyped sex roles.

Other theories, too, correspond in part, to Erikson's conception of life stages. In the realm of vocational behavior, Super and his associates employ a model of five developmental stages: (1) childhood, (2) adolescence, (3) young adulthood, (4) maturity, and (5) old age (Super and Bohn, 1970). The main task in the childhood (up to age 14) stage is growth. In this stage the person begins to fantasize about careers, and develops vocational interests and capacities. During adolescence, the person begins to explore his own interests and different specific career opportunities. This corresponds to Erikson's identity stage. In young adulthood (about age 25 to 44), the person may initially flounder a bit (as seen in the high initial turnover of recent college graduates), and eventually establish himself in a particular field. This corresponds to Erikson's intimacy stage with some hints of generativity later. In maturity (about 45 to 64), the person continues to hold his own in a sort of career plateau. This stage is probably when generativity concerns would be most important. Old age (65 and on) is a period of disengagement. This would be the time ego integrity would be achieved, if the person has resolved all the earlier stages. (The vocational stages defined by Super are shown in detail in Table 3–1.) Super's model has been supported in recent research on organizational careers (Hall and Mansfield, 1975).

Miller and Form's Occupational Stages

Miller and Form (1951) have described five stages based more on actual job behaviors than on the underlying developmental processes. The *preparatory work period* occurs in childhood. The *initial work period* (late teens) consists of part-time and occasional jobs. The *trial work period* starts with the person's first regular full-time job and continues until he settles into a stable field of work: (late twenties or early thirties). The *stable work period* extends from the thirties to the sixties, and is followed by retirement.

Typical career patterns tend to emerge, based upon the ways people have gone through (or have failed to go through) these work stages, with primary emphasis on the stability or security of the career. These patterns are as follows:

1. *Stable career pattern.* People in this category have gone directly from their schooling into work with which they stayed. Many managers and most professionals have careers of this type.
2. *Conventional career pattern.* In this pattern, the individual goes through the stages in the sequence listed above: initial jobs, trial jobs, and stable employment. This pattern describes most managerial careers.
3. *Unstable career pattern.* In this pattern the person never really becomes established in one area, going from trial jobs to a stable situation and then back to trial jobs again. She might be called *laterally mobile,* rather than upwardly mobile.
4. *Multiple-trial career pattern.* In this pattern the person does not stay in

1. *Growth Stage* (Birth–14)

Self-concept develops through identification with key figures in family and in school; needs and fantasy are dominant early in this stage; interest and capacity become more important in this stage with increasing social participation and reality testing. Substages of the growth stage are:

Fantasy (4–10). Needs are dominant; role playing in fantasy is important.

Interests (11–12). Likes are the major determinant of aspitations and activities.

Capacity (13–14). Abilities are given more weight, and job requirements (including training) are considered.

2. *Exploration Stage* (Age 15–24)

Self-examination, role tryouts, and occupational exploration take place in school, leisure activities, and part-time work. Substages of the exploration stage are:

Tentative (15–17). Needs, interests, capacities, values, and opportunities are all considered. Tentative choices are made and tried out in fantasy, discussion, courses, work, etc.

Transition (18–21). Reality considerations are given more weight as the youth enters labor market or professional training and attempts to implement a self-concept.

Trial (22–24). A seemingly appropriate field having been located, a beginning job in it is found and is tried out as a life work.

3. *Establishment Stage* (Age 25–44)

Having found an appropriate field, effort is put forth to make a permanent place in it. There may be some trial early in this stage, with consequent shifting, but establishment may begin without trial, especially in the professions. Substages of the establishment stage are:

Trial (25–30). The field of work presumed to be suitable may prove unsatisfactory, resulting in one or two changes before the life work is found or before it becomes clear that the life work will be a succession of unrelated jobs.

Stabilization (31–44). As the career pattern becomes clear, effort is put forth to stabilize, to make a secure place, in the world of work. For most persons these are the creative years.

4. *Maintenance Stage* (Age 45–64)

Having made a place in the world of work, the concern is now to hold it. Little new ground is broken, but there is continuation along established lines.

5. *Decline Stage* (Age 65 on)

As physical and mental powers decline, work activity changes and in due course ceases. New roles must be developed; first that of selective participant and then that of observer rather than participant. Substages of this stage are:

Deceleration (65–70). Sometimes at the time of official retirement, sometimes late in the maintenance stage, the pace of work slackens, duties are shifted, or the nature of the work is changed to suit declining capacities. Many men find part-time jobs to replace their full-time occupations.

Retirement (71 on). As with all the specified age limits, there are great variations from person to person. But complete cessation of occupation comes for all in due course, to some easily and pleasantly, to others with difficulty and disappointment, and to some only with death.

TABLE 3–1
Vocational
Life Stages

From D. Super, J. Crites, R. Hummel, H. Moser, P. Overstreet, and C. Warnath, *Vocational Development: A Framework for Research,* New York: Teachers College Press, 1957, pp. 40–41.

one field long enough to reach stability; he moves from one trial job to another. Many domestic and semiskilled workers would be in this category.

Hall and Nougaim's Stages in Management

In a study of young AT&T managers, Hall and Nougaim (1968) found some evidence to support a concept of *career stages*. In the first year of employment, there were strong concerns for safety—gaining recognition and establishing oneself in the organization. In year one, this need was second in importance only to the need for achievement and esteem, which was clearly of paramount importance to this group of executive hopefuls. However, by the fifth year, the need for safety had declined significantly and was the least important of the four needs measured. Furthermore, the managers who eventually attained the greatest success in the company were those with the lowest needs for safety in the first year. This result was consistent with other findings that tolerance of uncertainty was correlated with managerial success (Berlew and Hall, 1966). It seems that becoming established is a central concern when the young manager first enters an organization; and those who can feel the most comfortable with the insecurity and uncertainty involved can cope most effectively. This stage is described as follows:

> The beginning of the career is a new experience, and here the person is mainly concerned with defining the structure of his position and with feeling secure in it. At this point he is at the boundary of his organization, a very stressful location [Kahn et al., 1964], and he is searching for means of integrating himself into the system. Being new, he does not have a strong identity relevant to his particular organization, and he is struggling to define more clearly his environment and his relationship to it (Hall and Nougaim, 1968, pp. 26–27).

The next stage seemed to be advancement—promotion and achievement. At this point the person is not so concerned with fitting into the organization (moving inside) as he is with moving upward and mastering it. The young managers in the study showed a significant increase in the importance of the needs for achievement and esteem between the first and fifth years of the career. Furthermore, the most successful managers experience increased satisfaction in this need area, while those who were less successful showed less satisfaction. This was the only need area in which there were differences in satisfaction levels between successful managers in either the first or fifth year. Other studies have also shown increased concerns for achievement and autonomy between the first and eighth years of employment (Bray, Campbell, and Grant, 1974). Promotion was found to be a dominant intermediate career concern of scientists (Glaser, 1964).

In the AT&T study, it appeared that a maintenance stage might follow the advancement years:

Beyond the advancement stage we can only speculate, since our data cover only the first five years of the subject's careers. However, our subjective impression is that once the incumbent had cues that he was nearing the limit of this advancement, his career would start to level off, and the need— or opportunity—to compete would decrease. If he felt successful, he might become concerned with helping younger men—his successors—grow, in order to strengthen the organization and perpetuate his work. If he felt unsuccessful, he might still define his mission as helping these young men, or he might use his power to block their progress and thus punish them for his failure. Whatever the specific behavior at this later stage, the period does represent the onset of a terminal plateau. The man has achieved his own particular level of success, and he now must find some other means of gratification. The end, just as the beginning, can be a critical period, and the incumbent must adjust to a significantly altered self-definition (Hall and Nougaim, 1968, p. 28).

The safety and establishment concerns identified in the Hall and Nougaim study are clearly part of Super's *establishment* stage, representing an attempt at stabilization. The second Hall-Nougaim stage, advancement, does not emerge clearly in the Super model, but it is probably part of the process of becoming established in a career. The maintenance stage described by Hall and Nougaim fits well with the *maintenance* stage described by Super. It appears, however, that stabilization occurs earlier in managerial careers than for careers in general as described by Super, with advancement taking up the remainder of the years Super lists under stabilization.

The different models of career stages which we have discussed here are summarized in Figure 3-1. With the exception of the Erikson model, which deals with general life stages rather than work career stages, the models resemble general biological growth and decay curves: early period of exploration and trial, then growth, a stable period in the middle (maintenance), and a stage of decline and withdrawal from the work environment. Daniel Levinson refers to the exploration stage as "Getting Into the Adult World" (GIAW), to the growth stage as "Settling Down" (SD), and to the middle years as "Becoming One's Own Man" (BOOM), (Levinson et al., 1974). These different models can be synthesized graphically, as shown in Figure 3-2.

The dashed lines and question marks in Figure 3-2 reflect an unresolved question regarding the mid-career period. This appears to be a time when individual differences may be extremely noticeable. Why do some people continue to grow in mid-career, while others enter the maintenance plateau and still others begin to decline? This issue will be examined in more detail in the section on mid-career processes, later in the chapter.

Family Stages

A separate but related issue for married people with children is the fact that a family goes through life stages of its own. These

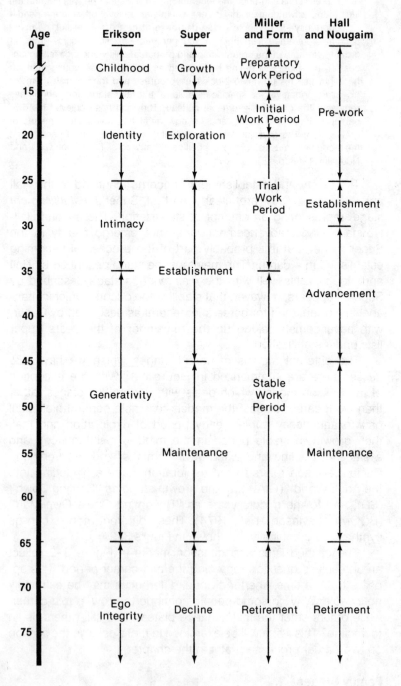

FIGURE 3–1
Summary
of Career
Stage Models

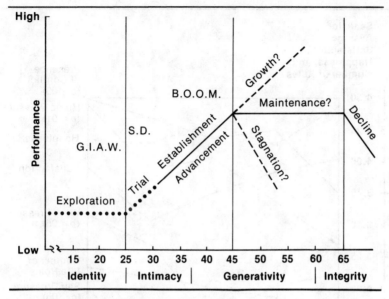

FIGURE 3–2
Stages in
Career
Development

family stages may be either compatible or in conflict with the career stages of the parents. The stages in the development of a family are as follows:

1. *Becoming a Spouse:* begins at marriage and ends with the birth of the first child.
2. *Expanding Circle:* begins with the birth of the first child and ends with the birth of the second child.
3. *Peak Stage:* the period in which the family has two or more preschool children.
4. *Full-House Plateau:* starts when the youngest child enters school and ends when the first child leaves home.
5. *Shrinking Circle:* starts when the first child leaves home and ends when the last child leaves home.
6. *Minimal Plateau:* when all children have left home.

Given our present norms, family role responsibilities (child care, domestic tasks, etc.) have traditionally fallen more heavily upon women than men. (This, however, is changing with the contemporary emphasis on women's liberation and the entry of more women into life careers in the "work world" outside the home.) A recent study examined the pressures, conflict, number of roles, satisfaction, and happiness of female college graduates in relation to the stages of their families. The results indicate that pressures from the home increase as the family grows (see Figure 3–3). Work pressures tend to decrease, probably because women with children withdraw from the labor force. The total number of roles the woman performs rises steadily with family stage (Hall, 1975).

This graph raises the question of how these family stages co-exist with the stages of a woman's work career. Just as she is getting into the hard-working establishment stage, her family **57**

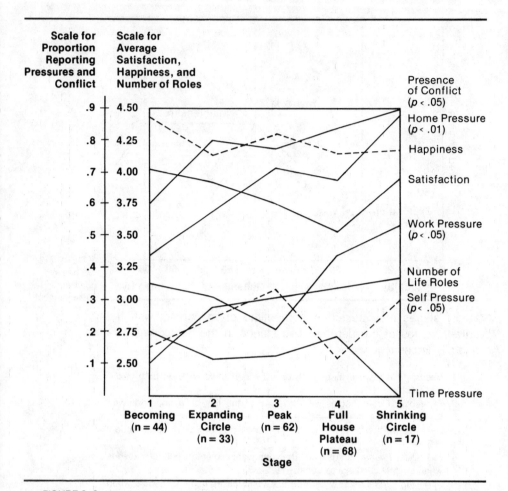

Scale for Proportion Reporting Pressures and Conflict	Scale for Average Satisfaction, Happiness, and Number of Roles				

Presence of Conflict ($p < .05$)
Home Pressure ($p < .01$)
Happiness
Satisfaction
Work Pressure ($p < .05$)
Number of Life Roles
Self Pressure ($p < .05$)
Time Pressure

1 Becoming (n = 44)	2 Expanding Circle (n = 33)	3 Peak (n = 62)	4 Full House Plateau (n = 68)	5 Shrinking Circle (n = 17)

Stage

FIGURE 3–3
Effects of Family Stage on Women's Role Pressures and Attitudes

From Douglas T. Hall, "Pressures from Work, Self, and Home in the Life Stages of Married Women," *Journal of Vocational Behavior,* 6 (1975), p. 127.

is growing and putting increased pressures on her time. These pressures and problems are coming to be increasingly shared by men as *dual-career families* become more common. (A dual-career family is one in which both partners maintain full-time work careers and also raise a family.) Joint husband-wife problem solving and role sharing are important ingredients in dealing with these role conflicts effectively (Fogarty et al., 1971).

SCHEIN'S MODEL
OF THE ORGANIZATIONAL CAREER

To be complete, a model of career development in organizations needs to describe the career from two separate but related perspectives—(1) the career as described by the characteristics and experiences of the person who moves through the organization, and (2) the career as defined by the organization (which involves policies and expectations about what people will move into what positions and how quickly, in relation to the organization's overall staffing needs).

A useful approach to understanding this relationship between the individual and the organization "sides" of career development has been proposed by Schein (1971), who views the organization as a three-dimensional space like a cone (or, in some cases, a cylinder) in which the external boundary is essentially round and in which a core or inner center exists. This model is illustrated in Figure 3–4.

The three dimensions represent three types of moves a person may make in the organization:

Vertical—moving up or down represents changing one's rank or level in the organization.

Radial—moving more (or less) "inside" in the system, becoming more (or less) central, part of the "inner circle" acquiring increased (or decreased) influence in the system.

Circumferential—transferring laterally to a different function, program, or product in the organization.

There are three types of boundaries which correspond to each type of movement:

Hierarchical boundaries—these separate the hierarchical levels from each other.

Inclusion boundaries—these separate individuals or groups who differ in the degree of their centrality.

Functional or departmental boundaries—these separate departments, or different functional groupings from each other.

Boundaries can vary in terms of the number of each type that exist in an organization; their permeability (ease of movement from, for example, production assignments to sales); and the type of filtering process (i.e., criteria for deciding who is transferred or promoted). All of these factors have bearing upon both the functioning of the organization and the course of the person's career. Other critical factors are the size of the organization and its shape. If it is more like a cylinder than a cone, there are more promotion opportunities for lower-level people. A steep cone means more competition for promotions, while a flat cone means few promotions will occur, with probably less competition.

The individual is seen as having (1) basic personality characteristics, which are probably unchangeable, and (2) constructed social selves which represent the differences in the way people present themselves in different social situations. These social selves are largely a result of socialization and are subject to change through resocialization, such as that which occurs when a person joins an organization.

59

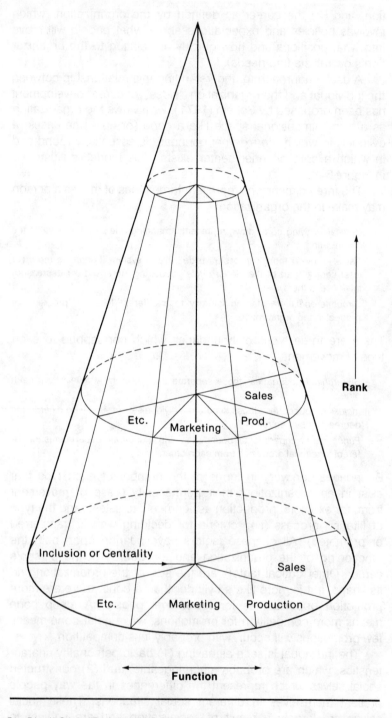

Rank

Sales

Etc.   Marketing   Prod.

Inclusion or Centrality

Sales

Etc.   Marketing   Production

Function

FIGURE 3–4
A
Three-
Dimensional
Model of an
Organization

From Edgar H. Schein, ''The Individual, the Organization, and the Career: A Conceptual Scheme,'' *Journal of Applied Behavioral Science,* 7 (1971).

These changes which occur in a person during the course of his career, as a result of adult socialization or acculturation, are changes in the nature and integration of his social selves. It is highly unlikely that he will change substantially in his basic character structure and his pattern of psychological defenses, but he may change drastically in his social selves in the sense of developing new attitudes and values, new competencies, new images of himself, and new ways of entering and conducting himself in social situations. As he faces new roles which bring new demands, it is from his repertory of attributes and skills that he constructs or reconstructs himself to meet these demands. . . .

When we think of organizations infringing on the private lives of their members, we think of a more extensive socialization process which involves changes in more stable social selves. Clearly it is possible for such "deeper" influence to occur, but in assessing depth of influence in any given individual-organization relationships, we must be careful not to overlook adaptional patterns which look like deep influence but are only the activation of and changes in relatively more labile social selves (Schein, 1971, pp. 308–309).

From the concepts and from the theory of *rites de passage,* Schein derives a series of stages for a person's career in a single organization, as shown in Table 3–2. It is important to note that the organizational career (the part of the person's career that is spent in one organization) is not the same as the person's career. Most organizational careers are much shorter than the person's total work career. For example, careers in many organizations are either "early-leaving" careers (e.g., airline stewardesses, professional athletes, prostitutes) or "late-entry" careers (judges, university administrators, physicians). Also, we may think of a person's experiences in any kind of system through which he moves in regularized status passages as constituting an organizational career. Thus, students go through their "college career"; the six-month volunteer has a "military career"; and Goffman has written a paper called "The Moral Career of the Mental Patient." In general, in those systems where people enter, move through, and leave in large numbers and through fairly regular transitions, the stages in the organizational career described in Table 3–2 can be found.

From these concepts, Schein develops five hypotheses about socialization and organizational careers:

Hypothesis 1. Organizational *socialization* will occur primarily in connection with the passage through hierarchical and inclusion boundaries; efforts at *education* and *training* will occur primarily in connection with the passage through functional boundaries. In both instances, the amount of effort at socialization and/or training will be at a maximum just prior to boundary passage, but will continue for some time after boundary passage.

The underlying assumption behind this hypothesis is that (1) the organization is most concerned about correct values and attitudes at the point where it is granting a member more authority and/or centrality, and (2) the individual is most vulnerable to socialization pressures just before and after boundary passage. . . .

61

Basic Stages and Transitions	Statuses or Positions	Psychological and Organizational Processes: Transactions between Individual and Organization
1. Pre-entry	Aspirant, applicant, rushee	Preparation, education, anticipatory socialization.
Entry (trans.)	Entrant, postulant, recruit	Recruitment, rushing, testing, screening, selection, acceptance ("hiding"); passage through external inclusion boundary; rites of entry; induction and orientation.
2. Basic training novitiate	Trainee, novice, pledge	Training, indoctrination, socialization, testing of the man by the organization, tentative acceptance into group.
Initiation, first vows (trans.)	Initiate, graduate	Passage through first inner inclusion boundary, acceptance as member and conferring of organizational status, rite of passage and acceptance.
3. First regular assignment	New member	First testing by the person of his own capacity to function; granting of real responsibility (playing for keeps); passage through functional boundary with assignment to specific job or department.
Substages 3a. Learning the job 3b. Maximum performance 3c. Becoming obsolete 3d. Learning new skills, etc.		Indoctrination and testing of person by immediate work group leading to acceptance or rejection; if accepted further education and socialization (learning the ropes); preparation for higher status through coaching, seeking visibility, finding sponsors, etc.
Promotion or leveling off (trans.)		Preparation, testing, passage through hierarchical boundary, rite of passage; may involve passage through functional boundary as well (rotation).
4. Second assignment Substages	Legitimate member (fully accepted)	Processes under no. 3 repeat.
5. Granting of tenure	Permanent member	Passage through another inclusion boundary.
Termination and exit (trans.)	Old-timer, senior citizen	Preparation for exit, cooling the mark out, rites of exit (testimonial dinners, etc.).
6. Post-exit	Alumnus emeritus retired	Granting of peripheral status.

TABLE 3-2
Basic Stages, Positions, and Processes in a Career within One Organization

From Edgar H. Schein, "The Individual, The Organization, and the Career: A Conceptual Scheme," *Journal of Applied and Behavioral Science,* 7 (1971).

Hypothesis 2. Innovation, or the individual's influence on the organization, will occur *in the middle* of a given stage of the career, at a maximum distance from boundary passage.

The person must be far enough from the earlier boundary passage to have learned the requirements of the new position and to have earned centrality in the new out-culture, yet must be far enough from his next boundary passage to be fully involved in the present job without being concerned about preparing himself for the future. Also, his power to induce change is lower if he is perceived as about preparing himself for the future. Also, his power to induce change is lower if he is perceived as about to leave (the lame duck phenomenon). . . .

Hypothesis 3. In general, the processes of socialization will be more prevalent in the early stages of a career and the process of innovation late in the

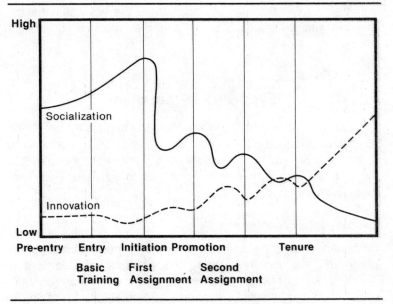

FIGURE 3–5
Socialization and
Innovation During
the Stages of the
Career within One
Organization

career, *but both processes occur* at all stages. [Hypotheses 1, 2, and 3 are illustrated in Figure 3–5.]

Hypothesis 4. Socialization or influence will involve primarily the more labile [changeable] social selves of the individual, while innovation will involve primarily the more stable social selves of the individual, provided the individual is not held captive in the organization. . . .

Hypothesis 5. A change in the more stable social selves as a result of socialization will occur only under conditions of coercive persuasion, i.e., where the individual cannot or does not psychologically feel free to leave the organization. Conditions under which coercive persuasion would operate can be produced by a variety of factors: a tight labor market . . . ; an employment contract which involves a legal or moral obligation to remain with the organization; a reward system which subtly but firmly entraps the individual through stock options, pension plans, deferred compensation plans, and the like (Ibid., pp. 314–16).*

Contrary to most views of organizational careers, which focus on the organization's influence on the person (socialization), Schein views the career as a two-way influence relationship between the person and the organization; the person influences the organization (innovates) as well as being influenced himself. This is a critical point to keep in mind, considering the great importance of organizational adaptation and renewal.

Given the importance of socialization and innovation, let us now examine in depth the two periods in the person's career when each process is most likely to be clearly shown. As we have seen, socialization is most likely to occur early—i.e., during the trial, stabilization, and advancement substages of the establishment stage. Innovation is more likely to occur in the later advancement

*See table source line in Table 3-2.

substage and in the maintenance stage. We will conclude this chapter with an examination of the pre-retirement or decline period.

THE EARLY CAREER YEARS:
BECOMING ESTABLISHED

Let us consider a person who has just completed her formal education and is about to enter the world of work. Perhaps the reader is at or near this career stage. It would probably be helpful for you to relate your own experiences to the issues we shall be considering here.

Training and Expectations

What happens during one's education and training for a profession? First, she acquires a body of specialized *knowledge* (e.g., business law, organizational psychology) and some technical *skills* (e.g., linear programming, accounting, marketing). According to research on law students, student teachers, and medical students, the person probably also acquires a certain set of professional *values and attitudes* imparted by her peers and faculty (Hall, 1968). Finally, she develops a set of aspirations and expectations about what she will encounter in her work. However, as we have seen, the career is a mutual-influence process, and the organization also holds certain expectations of the new recruit.

What are the expectations of the person as she enters her first job?* Perhaps most importantly, the young person usually expects *challenging work,* work that is meaningful and ability-stretching. She wants to be able to apply the knowledge and skills which it took so many difficult years to acquire. She wants to be able to test herself, to experience psychological success and a sense of competence. This need for competence, the need to have an impact on one's personal environment, is an important basic human need (White, 1959), and is especially important for young people.

Related to the desire for challenge is the need for *psychological involvement* in one's work. Young graduates tend to place increasing stress on intrinsic rather than extrinsic rewards for their work. Dissatisfaction with intrinsic work challenge seems to be especially strong in the first year of work, as we will see later. The return of many young people today to craft work is one reflection of this interest (and of the assumption that intrinsic involvement is hard to find in large organizations).

---

*The following discussion is based upon material from Hall, "Potential for Career Growth" (1971b), p. 20.

At this stage the young person also has a strong need for feedback in his performance. Without valid information on how you are performing, it is difficult to improve and grow. To take an extreme example, a person would not think of driving his car for even one block blindfolded, even if the block were straight and the car headed initially in the right direction. Outside factors, such as children playing, bumps in the road, other cars approaching, and unforeseen deviations from the original course all call for periodic braking, steering, and accelerating. Steering one's own career is far more complex than driving a car for one block, yet feedback is far more difficult to obtain.

Related to feedback, which often comes from the supervisor, is *coaching* and psychological support from the boss. There is a fine line between the supervisor's controlling and directing his subordinate's work and coaching him when he (the subordinate) requests it. Most supervisors either provide too much help or direction, and are perceived as overcontrolling; or they provide too little, letting the person "sink or swim."

A second aspect of the supervisor-subordinate relationship the young graduate probably desires is a collaborative authority relationship. He wants some say in making important decisions that affect his job and his career. He expects the boss to listen to his ideas and to apply them when they are good. He expects the boss to respect his opinion regardless of his age or seniority.

Finally, he expects a good salary and good promotion prospects. He expects to have these rewards contingent upon good performance on his part, but he does not want to see them blocked by factors beyond his control.

The following summary is based on surveys which have asked students what factors they consider in choosing their first jobs:

VERY IMPORTANT FACTORS

1. Opportunities for advancement
2. Social status and prestige—the feeling of doing something important and the recognition of this by others
3. Responsibility
4. Opportunities to use special aptitudes and educational background
5. Challenge and adventure
6. Opportunity to be creative and original
7. High salary

IMPORTANT, BUT LESS SO

1. A stable and secure future
2. A chance to exercise leadership
3. Opportunity to work with people rather than things
4. Freedom from supervision
5. Opportunity to be helpful to others (Schein, 1964)

So much for the individual's expectations. What does the organization expect to see in the new recruit?

Competence to get a job done—to identify the problem and see it through to solution.

Ability to accept organizational "realities"—to grasp those values which deal with non-technical factors, such as the need for stability and survival, recognition of group loyalties, informal power arrangements, office politics, and the like.

Ability to generate and sell ideas—to have in effect, a whole range of skills, such as

—ability to translate technical solutions into practical, understandable terms
—ability to diagnose and overcome sources of resistance to change
—patience and perseverance in gaining acceptance for new ideas
—ability to work through or around organizational "realities"
—interpersonal skills, or ability to influence others

Loyalty and commitment—to place the goals and values of the organization ahead of his own selfish motives and, if necessary, to sacrifice some parts of his personal life.

High personal integrity and strength—to stick to his own point of view without, however, being a deviant or a rebel (he must know how to compromise when necessary).

Capacity to grow—to learn from his experiences (mistakes are expected, but the repetition of mistakes is not tolerated); to demonstrate ability to take on increasing responsibility and maturity in the handling of interpersonal relationships (Schein, 1964, p. 70).

Reality Shock and Unused Potential

Now, what happens to these mutual expectations after the new recruit has been in the company for a year or so? Briefly, he experiences reality shock—the clash between high expectations and frustrating on-the-job experiences. A number of factors in the organization and in the recruit interact to produce a *syndrome of unused potential.* Let us consider the factors contributing to this syndrome.*

---

*The following discussion is based upon material from Hall, "Potential for Career Growth," pp. 21–24.

Low initial challenge. Results from a number of different studies (Berlew and Hall, 1966; Schein, 1967; Hall and Lawler, 1969; Campbell, 1968) show clearly that challenge is very important to the way a person's career develops. In a way, it is unfortunate that the word *challenge* has become a part of the rhetoric both for students criticizing organizations and for recruiters praising their organizations, because its overuse makes people lose track of just how important it really is. A study of young managers (Berlew and Hall, 1966) followed people at AT&T for five years and in another company for seven years. Performance was evaluated by salary scale and ratings from supervisors and other people, mainly in personnel, who were in a position to evaluate them.

The more challenging a person's job was in his first year with the organization, the more effective and successful he was even five or seven years later.

Unfortunately, the amount of challenge in initial jobs in most organizations is invariably low, despite the fact that it is very important. In a study of R&D organizations, there were only two companies out of twenty-two interviewed in which people described their first jobs as being moderately high or high on challenge (Hall and Lawler, 1969). There was only one company that had a conscious policy of making the first assignments difficult. Most companies felt that they should bring the person along slowly, starting him off on an easy project and cautiously adding more challenge only as the recruit proved his ability at each stage of escalation. This is a strategy to measure the person's ability by approaching it from below rather than by stretching it through high work goals and high standards of excellence!

A traditional problem is the expensive training which is invested in new employees before they can earn their pay. Research indicates that increased challenge and less formal training would increase the utilization of new people from the very beginning, benefiting both the individual and the organization (Hall and Lawler, 1969).

Another factor found to be related to performance was pressure on the person to do high-quality work and to assume a degree of financial responsibility in his work (Hall and Lawler, 1969). In the R&D setting this pressure was often associated with accepting responsibility, getting new projects for the organization, and obtaining outside funding for the work. This may have required direct contact with customers rather than being done through a supervisor. Organizations in which people felt personal pressure for quality work and attaining the financial goals of the organization were found to be highly effective. But again, we rarely found evidence of quality pressure or evidence of professional people being given financial responsibility in their work.

67

Low self-actualization satisfaction. A further problem was that the most important need for the job recruit specializing in research—self-actualization—was the least satisfied (Hall and Lawler, 1969). Further, we found that the longer researchers worked for an organization, the less important self-fulfillment was to them and the more important security was. Increasing tenure was also related to three significant changes in self-image: the people reported themselves as being less active, less strong, and less independent as tenure increased. There is an intriguing theory (Argyris, 1957) that predicts just this kind of human decay with increasing length of service in organizations. Because of the conflict between the needs of growing individuals and the requirements for organizations for tight control and uniformity, people become less concerned about their own growth and they become less independent, less strong, and less active as they spend more time in the organization.

Vanishing performance appraisal. Another finding (Hall and Lawler, 1969) that surprised the R&D managers in our feedback session with them concerned a communications gap—a disagreement between what the managers were doing and what their subordinates said the managers were doing. We asked everyone if the organization had a regular performance appraisal system and, if so, if the results were discussed with the man appraised. In most of the organizations, the directors said, "Sure, we do it every six months."

We talked to the employees we were studying. Not only did they generally report that the appraisals did not take place, but we even had to explain to some what a performance appraisal system was!

Because the appraisal system seemed to be there when we talked to the managers and not there when we talked to the employees, we called it the "vanishing performance appraisal." There was little feedback on how people were performing. We know that feedback is important for the learning and self-correction of any kind of system, and this resource was being lost to these R&D systems.

Unrealistically high aspirations. Another aspect of the syndrome of unused potential was a great sense on the part of the recent graduates that their important skills and abilities were not being used. New graduates possess high levels of training when they begin work. Indeed, the definition of education is to bring students to the frontiers of knowledge, the very latest techniques and theories. The college or university sends young men and women back into the society with this new knowledge. In this sense, new graduates are societal change agents. They come into the organization with new techniques, and they want to apply them. They find this difficult—first, because they lack the skills of applying what they know and second, because the organizations tend to resist innovation. This difficulty is compounded by the fact that people coming out of college usually have an unrealistically high aspiration level about the extent to which they are going to be using their new skills.

A man who had just finished his first year at the Harvard Business School exemplified this problem. He seriously hoped to begin his career as a vice-president of finance for a medium-sized organization. He was convinced that he had the ability to perform the job. Such an attitude on the part of a person just entering the job market creates anger on the part of superiors; and it also creates a certain amount of threat (more on this in a moment). In fact, however, developing this degree of confidence in students is one of the main socializing functions of many business schools.

Inability to create challenge.　Another problem is that the new recruit really does not know how to create his own challenge in a job. People who have been well-educated are accustomed to being given projects and challenging work. But they do not know how to take an unstructured and undefined situation and find something important in it, thereby defining the job for themselves. There is a contradiction—they want challenge and independence, but they don't know how to find these things by themselves. Research has shown that people tend to be rather passive about even major career decisions—the type of organizations they work for, whether or not to change jobs, and the type of jobs they accept (Roe and Baruch, 1967). Very often they respond to external challenge, demands, or changes more than they do to their own career blueprint—if they have one. Educational institutions are simply not teaching the student how to chart his own course and then follow it.

Sources of threat.　As we have mentioned, young graduates often threaten their superiors (Schein, 1968a); this threat is probably a major contributor to the syndrome of unused potential. There are different reasons why superiors may be threatened by a new person. For one, training programs are often defined so that the new recruit is seen as someone special—a "bright young person." However, the supervisor may be in a terminal position. He may have worked all his life to reach this position; now he may be confronted with a "young kid" who may soon be promoted *above* that same position.

Another cause for threat is that new people, coming in right out of college, may know more about a special area than the superior does. This may apply more in technical work than in general management. This threat is compounded when the superior has had to spend a great deal of time doing administrative work which kept him from upgrading his technical knowledge.

High starting salaries cause problems, too. The new employee **69** today makes far more than the boss did when he started his career; in fact, the new man's salary probably comes painfully close to what the boss is making right now. Personal styles are also different—the young recruit is probably more likely to rock the boat, make waves, and create pressure for change. All these personal threats created by young people can contribute to the syndrome of unused potential and in turn make later job experiences less satisfying.

Negative effect.   The overall result of this syndrome is that in the early career years there may be great changes in self-image, attitudes, aspirations, and motivation—all generally in a negative direction. The person is less optimistic about how he is going to succeed with the organization (Bray, Campbell, and Grant, 1974).

He sees himself as having less impact on the organization, and his values come to conform more to those of the organization. Schein's research (1967) shows how the values of business students tend to move toward those of authority figures in whatever system they join. Although the values of students in an MBA program tend to move toward those of the faculty and, interestingly, away from those of businessmen, when the career begins on the job, values move back again toward those of the managers and away from those of the faculty. Thus, with more integration into the organization, there is a certain amount of change toward organizational values. Educational institutions must become aware of their obligation to prepare students for such eventualities. A knowledge of the situations they will meet, the threats they may cause to managers, would be of great help in enabling new recruits to maintain their high aspirations, high values, high creativity. (More on solutions to these initial job problems will be presented later in this chapter and in Chapters 6 and 7.)

Problems with the recruit.   Not all the problems contributing to this unused potential syndrome lie with the supervisor or the organization. Many can be tied directly to specific shortcomings in the job performance of the new employee.

Schein found that many managers develop the following stereotype of the recent college graduate:

1. He is *overambitious* and *unrealistic* in his expectations.
2. He is too theoretical and naive to be given a challenging initial assignment; he must first be educated and "broken in."
3. He is too *immature* and *inexperienced* to be given much responsibility.
4. He is too *security-conscious,* unwilling to take risks.
5. He is *unskilled in communication.* He fails to see the difference between having a good idea and the process of selling it (Schein, 1964).

Of course, this stereotype may have some validity, depending upon the person. But the dilemma for the company and the new recruit is that if a manager holds this stereotype and trains new recruits in accordance with these assumptions, the new employee would never have an opportunity to prove the stereotype wrong. Thus, the stereotype can become a negative self-fulfilling prophecy, just as a challenging first assignment can be a positive one.

Attempts to influence the organization.   Individuals differ in the way they respond to these socialization forces in the first job. There are generally three categories of response (Schein, 1968b):

1. *Rebellion.* In this extreme form of reaction, the person rejects all of the organization's norms and values. She puts such a stress on her own individuality that she makes it very difficult for herself to remain in the organization. She is generally either successful in producing change, or she is dismissed!
2. *Creative individualism.* This is a more moderate reaction to the organization, in which the person accepts the most important or "pivotal" norms and values of the organization but rejects many of the less critical ones (such as norms about dress, lifestyle, or vocabulary). This is a difficult stance to maintain, but it often is the most successful form of adaptation for both the person and the organization, resulting in healthy organizational change and personal satisfaction.
3. *Conformity.* In this form of response, the person accepts uncritically *all* norms and values of the organization, pivotal and peripheral. In such a situation, the person is oversocialized and may have little creativity or initiative to offer the organization. His behavior will be quite dependable and predictable, however, he will generally play it safe and "not make waves."

Training

Now that we have seen something of the experiences and problems encountered by the new recruit during the establishment stage of his career, let us turn to the various strategies of development which are often employed to deal with these problems.

There are six common strategies which companies use to develop their new employees (Schein, 1964). First, the *sink or swim* approach involves leaving the person on his own with a fairly responsible, but unclear job assignment, with little guidance or support from the boss. The recruit is expected to define the task for himself and to work out his own solutions. Whether this approach succeeds depends upon how the organization handles success and failure:

Is he not punished for failure?
Is he given clear feedback on the degree of success or failure he attained?
Is he given clear feedback on why he succeeded or failed?
If he has failed, is he helped to see what should be done about it?

If the answer to these questions is affirmative, this strategy is more likely to be effective.   **71**

In the second approach, the *upending experience,* the person is given an assignment which he is virtually sure to fail. This leaves him depressed and chastised; he is "unfrozen" or ready to learn from his supervisor or trainer. In the third strategy, *on-the-job training,* the person is given regular assignments, perhaps especially challenging ones, with someone more experienced available to coach and support him when necessary. The success of this approach depends upon the quality of the job, the degree of learning expected, and the degree and quality of the coaching available.

The fourth strategy is *working while training.* Here the person is assigned to a full-time training program, but is rotated through short-term job assignments. Between assignments he may spend all his time on special training experiences. Training generally lasts from three to twelve months, after which the person is assigned permanently to a department. Working while training is a more formal, structured program than on-the-job training. Like on-the-job training, this approach depends upon the quality of the jobs and of the people the trainee works with. Because of the number and short duration of the job assignments, however, it is less likely that the person will feel greatly challenged by and involved in his work. Therefore, such programs are less likely to be effective means of developing successful managers.

The fifth approach, *full-time training,* is similar to on-the-job training. Here, however, the training department creates the job assignments (i.e., they are not "real" jobs and they are of little organizational consequence). Often, trainees are assigned to particular locations mainly to observe activities there. The idea of these programs is for the person to get a broad view of the organization, but they are often experienced by trainees as "make-work" or "Mickey Mouse" jobs.

The sixth approach is what Schein calls *integrative strategies,* in which each person's performance is first evaluated on the job, after which he is given training based on his needs and abilities. Schein (1964) describes an approach used at AT&T which employs three methods—sink or swim, training while working, and full-time training:

> When the man first reports for work, he is assigned to a regular supervisor and given regular work assignments for a period of a year. The supervisors who will have college graduates assigned them are given a special training program to help them deal realistically with the needs and capacities of the newcomers. All the new men in the program are evaluated on the basis of their job performance, and those with the greatest potential are then sent to a summer-long full-time training program at a university (p. 72).

In addition to the management-development strategies outlined above, two others can be identified. One is the *cooperative program.* This is an agreement between a university and various companies that a given person will alternate between being a full-time employee for one term or semester and a full-time student for the following term. Here the student acts as a kind of intern, applying his formal education to a real job as he acquires it, and using his job experience to facilitate his academic learning. Such programs give a realistic view of the work world to the person while he is still in school. It also helps him understand better what he needs to know to be well-prepared for work while he is still a student. Reactions to such programs have generally been quite positive, although they do call for a certain amount of extra administrative and coordinating work on the part of the company and the college.

The final form of management development strategy to be discussed here concerns the *assessment center,* a means of identifying managerial potential and predicting success (Bray, Campbell, and Grant, 1974). It can also be used as a basis of giving feedback to the participant and giving him training experiences. The basic idea is for a group of trainees to spend approximately three days together off-site, going through multiple methods of gathering diagnostic data: personality tests, tests of skills and abilities, and situational tests, simulations, and exercises.

An added benefit of assessment centers is the acquisition of new skills by the assessors, who are generally line or staff managers familiar with the positions for which the participants are being trained. At least 100 businesses and some government agencies now employ assessment centers, according to Golembiewski (1972), who lists five attractions and qualifications of this method:

1. The growing scale of the assessment problem has forced experimentation with new approaches.
2. Traditional measures of assessment have left much to be desired.
3. Several validation studies report the effectiveness of assessment approach for identifying organizational winners and losers.
4. The typical assessment-center design seems to deal with performance-relevant factors, although care is necessary to assure that its exercises and simulations do in fact elicit behaviors, skills, and attitudes appropriate to the target job or organization level. In particular, the assessment center is a method of employing performance-related criteria for assessing minority and female employees.
5. The use of assessor panels (e.g., line managers) from within the company has variously aided acceptance of the assessment-center concept, especially via greater understanding of its strengths and weaknesses.

TOWARD MORE EFFECTIVE EARLY CAREER DEVELOPMENT

One way to promote management development is to use career-development programs, such as those described above, in which the focus is on the individual and his or her training. One **73** of the problems we have seen with training programs is that very often they enable a person to acquire impressive new skills and attitudes only to return to a work environment that is not ready for these skills and, in fact, may be hostile to such changes. Organizational researchers now recognize that changes must be made in the work environment, in the rewards and opportunities it provides, if changes in persons are to continue and be productive.

Unfortunately, many top executives and personnel managers either have not received this message or find it difficult to implement. The fact is that much of the career-development activity in industry and government is still focused on the person (sending him off somewhere for three days or two weeks, putting him "through" a prepackaged program) rather than on the environment in which he works. In this section we shall consider how an organization might approach management development not through any new, extensive programs requiring expensive consultants, training sites, and time away from the job, but through the analysis and alteration of what is already there—the new recruit, his job, his supervisor, his peer group, and the organizational information system.* By working with what is already present, the intent is to show how feasible it would be to make changes that in sum could have tremendous impact.

What kind of changes might facilitate early career development? Probably the very first would be changes in schools and jobs. How does one change schools and jobs to get people into a positive cycle?

The Educational System

The first place to correct many of the problems in the first job is in the educational system—high school, college, or professional school. First, students need more information about occupations and jobs. Second, the information they get should be more realistic—positive and negative. Third, students of all types should receive more training in human relations in work settings. They need to realize that the technical side of their work is only part of their job; they need to learn how to "sell" their technical ideas and solutions to skeptical bosses, colleagues, and clients. They need to learn how to overcome resistance to change, how to diagnose and work around problems occasionally, rather than head-on.

One way to create these changes in schools and colleges is to introduce courses that deal with interpersonal and group relations. Most of our curricula could use real "beefing up" on

74 *The following discussion is from Hall, "Potential for Career Growth," pp. 26–29.

the social aspects of work. Co-operative programs, internships, required work leaves, and field projects are other ways of getting the student into the real world. Many students "step out" for a year or two on their own and then return to finish their degrees, which is another way to integrate school and work.

Another strategy is to get the faculty more exposed to the real world. This could be in the form of research, consulting, or sabbaticals in industry. Hiring executives or professionals in industry as visiting faculty on *their* leaves of absence is another way of bringing more experience into the classroom.

The First Assignment

The first step would be to analyze the initial jobs that new people are given in the organization. What happens to a young person when he walks in the door? If that first year is a critical period in which he is especially susceptible to learning new attitudes, what is happening to him during that important time? Is he just absorbing information and not really accomplishing important objectives? Is that time merely an investment that the company feels required to make in him? Or is it a time when the company really expects to challenge him? Does the company have some concrete goals for him to reach?

The ironic fact seems to be that organizations look at the first year as a necessary evil: an investment they have to make in the person until they can assign him an important project where he can make a valuable contribution. At the same time, the employee is impatient for something that has meaning and challenge.

Both the organization and the individual want and need the new person to have challenge and good performance, but for understandable reasons both are frustrated. It is not easy to make jobs more challenging when one gets down to the specifics of the task. It may mean hiring fewer people so the organization can do a better job on the assignments that they are given. One organization found that its turnover was so high that it had to hire 120 men each year in order to have 20 at the end of the year. So it took a gamble and figured that perhaps this attrition was because the first-year jobs were so unchallenging. The next year it hired 30 people and worked hard on upgrading first-year jobs. At the end of the year 25 people were employed and giving far better first-year performances.

Another recommendation related to early challenge is the elimination of job-rotating training programs. The first job ought to be a realistic, permanent assignment and not one seen as special or part of a training program. This generates job success rather than a succession of jobs. Moving through different short-term jobs means men are merely observers of different parts of **75** the organization rather than fully functioning participants. The term "rotation" literally means "going around in circles." Maybe that is one reason why young employees' self-perceptions tend to go down in the first year. The young person may feel that he is not doing anything really worthwhile, that he is just being paid to sit around and observe. If he stays, this is going to have an adverse effect on his self-image—he is being paid a lot for doing little.

The Supervisor

Another consideration is the superior to whom a new man is assigned. Probably the boss has the greatest impact on the definition of a job. Therefore, if management is going to redesign jobs, it must also redesign bosses or train them to deal with a new employee.

This was another realization of the company that tried upgrading first-year jobs. It learned in the first year that it had to work with the bosses as well as new recruits. In the second year it put the supervisors through a long training program before new people came into the organization. Then, as part of the training program for the new people, the company also involved the superiors, so that each recruit and his boss went through the program as a team.

This type of learning helps a superior develop a sense of what we call *supportive autonomy* (Hall and Schneider, 1973), so he can tread the fine line between allowing a man independence (i.e., sink or swim) on the one hand, and providing assistance with excessive control, on the other. The combination of autonomy and the supervisor's availability and willingness to work as a coach when the young person wants help may be the best combination for learning (Hall and Schneider, 1973; Pelz and Andrews, 1966).

Performance Review

Supervisors should also learn how to provide good performance reviews. If the new employee is left on his own to determine his performance, his conclusion may be based on highly distorted information. It is far better to have the feedback come through formal channels and get it straight rather than get it through indirect and unreliable means, such as the supervisors' manner of saying hello on a certain morning.

An important need for supervisors in this area is to develop skills in confronting interpersonal problems. If the new person is given autonomy, and if the supervisor sees himself as a bit more of a helper than he may have originally, this suggests that some new problems may arise. The new man is going to make mistakes, and he and his supervisor are going to have to learn how to get **76** through these problems and conflicts as a pair. Also, the supervisor has to learn to put on pressure at the appropriate times, when to exercise authority, and when to get tough. It is not only a matter of learning new values and attitudes about supervisory style, it is also a matter of translating these into specific interpersonal skills and knowing how to apply them at various times.

One way of achieving some of the necessary confrontation and problem-solving skills would be through a planned, structured exercise. A group of new employees could meet and draw up a statement describing their attitudes toward the organization, toward their supervisors, and toward their careers. Their supervisors would also meet as a group and draft a similar statement covering their attitudes toward the new men and their ideas of what the views of the new recruit are. These statements would then be used in diagnosing important career and organizational problems. The structured process and the group-level focus may be less threatening than unstructured or one-to-one encounters may be in confronting problems and working through to solutions.

The Recruit and His Goals: Career Planning

A third area of change concerns the organization's long-term plans for the new recruit. Perhaps most important would be the creation of a semi-annual work planning and review program, designed after the work of McGregor (1960) and the General Electric Company.

The purpose of such a program would be to establish collaborative goal-settings and more self-directed careers. However, the organization and the individual must be aware of and avoid the tendency for such programs to "vanish" in the sense we have used before. Such a program should allow for individual differences in administrative and interpersonal skills, which have been found to be related to career success (Campbell, 1968). Its focus should be on developing these skills in terms of specific day-to-day behaviors which can be measured and changed by the person and his supervisor.

Another useful exercise would be for the new recruit and his supervisor to examine the company's goals (or the department's or work group's goals) in relation to the recruit's personal goals and desires. One issue would be the attractiveness or "valence" of the organization's goals to the recruit. Can he identify with them? Are they important to him? How can they be made more important? The other issue is their instrumentality. Does he see his efforts toward the organization's goals as also leading to his own satisfactions? If not, how could this connection be better established?

The organization must be aware of the emotional development taking place in the recruit in his early career years. Organizations, like universities, have tended to see personal growth as being **77**

independent of or irrelevant to the "really important" career development changes—new skills, abilities, and knowledge. The bulk
of a person's career changes, however, are in the motivational
and attitudinal area (Campbell, 1968). Because motivation and
attitudes are related to performance and success (Hall, 1971a),
it is clear that organizations should see these personal changes
as relevant to their interests. In particular, one never knows when,
how, and what attitudes may be acquired by a new man. The
change may result as much from the climate of the organization
as from the work itself. Much personal stress may result from
the need to achieve and the relative lack of security in the first
year with a new organization. It would also be useful to be alert
for turning points which may help mark important career transitions—the first performance appraisal, the first completed project,
or a particular transfer or promotion. Certain events may have
symbolic value which make them far more important to the recruit
than the organization or the supervisor may realize, and it is important to attempt to see the recruit's career as it appears to him.

Family Changes

Along with recognizing the career as emotional change and identity development, it is also important to recognize the impact of
another important contributor to these changes—the family. Family
changes, such as marriage, children, relocation, or the death of
a relative, often have profound effects on a person's identity, attitudes, and motivation. If these family changes happen to be congruent with career changes, the mutually reinforcing effects could
be far more potent than the sum of the separate influences. An
example of congruent family and career effects might be the way
marriage and a significant promotion could contribute both to
increased career involvement and personal responsibility. On the
other hand, a problem in a critical family transition could greatly
disrupt a person's adjustment to an important career change. An
example here might be in-law problems in the new marriage and
problems with the supervisor in the recent promotion; both of
these might conceivably center on the issue of competence in
relationships with older people or authority figures. The combination of similar problems around the same issues in two central
areas of one's life could greatly compound any feeling of incompe-
tence or low esteem which might result from either problem separately. This interaction of family and career issues is discussed
in White (1952), Levinson et al. (1974), and Cox (1970).

The Organization Reward Structure

The fourth arena for facilitating career development concerns
78 characteristics of the organization itself. One important activity

would be the examination of the organization's reward structure in relation to the new recruit's path-goal profiles. Is the company using rewards that are valued by the new recruit? Also, does the recruit know what kind of behavior leads to these rewards? An example of a mismatch here occurred in the R&D labs studied. Here the most common rewards were money (pay raises); however, the scientists did not really understand what they had to do to get a pay raise. Furthermore, there was evidence that intrinsic satisfactions, such as greater challenge or autonomy, meant more to them than money. As a result the companies were trapped in an upward spiral of salaries with little apparent change in employee satisfaction (Hall and Lawler, 1969). Therefore companies should: (1) attempt to design jobs so that efforts toward company goals also contribute to satisfying employees' needs; and (2) clarify the organization's reward structure so that executives and lower-level employees are in agreement about the kind of performance that is expected and rewarded. Again, an examination of these issues through a structured exercise involving senior managers and recent graduates would probably be fruitful. Management by objectives (MBO) is another possible way to integrate the goals of the new employee with those of the organization.

Even before the recruit is hired, these organizational expectations should be communicated as well as possible to him, clearly and realistically. College students have become surprisingly accurate in diagnosing inflated or distorted recruiting information, and it usually backfires. This is especially important in view of the great sensitivity and value for openness found in today's students. Indeed, according to Schein (1968a), students report that the areas companies stress the most in their recruiting literature are often those about which they are most defensive; therefore, what are promoted as their strongest points often betray their weakest. For example, if a recruiter stresses all the freedom you will have in his organization, the reality may be that there are numerous rules and restrictions! In the insurance industry, an experiment revealed that recruiting information stressing both the pros and cons of selling life insurance attracted just as many new agents and resulted in lower turnover among the new employees and a concomitant reduction in training costs (LIAMA, 1966). A similar experiment was successful in reducing dissatisfaction and turnover for telephone operators (Wanous, 1973). Therefore to get and retain good people, "tell it like it is."

Impact of Peer Group

Another part of the individual's organizational environment with high potential for career impact is his employee peer group. Most of the new member's informal learning is communicated by this **79** group (Becker, Geer, Hughes, and Strauss, 1961; Becker, Geer and Strauss, 1969; Hall, 1969). The peer group can also provide important emotional support, coaching, and identification models to help the new recruit manage identity changes, difficult problems, and critical turning points (Hall, 1969; Schein, 1968b). Peer-group interaction is also associated with reduced turnover (Evan, 1963).

The peer group is often the employee's main emotional link to the organization; often he comes to value the organization only because of his regard for his peers. For example, much of the zeal and bravery of Marine troops is based on their devotion to their buddies rather than a general commitment to Marine Corps values (Stouffer, Suchman, DeVinney, Star, and Williams, 1949). Therefore, an organization would do well to examine the nature of work-group interaction patterns, norms, and values.

If these norms and values run counter to the organization's goals, a serious problem may exist, and an organizational diagnosis might be conducted to determine the probable reasons. If the work-group culture is supportive (or perhaps neutral) in relation to organizational goals, it would be useful to create structures that would encourage work-related peer interaction—such as weekly problem-solving sessions, an informal morning coffee break, team projects, or older "coaches" assigned to new men.

The important point here is that because the peer group is a potent force, there is a certain amount of risk attached to utilizing it. A group of employees can very accurately diagnose a "poor" organizational climate and can effectively transmit this awareness and quota-restricting pressures to new members. Thus, the peer group can be either strongly functional or strongly dysfunctional for organizational identification.

MID-CAREER MAINTENANCE AND RE-EXAMINATION*

Once a person has become established in his or her career, the next stage, from the forties to retirement, is, as we have seen earlier, often called a maintenance period. In contrast to the fierce strivings and achievements of the trial and establishment periods, the maintenance period is more like a plateau; holding your own, maintaining what has already been achieved. As Super says, it is not a time for breaking new ground.

Does this maintenance stage sound like a fairly tranquil period, one of reaping the fruits of earlier labors and achievements? There is a growing body of evidence that the transition into this stage

---

*A more detailed discussion of the nature of and possible cures for mid-career stress is found in Stoner et al. (1974).

is not at all smooth in many cases; furthermore, for many people this is a period for embarking on a new career rather than maintaining the old one. In many ways it appears that the transition into mid-career is perhaps even more stressful than the move from the educational institution in early career years.

Elliott Jacques (1965), in a classic paper, has referred to this stage as the *mid-life crisis*. He noted that 37 seemed to be a critical age in the lives of creative artists. In a random sample of 310 great painters, composers, poets, writers, and sculptors, Jacques found a sudden surge in the death rate between 35 and 39, far above the normal rate. Then he found a drop in the death rate between 40 and 44, followed by a return to the normal rate. It appeared that the greater the artists' genius, the more pronounced was the peak in death rate. These figures are compatible with the peaks found in the scientific contributions of scientists in the late thirties and early forties (Lehman, 1953; Pelz and Andrews, 1966). For scientists, the peaking is also more pronounced for more major achievements, and the time of the peaking later in life for less abstract fields. This would indicate that the peak performance/crisis would come for managers and other more applied professionals in the forties rather than the thirties.

Later research has found that mid-career changes are not restricted to great artistic and scientific geniuses. It is becoming clear that as people move into the maintenance stage of their careers, they experience a variety of physiological, attitudinal, occupational, and family changes:

Awareness of advancing age and awareness of death. At 40, many people report the sudden feeling that "life is half over," that they now have as much or more time behind them than ahead of them. They are now symbolically "middle-aged." Time now feels like a scarcer resource.

Awareness of physical aging. The person becomes aware that his endurance in sports is decreasing, while his recovery time is increasing. Aches and pains become more frequent, and physical performance (e.g., reaction time, running speed) drops off. One review of the literature on aging (Kutner, 1971) cites a depressing list of physical changes which occur in the forties and fifties:

—Change in pituitary secretions, so that body fat doubles
—Decline in metabolic rate
—Decline in secretion of dominant sex hormones, which allows opposite-sexed hormones to have more influence
—Decreased energy: lungs have less capacity and heart pumps less blood
—Decrease in muscle tone
—Rapid increase in disability and invalidism

—Arteries harden, blood pressure increases, and coronary problems occur

—Visual efficiency declines rapidly after 40

—Hearing gradually diminishes, starting with higher frequencies

—Skin loses its elasticity, becomes coarser, shows wrinkling; results in "flabby skin hanging in loose folds"

—Skin shows discoloration (pale or yellow), dark circles appear under eyes, varicose veins appear

—Men's hairlines recede, stiff hair appears in nose and ears, women develop more facial hair and men less

—Weight shifts downward from chest to abdomen, so torso looks pear-shaped. (As a wag once said, "Middle age is like the stock exchange in bad times—it's all still there, but lower.")

—Following ejaculation, it takes a 40-year-old man two days to regenerate a full sperm count, while it takes a 15-year-old boy half an hour.

The person knows how many of his career goals he has or will attain. By the time a person reaches his forties in a managerial or professional career, he has a pretty good idea of how far he will advance—he knows if he is going to become a vice-president or not. If he has not attained his important goals, he needs to adjust his level of aspiration or find a new field of work. Even in mid-career, managers find themselves confronted with unrealistic expectations regarding promotions and career advancement (Buchanan, 1974). Ironically, the stress may be greater if he has achieved his career goals; then he may wonder, in the words of a recent popular song, "Is that all there is?" In either case, the goals that have formerly guided the person's work life are no longer operative. Even Catholic priests aren't immune to this mid-career letdown (Hall and Schneider, 1973.)

There is a search for new life goals. With the former goals either achieved or unattainable, and with time seeming suddenly short, the person may begin to search for new values, goals, and meaning in life. There is more concern to produce something lasting and worthwhile. Often people make complete breaks with their old lives and careers and embark on totally different courses. One marriage counselor quoted a statement often heard among his colleagues: "Between the ages of 40 and 50, a man changes jobs or changes wives." The result of this search could be, of course, a reaffirmation of one's present goals.

There is a marked change in family relationships. Children are now teenagers, in need of authority figures to rebel against. The person's spouse is not quite the dashing young thing he or she was twenty years ago, physically or emotionally. People's values, needs, and interests change as they mature, and what was a good match in 1955 may have become a mismatch. Women in general have experienced greater freedom as a result of the women's movement, and this can also put strain on the marriage contract. The apparent weakening of these family bonds may cause the person to ask what life is all about.

There is a change in work relationships. The person is no longer a "bright young man/woman" on the way up. He or she may now have advanced to a position of influence, with authority over younger people who are competing for promotion and perhaps for the person's job. These young subordinates may be questioning the person's authority, much like the kids are at home. Not only does this make a person feel older, but it also leads one to question occasionally one's own competence and purpose.

There is a growing sense of obsolescence. The bright young subordinates and their more recent technical knowledge and skills may present a sharp contrast with the middle-aged manager, who may not have learned much of today's technology and has perhaps forgotten a great deal of what he did learn. With all the increased administrative demands on the person in mid-career, he has little opportunity to bring himself up to date. This contributes to the gnawing anxiety that someday he will be "found out." As Satchel Paige said, "Never look back; someone might be gaining on you."

Kaufman (1974), in an impressive review of the literature, defines obsolescence as "the degree to which organization professionals lack the up-to-date knowledge or skills necessary to maintain effective performance in either their current or future work roles (p. 23). Or, as someone described the condition recently, "There's been an alarming increase recently in the number of things I know nothing about." Several surveys indicate that obsolescence is seen as a serious problem for technical professionals (as indicated by 9 out of 10 respondents, on the average), and less of a problem for managers (rated a problem by anywhere from 38 percent [computer marketing managers] to 86 percent [engineering managers] of the respondents).

The person feels less mobile and attractive in the job market and therefore more concerned about security. Many companies are reluctant to lure a manager in his forties or older for various reasons—they feel he is untrainable, obsolete, has too little time left, is too expensive, etc. Furthermore, in the recent recessions, many firms found they could make great savings by cutting back in their middle-management ranks. Therefore, the middle manager may feel more dependent upon (or perhaps trapped in) his present organization.

Referring back to Erikson's model of life stages, in theory the mid-career person should be in the generativity stage, concerned about what he is producing of lasting value for future **83** generations. The changes reported above indicate that this is the case for many people in mid-life. They are experiencing a *generativity crisis,* directly analogous to the identity crisis experienced by many adolescents. Although the mid-life phenomenon may appear to be an identity crisis, with concerns about goals and questions like "Where am I headed?" we can see that it has more to do with leaving one's mark on future generations, as well as an awareness of limited time.

One way all these problems show up is in physical indexes of health. One study indicated a sharp rise in specific symptoms, such as extreme fatigue, chest pains, and indigestion, in young executives on their way into top management. Only one-third of these symptoms among managers aged 31 to 40 could be linked to organic causes (Levinson, 1969). It appears instead that many of the symptoms are caused by depression associated with mid-career changes.

Changes in the Work Environment

What are some of the changes in the work environment which contribute to the mid-life crisis? Harry Levinson cites seven factors:

1. *Increasing contraction of the hard-work period.* The average age at which people become company presidents is decreasing, while people start their careers later owing to increased training (e.g., MBA programs). Therefore people have less time to "make it."
2. *Inseparability of life and career patterns.* For many young professionals, their careers are their lives, and they live on a self-made time schedule. Time spent in each level is critical, and each passing year is a milepost.
3. *Continuous threat of defeat.* With the pressures, competition, and need for success so intense, the thought of defeat (psychological failure) can be devastating.
4. *Increase in dependency.* To remain successfully competitive, the professional, especially the technical specialist, must come to depend increasingly upon subordinates and support personnel. However, he may not fully understand the data, the subordinate, or the process by which the data were generated. "He is therefore often left to shudder at the specter of catastrophe beyond his control."
5. *Denial of feelings.* The executive career involves self-demand, self-sacrifice, guilt about making decisions affecting others' decisions and anger at himself and the organization for the other life goals he must sacrifice. He often cannot allow himself to get close to superiors, subordinates, or peers (competitors). Therefore, he must repress his feelings, which drains energy.
6. *Constant state of defensiveness.* As in the child's game, "King of the Hill," the person is busy either fighting his way to the top or defending it. There is no respite, which means being constantly in a state of emergency, a very stressful condition.
7. *Shift in prime-of-life concept.* Because society now values youth more than in the past, the attainment of success is partially offset by the loss of youth. "Since only rarely can one have youth and achievement at the same time, there is something anticlimatic about middle-age success" (1969, pp. 52–53).

HOW TO COPE WITH MID-CAREER STRESS

The preceding ideas sound sort of gloomy for the poor, decaying 40-year-old, don't they? One bright spot is our knowledge that having realistic expectations about impending crises and transitions can actually ease the stress and pain. This is true as much for students embarking on their first jobs as for the hospital patients about to undergo surgery. Therefore, if the reader does some thinking about these mid-life changes and prepares for them, this can be one effective way to cope.

Training for people in mid-career should give them an exposure to new skills and ideas, but only enough to make them appreciate how they can be used. By this time, they are often managers of people with these skills, not specialists themselves. This exposure should help remove some of the personal threat and anxiety that has been caused by their lack of knowledge.

More importantly, the person should learn more about the processes of mid-career change to help understand what is going on inside him. He should be encouraged to face up to feelings of restlessness and insecurity, to re-examine his values and life goals, and to set new ones or recommit himself to old ones. Life planning and career planning exercises have been devised which are extremely helpful for people in mid-career. In fact, an organization, Forty-Plus, provides professional assistance on mid-career processes to individuals and organizations on precisely these problems.

The mid-career employee should also be trained to help develop younger employees in the service of his own growth as well as the younger person's. By working closely with younger people, he keeps himself up-to-date, fresh, and energetic. Because he has enough experience to identify more with the organization and to be more aware of the "big picture" he is also in an ideal position to serve as a link between the young person and the rest of the organization. One of the psychological needs of middle age is to build something lasting, something that will be a permanent contribution to one's organization or profession. The development of a future generation of leaders could be a significant lasting and highly satisfying contribution. By pooling the resources of its young and middle-aged employees, the organization can literally combine the forces responsible for yesterday's and tomorrow's successes.

Another way of dealing with the anxiety experienced by some people at mid-career is to deal with the problem of obsolescence. One way as we have mentioned, is to send people back to school for seminars, workshops, courses, degree programs, and other forms of "retreading." But a better approach is to *prevent* obsolescence from occuring in the first place. This can be done by giving **85** the person assignments throughout his career which force him to develop new skills and learn about new developments in the professional field. The job itself probably has more impact on the person than most off-the-job activities which are billed as professional development experiences. If the person is assigned to a job on which he is working with recent graduates, mutual learning and a trading of experience for new ideas may occur. If the job requires use of computer operations, the person will learn more about the computer than in a special two-day seminar. We tend to think of job transfer into new areas as something that only happens to new employees. If transfers were expected to continue throughout the career, as is true in many organizations, more use could be made of the learning potential in new jobs and new people, and obsolescence could be reduced.

In a comparison of adaptive and nonadaptive mid-career managers, Morrison (1975) found more exploratory behavior (i.e., self and career inquiry) among the adaptive group. It is not clear whether the adaptive managers have not "completed" the exploratory stage in their careers (which, theoretically, should occur in the early twenties), or if they have "recycled" and are now reexamining their careers. Morrison's hunch is that "people never 'finish' exploration once and for all today as much as they did possibly two decades ago" (personal communication, 1975).

Kaufman's (1974) review identified three additional personal characteristics associated with low obsolescence: high intellectual ability, high self-motivation, and personal flexibility (lack of rigidity). Similar findings are reported by Shearer and Steger (1975). The first may be hard to do much about for most people, but self-motivation and flexibility can probably be developed. On the organization's part, effective personnel policies, such as selection for long-range needs, good assessment and testing, and career counseling, are recommended by Kaufman for resisting obsolescence. Key factors in the organizational environment are: challenging initial jobs, periodic job changes, work climates containing communications, rewards for performance, participative leadership, and matrix structures. Kaufman concludes that common remedies for mid-career problems, such as dual ladders and continuing education, tend to be ineffective, although integrating continuing education with demands for innovation from the work itself is useful. Dubin (1973) reports similar conclusions regarding effective means of mid-career updating.

ADJUSTMENT INTO RETIREMENT

The third critical adjustment for most workers (after the early career years and the mid-career crisis) is the transition from the status of working person to retired person. Because work is such an important part of one's identity, especially for highly job-involved people like managers and professionals, the loss of one's work role (and, therefore, one's work subidentity) feels like part of one's self being removed.

On the other hand, retirement can mean escape from a frustrating job and other positive rewards for a lifetime of hard work. As Super points out,

> Retirement means different things to different people. It may mean unwelcome activity, or freedom to do things one has not had time to do, or escape from pressures that are too great. Retirement requires changing the habits and daily routines of a lifetime, changing a self-concept which has been relatively stable even over a long period of years, and changing a role which has been played for more than a generation (1957, p. 159).

Super goes on to illustrate the meaning of retirement with an example of a retired man and his wife, a full-time housewife. After the man retires, he has no need to get up at a certain time in the morning, he has no place to go, and has nothing he must do.

> His wife, on the other hand, still has a job. The home is still there to be taken care of, dusting and straightening up must be done, . . . She has already adjusted to a reduction of roles, for the children left the home when she was in her forties. As she goes about her daily routines the husband is occasionally in her way, and both of them become uncomfortably conscious of the fact that she belongs there, that—whereas she has a role to play and ideas as to how she should play it—he does not belong there, he has no role to play. His role has changed from that of breadwinner to that of do-nothing, while his wife is still a homemaker. The self-concept which goes with the role of do-nothing is not a comfortable one to try to adopt after thirty-five years of working and being a good provider (Ibid.).

What exactly is it in a person's life that changes when he or she retires? The various functions served by work have been summarized by Sofer; these functions also indicate the extent of the emotional losses accompanying retirement:

1. Work roles provide economic returns that are a means to other ends, ends distinct from the work itself; notably work is instrumental for survival.
2. Work provides the individual with opportunities to relate himself to society, to contribute to society, or view himself as contributing to society, through providing needed goods and services.
3. Having a work role enables a man to sustain status and self-respect.
4. Work roles provide opportunities for interaction with others.
5. Work roles contribute to personal identity.
6. Work roles structure the passing of time for one, through scheduling, time tabling, requiring that one must be at a particular activity at a particular time.
7. Work helps ward off distressing thoughts and feelings (loneliness, isolation and thoughts of death . . .).
8. Work roles provide scope for personal achievement—meeting and surpassing objectives recognized by others as valuable or praiseworthy.
9. Work provides for assuring oneself of one's capacity to deal effectively with one's environment and developing that capacity (Sofer, 1970).

87

One manifestation of the importance of work in a person's life is the fantasy of many workers that they would soon die following retirement; this is one of the "distressing feelings" described in point 7 above. The following interview illustrates the connection between employees' perceptions of retirement and fear of death:

> *Question* (to a 64-year-old stock marker): Why should you want to keep on working?
>
> *Answer:* Why? I'll tell you, last year a man I know reached 65. Then, they had to retire, even the big shots. But, he told the foreman he wanted to go on working. The foreman told him: "Why the hell should you go on working? You have the house, the car, the family, the money—why don't you want to quit?" He answered: "Sure I have the money and the car, but I'm used to working. If I quit, I'll die in a little while." The foreman told him he had to quit anyway, and three months later he was dead. When a man's used to exercise and work, he can't just quit and do nothing. The only way to stay alive is to keep working (Friedman and Havighurst, quoted in Sofer, 1970, p. 95).

This man and others interviewed in a study by Friedman seemed to have "equated 'keeping busy' with 'keeping alive' and feared that their failure to keep busy would result in death" (Ibid.). On the other hand, having a variety of roles and being highly involved in one role are strongly related to happiness in old age (Sofer, 1970).

In theory, this stage should be one of decline (Super and Bohn, 1970), both in physical capability and in work involvement. However, job involvement continues to increase in late career for research and development professionals (Hall and Mansfield, 1975). Research on IQ and aging also casts doubt on the decline notion (Baltes and Schaie, 1975). Among Catholic priests, the late career years involved a "mixed bag" of fairly stable work activities, increasing satisfaction, and declines in skill utilization and in self-image (Hall and Schneider, 1973). A survey of retired professors reports a similar mix of positive and negative reactions during the move into retirement (Ingraham, 1974). Whether late career is a period of decline remains to be determined by future empirical work.

The difficulty of the transition into retirement may be eased in various ways: part-time work, hobbies, and preparation for retirement. Because we seem to be entering an era of multi-career lives, the person at retirement age (which has been decreasing in recent years) may simply switch to a different employer or a different type of work. Indeed, the greater amount of leisure time people enjoy now, with increased holiday benefits and four-day weeks, is forcing people to plan more creatively the use of leisure time; this could be a good form of preparation for retirement.

There appears to be a trend toward earlier retirements as both a benefit to older employees and an opportunity to provide faster advancement for younger, lower-level employees. This means that adjustment to retirement will become more of a problem; if a person retires at 50 (a possibility being seriously considered in some occupations today), he could have another 25 years (50 percent of his present age) still ahead of him. In some way, a sense of meaning and purpose will have to be found. But if second (or third) careers become a concomitant of early retirement, then the concept of retirement changes. We would not in this case be talking about retirement from work, but retirement from a particular occupation as a prelude to a career shift, much as professional athletes and stewardesses now "retire." If multiple careers become more widespread, retirement as we know it today and its concomitant role-removal problems may become a novel experience.

DEVELOPMENTAL NEEDS IN EARLY, MIDDLE, AND LATE CAREER

As a way of tying together what we have been saying about early, middle, and late career, let us consider the practical question of how organizations can facilitate the person's development in different stages. Table 3–3 summarizes what has been said earlier in this chapter about the developmental needs which arise at each stage.

Early career, as we have seen, is a time when the person needs to develop action skills, so that he or she can apply the concepts and learnings obtained in school. These are good years for creativity and innovation, qualities which should be developed. The person should be encouraged to go into depth in one area and develop a specialty. However, this specialty could easily become a trap if the person becomes too indispensable in this area. Therefore, in some cases, rotation to a new specialty after a few years is advisable to avoid becoming too narrow, or even obsolete, as the specialty changes. The socio-emotional needs in early career call for a combination of support and freedom (supportive autonomy)—freedom to make mistakes, learn, and develop confidence that one's successes are one's own, but help and support when needed. Feelings of rivalry and competition toward other fast-moving young colleagues must also be managed.

In mid-career the person needs to redefine his or her task role. First, there is a need to move somewhat from "player" to "coach" and to develop more of a broader view of the organization and one's identification with it. Second, the person needs to update and develop new skills, ideally through new job assignments which require him or her to go on learning continually. If this job rotation continues in mid-career, obsolescence may be pre- **89**

Stage	Task Needs	Socio-Emotional Needs
Early Career	1. Develop action skills. 2. Develop a specialty. 3. Develop creativity, innovation. 4. Rotate into new area after 3–5 years.	1. Support 2. Autonomy 3. Deal with feelings of rivalry, competition.
Middle Career	1. Develop skills in training and coaching others (younger employees). 2. Training for updating and integrating skills. 3. Develop broader view of work and organization. 4. Job rotation into new job requiring new skills.	1. Opportunity to express feelings about mid-life (anguish, defeat, limited time, restlessness). 2. Reorganize thinking about self (mortality, values, family, work). 3. Reduce self-indulgence and competitiveness. 4. Support and mutual problem solving for coping with mid-career stress.
Late Career	1. Shift from power role to one of consultation, guidance, wisdom. 2. Begin to establish self in activities outside the organization (start on part-time basis).	1. Support and counseling to help see integrated life experiences as a platform for others. 2. Acceptance of one's one and only life cycle. 3. Gradual detachment from organization.

TABLE 3-3
Developmental
Needs in Early,
Middle, and Late
Career

ventable. On the socio-emotional side, the person needs to have opportunities to express feelings about mid-life, gradually re-work his or her self-image, and engage in mutual problem solving for coping with mid-career stress.

In late career, the person's task and socio-emotional needs both revolve around his or her gradual withdrawal from the work organization into some other setting—another job, retirement, volunteer work, etc. This is a time when the person's experiences can be a useful source of wisdom and guidance to younger people. The central emotional need is to develop what Erikson calls a sense of integrity, an awareness of the integration and value of one's life.

SUMMARY

The central point of this chapter has been that people experience changes in their needs, expectations, abilities, and behavior as they go through different stages of their careers. Therefore, the career stage is a critical individual characteristic which can explain differences in behavior and attitudes among different people in organizations, although the concept has not been widely used in organizational research. For example, the response of a 60-year-old employee to increased responsibility and challenge may be less positive than that of a 25-year-old, even though it might benefit each of them. Administrators seem to have been more aware of the impact of age and career stages than have researchers.

Because age and career stage influence the person's responses to the job and organization, employees have different needs regarding career development, as we have seen. Programs for career development should obviously be designed to provide different experiences for people in different career stages. Some possible differential training experiences for people in different career stages are proposed by Hall and Mansfield:

> If the younger person is in fact in a trial period, he or she should be hired for jobs in which turnover may be desirable—for example, specific time-bounded projects, experimental programs, or visiting positions. These ad hoc activities may be sufficiently exciting to test his or her creativity and meet some self-fulfillment needs, without obligating the person or the organization to a long-term commitment. Once hired, the early career person will be motivated more by challenge and variety than by security and long-term benefits. Investments such as training and development should be made carefully because of the employee's high mobility at this stage.
>
> The mid-career researcher is ready to settle down and advance in a more stable, long-term relationship with an organization. The prospects of long-term development and advancement will be strong inducements in hiring, rather than the excitement of the immediate assignment. Organizational recognition and esteem for the researcher's accomplishments will be powerful motivators.
>
> The late-career researcher is motivated by a steady, secure position. Job offers are few and far between at this point, and the person becomes increasingly involved in his or her present job and organization. Good job security, recognition of the person's continuing value to the organization, and health and pension benefits would be effective inducements in hiring and motivators on the job.
>
> It would also be wise to seek people at eacn stage who have qualities not normally found at that stage—for example, a ''settled down'' young researcher or a late-career person who is still oriented toward growth. Such individuals would probably embody the best qualities of several stages. Another way to combine the strengths of different stages is to assign people at different stages to the same project. The younger researcher would bring his or her new ideas, energy, and growth drive while the older person would bring maturity, stability, more concern for the organization's goals, and an established ''track record.'' Such a combination could aid performance as well as each person's career development, as the young person learns maturity and how to work within the organization from the older professional, and the older absorbs some of the new ideas, techniques, and zeal of the younger (1975, pp. 209—10).

Now that we have seen the general and common experiences that are found in most careers, let us move back again to individual differences in career experiences. In the next chapter we will examine the factors that account for differences in a critical career outcome, the degree of success the person achieves as the organizational career progresses. Here, however, the important predictors are not solely characteristics of the individual alone. As we will see, success is also largely determined by features of the **91** organization and work environment as well as by the interaction of personal and environmental characteristics.

Discussion Questions

1. How would you define the term *career stage*?
2. How are adult life stages different from those of children?
3. What are the stages of the adult work career? What are the characteristic developmental needs within each stage?
4. What organizational actions (programs, policies, etc.) would improve the career development of individuals at various career stages?
5. Although it is clear that events of the early career years, especially the initial job assignment, are critical to the person's career development, organizations have been reluctant to provide more challenging initial assignments for new employees. Why do you think this happens?
6. Why do some people experience a crisis in mid-career? What do you think could help prevent mid-career crises?
7. Why is retirement such a difficult transition for many people? How can the effects of this transition be eased?

PREDICTING CAREER OUTCOMES: Performance

4

Now that we have explored common elements in organizational careers as they develop over time, let us turn to the issue of individual differences in this career process.

Related to these questions is one critical to organizations: How can knowledge about these career-affecting factors be applied to facilitate the development of careers in organizations? To help answer this question, we will examine a number of points in the unfolding of a person's career where attempts at development have been—or could be—made and then draw conclusions about what seems to work best.

FACTORS RELATED TO CAREER EFFECTIVENESS

It is possible to identify at least five basic types of information with which to predict career effectiveness:

1. *Background or biographical data*
2. *Assessment* (a combination of several types of data)
3. *Personality characteristics* (motives, interests, values, etc.)
4. *Career processes* (work environment)
5. *Person-job fit* (or person-organization fit)

Each of these sources of information represents, in effect, a strategy for conducting research on careers and an implicit theory of what influences career development.

What is Career Effectiveness?

Before discussing the factors that influence career effectiveness, let us pay some attention to our criterion—what exactly do we mean by career effectiveness? Generally, in the research literature, career effectiveness has been defined in terms of *performance* and the popular symbols of success—money and position. Position has been employed in the following ways: rank or level in an organizational hierarchy, number of promotions received over a given time period (i.e., rate of advancement), or conversely, length of time in present position. Typical financial indicators are present salary, average yearly salary increases (often expressed as average percentage increases), or salary in relation to other people with equivalent length of service or of similar age. Other measures of effectiveness in this category are supervisory ratings of performance, success, or contributions, number of employees for whom the person is responsible, size of the budget for which the person is responsible, revenue accounted for by the organization unit which the person manages, and so forth.

Another important measure of career effectiveness is the way the career is perceived and evaluated by the individual himself or herself. This personal evaluation is part of a broader class of outcomes called *career attitudes*, which will be discussed in the second section of this chapter.

A third criterion, seldom employed in the past, but becoming increasingly crucial, is *adaptability*. As job mobility and technological and social change continue to increase, obsolescence in mid-life becomes ever more threatening. In order for a person to provide for long-term performance, he must learn the skills of adaptability.

The fourth and final measure of career effectiveness is the person's *sense of identity*. Identity has two important components. First, it entails the person's awareness of his values, interests, abilities, and plans. The clearer and more internally consistent this awareness is, the clearer is his self-concept and the greater his identity resolution. If his values, interests, abilities, and plans seem undefined or unclear to a person, or if he has internal conflict about them, we would say he is experiencing identity confusion. The second important facet of identity is the degree of integration between past, present, and future concepts of self— the person's sense of continuity and sameness. A person may see that his values and interests have changed quite drastically over the years, but if he sees how the "old self" relates to and helped create the "new self," his sense of identity will remain strong. If, on the other hand, he sees his present values and interests as being totally distinct from those of a previous age, he may feel alienated from his past, and his identity will be weakened, since he is now essentially two people—the one he used to be and the one he is now.

94

Identity, then, is a measure of wholeness, of how well integrated the person's life is. It tells how well the pieces (values, interests, etc.) fit together in the present, and how well the present fit is linked to that of the past and the future. Erik Erikson, the psychologist most closely identified with the concept of identity, explains the term as follows:

> [Ego identity] is the accrued experience of the ego's ability to integrate all identifications with the vicissitudes of the libido, with the aptitudes developed out of endowment, and with the opportunities offered in social roles. The sense of ego identity, then, is the accrued confidence that the inner sameness and continuity prepared in the past are matched by the sameness and continuity of one's meaning for others, as evidenced in the tangible promise of a "career" (Erikson, 1963, pp. 261–62).*

In view of the widespread use and misuse of the term, it is important to reiterate that identity is based upon the person's awareness of his values, his interests, his abilities and opportunities, and his plans for the future. Identity is often seen incorrectly as something that can be measured with the simple question, "Who am I?" Erikson has no patience with this misuse of "his" concept:

> I can now register a certain impatience with the faddish equation of the term identity with the question, "Who am I?" This question nobody would ask himself except in a more or less transient morbid state, in a creative self-confrontation, or in an adolescent state sometimes combining both; wherefore on occasion I find myself asking a student who claims that he is in an 'identity crisis,' whether he is complaining or boasting. For most, the pertinent question really is "What do I want to make of myself—and—what do I have to work with?" (1966, p. 148).

Parallels between Career and Organizational Effectiveness

The four dimensions of ascertaining career effectiveness used here and the criteria of effectiveness for organizations are remarkably similar. When one considers the close interdependence between the individual and his employing organization, this parallelism is perhaps not as coincidental as it may initially appear.

An organization consists of a number of individuals whose activities are structured and controlled through a system of authority for the purpose of attaining task goals. According to Argyris (1964), an organization must perform three core activities in order to be effective: adaptation, goal attainment, and integration of individuals into their work roles. In the literature on systems theory, Parsons (1960) states that any social system (of which an organi-

*Reprinted from *Childhood and Society,* 2nd ed., by Erik H. Erikson. By permission of W.W. Norton & Company, Inc. and The Hogarth Press. © 1950, 1963 by W.W. Norton & Company, Inc.

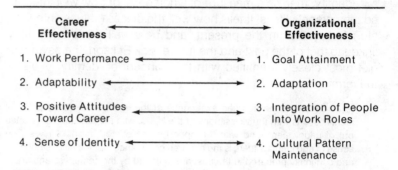

FIGURE 4-1
Relationship
Between
Career
Effectiveness
and
Organizational
Effectiveness

Career Effectiveness	Organizational Effectiveness
1. Work Performance ←——————→	1. Goal Attainment
2. Adaptability ←——————→	2. Adaptation
3. Positive Attitudes Toward Career ←——————→	3. Integration of People Into Work Roles
4. Sense of Identity ←——————→	4. Cultural Pattern Maintenance

zation is a particular type) must perform four functions if it is to survive: goal attainment, adaptation, integration of individuals into work roles, and pattern maintenance. The first three functions are the same as Argyris' core activities; the fourth, pattern mainten-ance, refers to the preservation of cultural patterns, norms, and values over time.

How do the criteria for individual career effectiveness corre-spond to those for organizational effectiveness? Maintenance of the organization's cultural patterns is analogous to the develop-ment and maintenance of the individual's identity over the years. Both refer to the degree of continuity in the values and goals of the person or organization. Goal attainment at the organiza-tion level is analogous to the work performance or task accom-plishment of the individual; both measure the extent to which the person or system is moving toward some objective indicator of achievement. The adaptation of the organization is clearly related to the adaptability of its employees; both indicate an ability to respond quickly and appropriately to changes in the demands, opportunities, and constraints imposed by the environment.

The integration of people into organization work roles is relat-ed to career attitudes in that the latter comprise one indicator of the former. Some examples of career attitudes are job involve-ment, commitment to the organization, and feelings of psycholo-gical success. The more positive these attitudes are, the more strongly the person is committed to or integrated with his work life, i.e., the more strongly the satisfaction of his needs is integrat-ed with the goals of the organization.

This connection between organizational and career effective-ness is shown in Figure 4–1. Each criterion of career effectiveness is actually a contributor toward the effectiveness of the organiza-tion. The overall goal attainment of the organization depends upon good work performance from its employees. Similarly, the more adaptable its employees are, the better the adaptation of the orga-

nization will be, and so forth. In sum, the more effective the careers of its employees are, the more effective the total organization will be.

These four criteria of career effectiveness represent four conceptually meaningful dimensions along which to analyze careers. Not all dimensions, however, have been equally represented in the research literature on careers. As we will see later in this chapter, an inordinate proportion of career research, particularly research on management careers, has dealt with performance and attitudes; very few of the studies have dealt with the more self-related dimensions of identity and adaptability. This bias is understandable, given the past preoccupation of industrial and organizational psychologists with aiding organizational performance and profits. However, now that there is more concern in government, industry, and the media for the individual's total life, the quality of life, and how quality of life is affected by quality of work life, there will undoubtedly be more concern in the future for the identity and adaptability.

METHODS OF STUDYING CAREER DEVELOPMENT IN ORGANIZATIONS

Before examining factors related to the effectiveness of a person's career, let us first consider an important issue in the research literature—methods of investigating careers. At the risk of oversimplifying, we can identify five general methods, using four types of data:

1. *Background* (pre-hire) data
2. *Assessment data*
3. *Personality data*
4. *Career process data*
5. *Person-organization fit data*

Each method, in turn, involves an implicit assumption about what forces and experiences affect and predict the way a person's career develops.

Background data. Background data include any information related to the experiences of the individual prior to the commencement of either his work career (if the focus is on his entire work career) or his career in a particular organization. In the psychology literature, background information is usually called biographical data. Examples are level of education, parents' education and occupations, parents' income, region or country of origin, birth order, number of siblings, and size of home town or city. Other examples of background data would be academic performance (e.g., high school or college grades or class standing), extracurricular activities while in school, quality of college or university, military service or not, military rank attained, and so forth. In the sociological literature on careers, these background data are sometimes transformed or coded to yield various indices, such as socioeconomic status (often based on income, education, and occupation of father or of both parents) and career or geographical mobility or stability. The attitudes of the person's parents, such as attitudes toward the person's education or career, have also been employed, either obtained directly from the parents themselves, or more frequently, from the person's reports of his parents' attitudes. These attitudinal measures are often combined to form an index such as "parental pressure to attend college" or "parental support."

The assumption underlying the use of background data in career research is that the person's previous experiences will in some way affect his future experiences—either his performance, career attitudes, adaptability, or identity. Often this assumption is only implicit, because there is little theoretical or conceptual grounding to studies employing background data, particularly in the case of psychological studies. Research with biographical data typically includes a host of background factors, which are then correlated with, or in some other way compared to, various career criteria. If significant relationships are found, the theorizing is generally *post hoc*; often the reader is left with knowledge such as "first-born children and people from the Northeast attained middle-management positions most rapidly."

This empiricism is tempered somewhat in the sociological literature. Here one often finds hypotheses derived from implicit or explicit theories of social class and stratification. For example, if one theorizes that social strata tend to remain generally stable over time, one would hypothesize that the status a person attained in his own career would be strongly related to that attained by his parents. If one assumes we live in a male-dominated society, one would predict that the father's occupational status would predict his son's attainment better than the mother's status. Similarly, if the researcher has a social theory that views the educational system as preparing people for the occupational system, then she might hypothesize that the quality of school or university and the level of education attained would predict the person's later occupational attainments. In these sociological analyses the background variables are selected for their theoretical relevance as well as for their predictive power, in contrast to the psychological use of background and biographical data.

Assessment data. The second method used to study and predict career outcomes is the *assessment-center approach*. This method entails collecting large amounts of information on each person early in his training and using this as the basis for assessing his or her future potential for success in the organization.

98

According to Bray and Grant (1966, p. 2), assessment centers in different organizations vary in their methodology, but generally three common procedures are found:

1. The use of multiple methods for obtaining information on individuals
2. Standardization of these methods and those for making inferences from them
3. The use of several assessors whose judgements are pooled in arriving at evaluations of the persons assessed

Examples of some of the multiple methods employed might be paper-and-pencil ability measures, projective techniques (such as the Rorschach and Thematic Apperception Test), simulated job experiences (such as role playing, leaderless group discussion, and In-Basket), and interviews. Typically a candidate spends a number of days at the assessment center, interacting with a group of other candidates and staff members. After all the data have been collected, the staff would meet and discuss each candidate in depth, reviewing all the data generated during the assessment process. Then staff members would arrive at a pooled judgment, rating the person on a number of relevant dimensions, such as his likelihood of attaining a given level of management in the firm, and his personal characteristics (such as administrative skills, interpersonal skills, work motivation, independence, etc.). The personal attributes on which staff judgments are made would of course depend upon the particular organization and the qualities it requires in its managers.

The multiple-assessment approach was employed by German, British, and American military psychologists for the screening of officer candidates and intelligence men. These activities, and in particular the screening of U.S. intelligence agents, is reported in a volume written by the staff of the U.S. Office of Strategic Services (OSS, 1948). Because of both the importance of actual, "live" experience in training people in intelligence and the high risk of "on-the-job" espionage training, the simulation of experience through an assessment center was an excellent way to select candidates. Summaries of the many applications of this technique can be found in Taft (1959) and Cronbach (1960).

Although the assessment approach has been applied to personality research, selection, and prediction of later performance, most of the work has been in the third area, prediction. Although the results of different assessment attempts have varied, it is possible to describe factors which tend to increase our powers of prediction with this approach, according to Bray and Grant (1966, p. 2) under the following conditions:

1. When the performance to be predicted is clearly defined
2. When the assessment results do not restrict the range of subsequent criterion performance

99

3. When the criterion measures employed are not limited by low reliability and questionable validity

Personality data. A third method of studying careers in organizations involves the use of *personality characteristics*, such as values, interests, needs, self-conceptions, and the like. Generally, personality variables have been used more to predict occupational choice rather than career outcomes such as performance or attitudes. The underlying assumption is that certain personal qualities are best suited for particular occupations, and that the process of choosing and succeeding in an occupation often involves matching one's personal qualities with those required in a given line of work. Two of the most familiar measures of personal characteristics (in this case vocational interests) are the Strong Vocational Interest Blank (SVIB) and the Kuder Preference Record.

Generally, the method employed to study personal characteristics is to test people while they are students or new employees and then to relate the data to occupational experiences in later years, to see if personality variables can predict career effectiveness. Another approach is to compare the personality characteristics of successful and less successful people, to identify the personal qualities which discriminate between the two.

Career process data. The fourth method of studying and predicting career outcomes involves the use of career process data. Career processes are actual events and experiences the individual encounters during his career. The underlying assumption here is that what happens near the beginning of a process involving feedback, learning, and cycles of behavior will have a continuing impact on the person and will be a good predictor of what will happen later in that same process. This is analogous to the old notion that one of the best predictors of future success is past success. Examples of career process variables studied might be the challenge of one's initial job, the person's relationship with his first boss, and the number and nature of job changes he made in a given period of time.

Person-organization fit data. A fifth type of career-relevant data is that measuring the degree of person-organization fit. To some extent this is analogous to the personal characteristics approach, but a more refined assumption is made here; it is assumed that within a given occupation, employing organizations vary widely, and the extent to which a person develops his abilities and succeeds will depend upon the extent to which his personal qualities are in tune with the characteristics of the organization. For example, a person with strong needs for achievement may be far more successful in a company whose climate values achievement than in a company whose climate stresses affiliation. Similarly, the affiliation-oriented person may "shine" in the latter firm.

Type of Data	Performance	Attitudes	Adaptability	Identity
Background Characteristics	√			
Assessment Data	√	√		
Personality Characteristics	√	√		
Career Processes	√	√		√
Person-Organization Fit	√	√		

Career Criteria

Key: A check mark (√) in a cell indicates that some or considerable research has been done in that area. Absence of a check mark indicates that little or no research has been done in that area.

FIGURE 4-2
A Matrix
or Career
Analysis

Therefore, by this view, success is not a matter solely of what kind of person the individual is, or what kind of experiences he has had, but rather a matter of how well he fits the climate or other characteristics of the employing organization.

A MATRIX FOR CAREER ANALYSIS

To this point we have discussed four criteria for evaluating the effectiveness of a career and five methods and types of data that can be used to study careers. If one relates the career criteria to the five types of career data, the result is a 4 × 5 matrix in which to classify career research (see Figure 4–2). The check marks in the cells give a very rough indication of the areas in which career research has been done to date. The blank cells, conversely, indicate gaps in our knowledge of careers. As was said earlier, virtually no work has been done on career adaptability, and relatively little on career identity. The background data approach has been applied to the smallest number of career criteria, while the career process approach seems to have covered the greatest range of outcomes. Obviously these are subjective impressions, subject to debate. However, in the following sections we will review some of the research in these various cells of the career research matrix and attempt to support the summary ratings shown in Figure 4–2.

RESEARCH ON CAREER EFFECTIVENESS

In the following sections we will review research and theory on each of the four criteria of career effectiveness: performance, attitude, adaptability, and identity. Because so many of the research studies available have focused on performance, in contrast to the other three criteria, our discussion of the correlates of career performance will be organized in terms of the types of research conducted—background studies, assessment research, job process research, etc. This breakdown of studies is neither necessary nor possible in reporting research on the other three career outcomes.

When we consider what factors lead to career success, in contrast to issues such as career stages and career choice, we find that the critical factors vary somewhat from one occupation to another. Furthermore, because of the vast literature on career success which exists if all occupations are considered, it is necessary to restrict our review here to one particular occupation. Because of its probable relevance to all types of organizations, the profession of management was chosen for purposes of illustration. All types of organizations—hospitals, businesses, churches, schools, government agencies, and voluntary associations—have managers and administrators, and the paths of many careers in organizations eventually lead into management.

To simplify the presentation, the remainder of this chapter will examine research only on one of the four career criteria, work performance. Factors related to career identity, attitudes, and adaptability will be discussed in the following chapter.

Personality Characteristics versus Performance

Of all the reserach conducted on managerial careers, more have dealt with performance than with any other career outcome. This probably reflects both our traditional cultural bias toward achievement as an ultimate indicator of the quality of a person's life. It probably also reflects the fact that most research on management careers has been sponsored by or required the blessings of the top management of the organizations involved in the research. Attaining top management support generally entails relating the research to criteria which are consistent with the organization's goals of profitability and success, and nothing could be more congruent with corporate success than the early identification of people destined to become effective performers.

Within this great bulk of research on performance, there is a further bias toward research using personal characteristics (often referred to as "individual difference" variables) as potential predictors. This is quite reasonable, considering the fact that most of the researchers interested in predicting individual differences in performance were industrial and vocational psychologists, rather than social psychologists or sociologists. Traditionally, industrial psychology has viewed the interaction between the person and the organization as one in which the person is the only variable component, the environment generally considered fixed. Thus, most of the research dealt with characteristics of individuals, such as values, interests, needs, abilities, and personality. In recent years psychologists have shown greater interest in environmental variables, but there has not been enough time for this change to show up yet to any degree in the research on careers. Sociologists, who are more accustomed to studying the work environment, have unfortunately shown little interest in studying career performance.* Therefore, research on the important process of how the work environment affects the unfolding career of the individual falls in the gap between the two disciplines and remains largely unexplored.

Interests. Now, let us proceed to the research. We shall begin by looking at *interests*. As was reported earlier, an interest is an expression of liking or disliking for a particular object, such as an occupation, activity, or type of person. Strong was unable to identify interest patterns that characterized managers in general, although he was able to derive scales for managers in specific functions, such as personnel, production, and advertising. He was also unable to report much evidence of a relationship between interests and success in management. This may have been due more to a lack of research on his part than to a lack of results. The fact that he did not devote much energy to the interest-success relationship was due to two methodological difficulties: (1) securing enough cases of successful and poor performance within each occupational group, and (2) the lack of an adequate criterion of success. In the limited research he did report, he found moderate relationships between the appropriate interest scores and rated performance for advertising account executives and foremen, as well as for life insurance agents, engineers, janitor-engineers, and policemen. No other managerial groups were studied

In theory, Strong argued that a relationship between career interests and later career performance might not be entirely meaningful.

> . . . those with interests characteristic of an occupation should like that occupational environment and those without such interests should not enjoy doing what that occupation requires. Consequently, scores on an occupational-interest scale might correlate not with measures of ability but with measures of adjustment to varied aspects of the occupational environment (1943, p. 512).

---

*An exception here is the work of Slocum (1966).

I agree with Strong's conclusion and would argue that variables such as needs and interests would best predict how well-suited a person is for a particular occupation. These personal characteristics should predict the person's *choice* of occupation, his *satisfaction*, and his continuation in the occupation better than they predict his *performance* in that occupation. Unfortunately, this quite straightforward hypothesis has never been tested, to this writer's knowledge.

In the years after the publication of Strong's book in 1943, some progress has been made in identifying interest patterns that correlate with managerial effectiveness. In a review of the literature in this area, Nash (1965) found some evidence that vocational interests relate to managerial effectiveness, and he identified four clusters of interests which seem to be associated with success in a managerial career:

1. Social service, humanitarianism, and people-oriented interests
2. Persuasive, verbal, and literary interests
3. Dislike of exclusively scientific, technical, or skilled trades pursuits
4. Business contact and business detail activities

In his own research, Nash was able to develop and cross-validate a special scoring key for the SVIB (Strong Vocational Interest Blank) which correlated reasonably well with effectiveness in a sample of 159 executives from 13 companies. This study identifies the following profile of the preferences of the effective manager:

1. Prefers activities requiring independent, intense thought, some risk, and little regimentation
2. Dislikes technical and agricultural activities, involving spending long times concentrating on close or detailed tasks
3. Enjoys being with other people, especially when he is dominant to them
4. Prefers physical and social recreations as opposed to aesthetic or cultural forms of entertainment (Nash, 1966)

The usefulness of this key was supported in subsequent research by other researchers (Johnson and Dunnette, 1968).

An important characteristic of vocational interests, at least as measured by the SVIB, is their remarkable consistency over time. Interests are relatively unaffected by training or experience for college students; they may be more susceptible to influence among juniors and seniors in high school. These results held true for both men and women. Therefore, the older the person becomes, the more stable and uninfluenceable his or her interests become (Strong, 1943; Johansson, 1966).

It appears, then, that vocational interests comprise an important and quite stable personal characteristic relevant to career development. Research like Nash's suggests that such interests may be used to predict managerial success. It would seem, however, that interests have a far greater potential for predicting career attitudes, such as satisfaction, involvement, and perceived quality of work life. This statement is more of an hypothesis for future research, however, than a conclusion based upon actual research evidence.

Values. Closely related to interests is the concept of *value*, the person's conception of what to him is desirable and "good." A person's values guide his actions in two ways. First, they provide a kind of moral "road map" for a person, representing internalized guidelines about morally or ethically good or bad ways to behave. Second, values indicate the attractiveness to the person of various objects, behaviors, and experiences, not so much in moral terms as in terms of the amount of pleasure (or pain) or satisfaction (or frustration) they provide him. Values have seldom been employed as predictors of success in managerial careers. Rather, they have been used more commonly to predict career choice.

One of the important value issues in the career literature deals with the object of the person's career commitments. Where is the person most ego-involved—in his organization, his profession, his present job, his industry, or in some other aspect of his work? Most of the research on career commitments has involved professional employees (scientists, engineers, professors, and physicians). The most widely studied orientations are commitment to the organization (termed *localism* by Alvin Gouldner), and commitment to the profession (termed *cosmopolitanism*). (These concepts will be discussed further in Chapter 5.) The "local" is concerned mainly with managing a successful career in his present organization, and he invests himself heavily in organizational activities—committees, establishing a wide network of relationships throughout the organization, and working hard on his job as opposed to outside professional societies and activities. The "cosmopolitan" is concerned mainly with his performance in his technical professional work, and his important reference group is his professional colleagues in a number of different organizations; he would show more interest than the local in attending professional society meetings, presenting and publishing papers, and holding office in his professional societies.

Originally, localism and cosmopolitanism were thought to be inversely related to each other, so that a person with a strong local orientation would necessarily score low as a cosmopolitan. However, research has indicated that these are independent dimensions and that a person can have both a strong local and a strong cosmopolitan orientation. In fact, for scientists and supervisors of research, Glaser (1964) found that the highest performers were those with just such a dual orientation, people whom he called local-cosmopolitans. This issue of where one's commit- **105** ments lie has not been studied frequently in the case of the manager, however. The area of career commitments obviously calls for research as managers become increasingly mobile and professionalized. If mobility is associated with cosmopolitanism, then Jennings' work, to be examined later, would suggest that cosmopolitan managers are more successful than locals. (His data show a correlation between mobility and success.) Obviously the organization needs a combination of professional skills and a certain amount of local commitment from its managers. We need to know more about how a manager deals with dual loyalties and how various combinations of commitments relate to career outcomes. Research on women's careers, and ways women cope with the dual commitments of family and career, may yield solutions that can be applied to managers' dual loyalties.

Although they were not examining local and cosmopolitan involvements per se, Zalesnik and his associates (1970) examined a highly related pair of value orientations in a sample of research professionals and managers—the theoretical and the economic scales of the Allport-Vernon-Lindzey Study of Values. They defined those research managers whose economic values were stronger than their theoretical values as "oriented"—that is, their values would be congruent with their managerial job demands. If, however, the managers' theoretical scores were higher than their economic scores, they were designated "conflicted." Interestingly, the "conflicted" managers were rated higher on overall performance by their superiors than were the "oriented" managers.

There is, however, some question as to the appropriateness of the term "conflicted" as used in this study. It seems entirely reasonable that if a research professional can maintain a strong theoretical orientation even after being promoted into management, he will be motivated by both economic and theoretical values—the former because of his managerial job pressures and the second because of his own values. If, on the other hand, the research manager has higher economic values than theoretical (i.e., if he is oriented), he will be economically motivated by two sources (job and values) and scientifically motivated by neither, relatively speaking. The conflicted manager, then, corresponds to Glaser's local-cosmopolitan, with his dual orientation, who Glaser also found to be the more effective research manager.

Needs. When we think of factors affecting success in management, perhaps one of the first to come to mind is that of personal *needs, drives,* or *motives*—the what-makes-Sammy-run approach to career success. According to Atkinson:

> a need, or motive, [is] a relatively enduring disposition of personality . . . to strive for a particular kind of goal-state or aim, e.g., achievement, affiliation, or power. The aim of a particular motive is a particular kind of *effect* to

be brought about through some kind of action. The aim of a motive defines the *kind* of satisfaction that is sought, e.g., pride in accomplishment, a positive affective relationship with another person, a sense of being in control of the means of influencing the behavior of other persons (1958, p. 597).

Needs are often assessed through projective techniques, which present a person with ambiguous stimuli (e.g., an ink blot in the Rorschach Test or a picture in the Thematic Apperception Test, or TAT) and ask him to respond to it. In the case of the Rorschach or TAT, the response consists of the person's describing and explaining what he sees. Although personality and needs have been measured extensively in industry for use in selecting and promoting managers, little research has been conducted on their relationship to managerial success. A review of the use of projective techniques in personnel psychology since 1940 reports only eleven studies of managers or supervisory personnel; of these, nine showed that some indicators from the projective tests distinguished between more and less successful managers (Kinslinger, 1966).

There is some evidence that the needs for achievement and dominance, more than the need for affiliation, do relate to managerial success. Grant, Katkovsky, and Bray (1967) found that achievement motivation and leadership needs correlated moderately well with salary progress in AT&T college and noncollege samples. The achievement and dominance needs were also significantly related to assessment-center ratings of management potential.

In a study of research and development entrepreneurs, Wainer and Rubin (1969) examined the personality of fifty-one company presidents to the sales growth rate of their firms. The entrepreneurs' needs for power and affiliation were not significantly related to company performance. The highest-performing companies were led by men with a high need for achievement and a moderate need for power. The importance of high achievement seems logical enough, and the moderate power need is seen by Wainer and Rubin to lead to a democratic leadership style—whereas high need for power might lead to autocratic behavior and low need for power to laissez-faire leadership.

These studies suggest that achievement motivation plays a key role in managerial success. The need for power also seems important, in the sense that the manager's power needs should not be extremely high or low. The need for affiliation seems to have little to do with success in management.

Because achievement motivation is so important in the managerial career, let us turn briefly to the work of David McClelland, who is probably more strongly associated with this topic than any other psychologist. In his book, *The Achieving Society,* McClelland **107** develops a strong case for the impact of the achievement needs of the people in a society with the economic development of that society. McClelland reasoned that it must be possible to train managers to increase their achievement motivation and thus help them become more successful in their careers.

In his achievement training programs, McClelland took an eclectic approach and used the results of a wide range of research studies on personal change to come up with career development activities such as goal setting, knowledge of progress, personal warmth and support, etc. He also taught people the language of achievement—how to code for achievement motivation, how to write stories "dripping" with achievement imagery, how to take moderate risks in action situations, etc.—so that achievement thinking permeates their everyday lives. In fairly well-documented research on achievement motivation programs in the U.S., Mexico, and India, McClelland (1965) has shown relationships between the achievement training and career development of groups of executives and the economic development of the regions in which they work. This program is being offered now by a consulting firm, which finds a wide market for its services. To date, little research has been conducted on the effects of achievement motivation training within a particular organization, however.

Questionnaire measures of needs and personality, such as the MMPI,* have shown little promise as predictors of managerial success, according to reviews by Guion and Gottier (1965) and Hedlund (1965). Guion and Hedlund suggest that personality measures designed for a specific situation may be more effective than a standard test with a standard scoring system. In another literature survey, Ghiselli (1966) reports modest correlations between personality measures and success, a finding later supported by his own research (Ghiselli, 1971).

In a third review, Korman (1968b) concludes that objective personality inventories have generally not shown predictive ability. In the AT&T research, in which objective test measures, as well as projectives, were used, the objective measures did not fare too well. It would appear, then, that the basic needs for achievement and power, measured projectively, hold promise as predictors of managerial success, but that other needs, and questionnaire measures of needs, are less fruitful.

Ability. So far we have examined interests, values, and needs as predictors of managerial success. Let us shift to a different type of characteristic—*ability.* Most of the management research has focused on mental ability or IQ. As one would expect, there seems to be a consistent tendency for mental ability to correlate positively with success. In the AT&T Management Pro-

*Minnesota Multiphasic Personality Inventory.

Andy Capp

9-10

gress Study, verbal scores on the School and College Ability Test (SCAT) showed generally high correlations with salary progress for seven samples from five companies reported by Bray and Grant (1966). Reviews by Korman (1968b) and Ghiselli (1966) also conclude that measures of intelligence relate to success.

Cognitive skills such as perceptual accuracy, tolerance of ambiguity, and divergent and convergent thinking have rarely been studied in relation to managerial success. A study of R&D entrepreneurs found that company presidents with skills in veridical (accurate) perception had more successful firms than men lacking these skills (Schrage, 1965). In a similar vein, Ghiselli's (1966) review indicates that perceptual accuracy is related to success for executives, but not for foremen. These results seem reasonable in light of emerging research showing the importance for the manager in accurately "reading" the uncertain and rapidly changing environment, the technology of his work unit, and the characteristics of subordinates (Fiedler, 1967). According to Schein (1970), the effective manager must have *diagnostic sensitivity* and *behavioral flexibility* to understand and react to changing situations and conditions. Ghiselli's findings fit well with the fact that executives have to deal with more uncertainty than do foremen.

Another important skill is tolerance of uncertainty, which was found to be related to success by Berlew and Hall (1964); similarly, Bray and Grant (1966) found that a scale combining tolerance of uncertainty and resistance to stress was related to salary progress in three of seven samples they studied.

Given the importance of environmental conditions such as uncertainty and change in the contemporary management literature, it would seem that cognitive skills, such as tolerance of uncertainty, in interaction with measures of environmental uncertainty, would be promising personal characteristics for further study. For example, one would expect tolerance of uncertainty to be a better **109** predictor of success for research managers (in their highly uncertain, changing environment) than for production managers (who operate in a more stable, predictable environment). Similarly, measures of personal flexibility should predict success better in the relatively turbulent electronics or plastics industry than in the relatively stable glass container or plumbing industry.

Leadership. One final personal characteristic to be discussed as a possible factor in managerial success is *leadership style.* Because management involves influencing and leading subordinates, a person's leadership style or skill should be a logical predictor of success. But it isn't. Probably the most thoroughly studied measures and dimensions of leader style are those growing out of the Ohio State leadership studies, conducted by Hemphill, Stogdill, Coons, Fleishman, and others. The dimensions of initiating structure and consideration have shown inconsistent relationships with managerial performance. Recent work by Evans (1970) and House (1971) indicates that leader behavior may be a better predictor of managerial success if we pay more attention to the effect of leader behavior on the rewards and the subordinate's perceptions of the links between effort, performance, and rewards. In this view we are not viewing the leader's style as having a direct bearing on his own success or failure, but as affecting intervening variables such as subordinate attitudes, perceptions, and motivation, which in turn affect subordinate performance and satisfaction, which in turn affect the success of the manager. The two models, illustrated in Figure 4–3, show the assumed link between leader style and success in most research to date, as contrasted with the approach of contingency theorists such as Evans and House.

The impact of leader style, in House's theory, is in turn moderated by such factors as task structure and personal characteristics of subordinates. For example, in a task with low structure and high ambiguity, a boss who is high on initiating structure would be more effective than one who provides little structure, while the latter boss would be more effective on a more highly structured task.

In sum, then, although the contingency approaches which integrate leadership theory with motivation theory appear promising as means of predicting the career performance of managers, there has not been sufficient research to test these models adequately yet. We are even farther from being able to apply them to the problem of selecting and developing effective managers.

As a concluding note on the topic of personal characteristics in relation to managerial performance, let us benefit from the experiences of researchers in the area of leadership. Originally, researchers reasoned that there were particular traits, needs, or

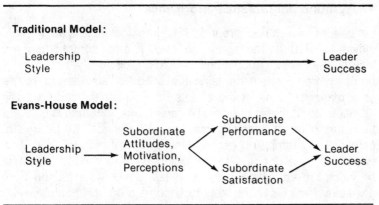

Traditional Model:

Leadership Style ⟶ Leader Success

Evans-House Model:

Leadership Style ⟶ Subordinate Attitudes, Motivation, Perceptions ⟶ Subordinate Performance / Subordinate Satisfaction ⟶ Leader Success

FIGURE 4-3
Two Models
of Leader
Effectiveness

Model of leader effectiveness, adapted from Evans (1970) and House (1971).

other characteristics which made people good leaders—the "great man" approach. Many studies found particular traits that correlated with leader effectiveness, but unfortunately, each study seemed to report a different set of traits. About all we can conclude about traits of good leaders is that perhaps they are a bit taller and a bit smarter than the rest of us.

Other approaches to leadership have emerged, and we have now reached some consensus in the field that some sort of situational or contingency approach can best explain leadership. The personal qualities and skills of the leader must be appropriate for the characteristics of task, his followers, his relationships with them, the time available, and the environment. Similarly, managerial success undoubtedly depends upon characteristics of both the potential manager and the organizational situation in which he works. (We will say more about this when we examine the career process and person-organization fit as predictors of success.) I mention it at this point to caution the reader that attempts to identify personal characteristics that account for a great deal of variance in managerial success are probably hopeless, because there are so many different types of managerial jobs and job demands.

This concludes the section on the relationship between personal characteristics and career performance. So far, we have discussed just one cell of the matrix for classifying career research in Figure 4–2. If this material were being presented in a seminar, you would probably be frantically checking your watch about now. The fact is simply that we have already reviewed a significant portion of what is known about managerial careers, since the most popular criterion in the literature has been performance, and the most popular class of predictors has been personal characteristics. **111**

Background Data versus Performance

Let us turn now to background or biographical factors as possible indicators of future managerial success. Is there something in the history of a person, such as his education, his family, or his childhood community that contains the seeds of success or failure as a manager? One of the effects of a person's background is its influence upon his *choice* of a career; this of course is different from the issue of how effective his performance will be in that career. For example, a person lacking a high school education could not be a doctor (without going back to school), because he lacks the educational prerequisites. Similarly, a person from a wealthy family is more likely to become a doctor than one from a poor family, because of the financial difficulties in obtaining sufficient education. However, once the rich young man or woman and his or her poor colleagues have become doctors, their backgrounds may have less impact on how *successful* they are as doctors.

Most of the sociological literature on background factors has dealt with the occupational (or status) level attained as an indicator of career performance. Criteria such as superior's ratings of effectiveness or salary progress have typically not been used. This is in part because the sociological research has employed either pre-existing data or extensive mail surveys, making boss ratings difficult to obtain and making salary information not comparable because of differences in employees, ages, occupations, etc. The more important factor, however, is that sociologists are interested in social structure, and occupational level is a measure of how far a person has advanced within one aspect of that structure; variables like salary and effectiveness ratings are less relevant when we are talking about social status.

The Warner and Abegglen study. The most extensive study of background factors in the managerial career was Warner and Abegglen's (1955) classic, *Occupational Mobility in American Business and Industry.* The question they addressed was: What are the backgrounds of the American business elite? Their sample was 8,300 men holding chief executive jobs in the largest firms in each type of business and industry in the United States. They also included results of a similar study originally reported in 1928, to see if there had been any changes in the impact of background factors. The rate of response to their mailed questionnaire was 47.6 percent (versus 48.8 percent in 1928), and it showed no apparent bias by level, geographical area, industry, or personal background.

To establish a profile of the elite manager, Warner and Abegglen computed the percentage of their sample who had particular background characteristics and compared these with what would be expected in the general population of the United States. Their results showed that these business leaders had the following characteristics (versus the population at large):

1. Their fathers were more likely to be business leaders themselves, or small businessmen, or professional men.
2. They were more likely to have been born in: (a) the middle Atlantic States, (b) the New England States, and (c) the Pacific Coast States (in that order of probability).
3. They were more likely to have been born in big cities.
4. They have been highly spatially mobile (i.e., they have moved around the country a lot).
5. 57% were college graduates (versus 7% of the general population).
6. They averaged 53.7 years of age.
7. They entered business at an average age of 24 years. It took almost 24 years to reach their present positions. (The sons of major executives took only 20.6 years, while sons of laborers took 26 years.)
8. They moved from one firm to another (only ¼ of them spent their full career in one firm, 23% worked for 2, 22% for 3, 30% for 4 or more). (One suspects these mobility rates would be higher today.)
9. They started their careers in white-collar and professional jobs (not labor and blue-collar jobs).
10. The majority of the elite in slowly expanding businesses were college graduates. Men with less formal education were more often found in more rapidly growing businesses.
11. Having relatives in the firm reduced the time to reach the top (19 to 20 years, versus 24 years). Having friends in the firm did not help advancement.
12. They tended to marry women from their own occupational level.
13. A college education increased the chances of marrying at higher levels.
14. The status of the wife did not seem to have a direct effect on accelerating the career of the business leader.

A comparison of the 1928 data (Taussig and Joselyn, 1932) and the 1952 figures shows that in 1952 there was relatively more opportunity for the sons of laborers and clerks to reach top management and slightly less for the sons of major executives and owners of large businesses. On the basis of their study, Warner and Abegglen conclude the following:

> . . . the operation of rank and the effects of high birth are strongly evidenced in the selection of the American business elite. Men born to the top are more likely to succeed and have more advantages than those born further down. . . . Nevertheless, they do so now in decreasing numbers. The sons of men from the wrong side of the tracks are finding their way increasingly to the places of power and prestige (1955, p. 36).

How background operates. More recent work in sociology has moved away from descriptions of mobility rates and toward explanations of how this strong connection between inherited and attained status occurs. Most of the theory and research on the process of status attainment has been provided by two groups of researchers, headed by Blau and Duncan, on the one hand, **113**

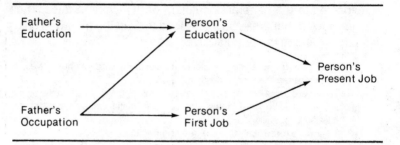

FIGURE 4-4
The
Blau–Duncan
Model

and a group at the University of Wisconsin (Haller, Sewell, and others), on the other. The work of Blau and Duncan (1967) suggests that main impact of family background is that of the father's occupation and education on the educational attainment of the person. Educational attainment, in turn, strongly influences one's initial job, which, with education, is the main determinant of final occupational attainment. This model is shown in Figure 4–4.

The model of Sewell and his colleagues at Wisconsin (Sewell, Haller, and Ohlendorf, 1970) places more stress on the impact of inherited status social psychological factors, such as level of aspiration and the influence of significant others. These act as intervening variables, in turn affecting educational attainment and occupational attainment. The Sewell et al. model is shown in Figure 4–5. Note that the model also contains an important "individual difference" variable, mental ability.

This research in the process of status attainment indicates that it is not "high birth" per se that facilitates career success, but rather the intervening attitudes, environmental influences, and educational attainments which do seem to stem from inherited status. As Haller and Portes (1973) conclude:

> . . . Wisconsin results indicate that practically all the effect of family's position on educational and occupational attainments is due to its impact on the formation of status aspirations and significant others' encouragement of their enactment. Once these variables are controlled, family's position has no direct effect as a facilitator of status attainment. This runs contrary to a widespread imagery of ambitions, especially among lower-class groups, frustrated by lack of means. Inheritance of poverty has often been blamed less on psychological than on economic limitations. In contrast, findings presented above seem to emphasize the importance of psychological formations and their consistent support from those youth considers important (p. 88).

Psychological research. Psychological studies of background factors also show promise in influencing managerial success, if somewhat less promise so far in explaining the theoretical processes by which background factors influence success. In his review, Korman (1968b) concludes that personal-history data are fair predictors of first-line managerial success, although less so for higher-level managers. In their later review, Campbell et al.

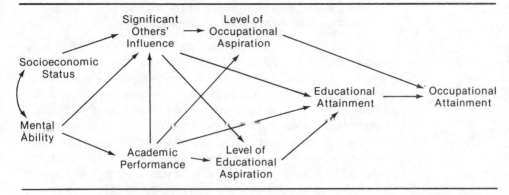

Significant
Others'
Influence

Level of
Occupational
Aspiration

Socioeconomic
Status

Educational
Attainment

Occupational
Attainment

Mental
Ability

Academic
Performance

Level of
Educational
Aspiration

FIGURE 4–5
The Sewell Model

(1970) are more optimistic. They present the following background portrait of the successful manager:

> . . . men rating high in overall success report backgrounds suggesting a kind of "life-style" of success—excellent health, scholastic and extracurricular leadership in high school and college, assumption of important responsibilities rather early in life, high ambition, and active participation in religious, charitable, or civic groups. . . . What is impressive is that indicators of past success and accomplishment can be utilized in an objective way to identify persons with different odds over the long term in their management career (p. 196).

Assessment Data versus Performance

The use of assessment data in predicting management performance holds great potential. The advantage of the assessment approach is that it uses multiple methods of measurement and thus can benefit from the best of the variety of methods and instruments available in the literature. Typically, a number of situational performances, background data, questionnaire, projective tests, and ability measures are used to obtain a file of data on each person. Using those data as inputs, a staff of assessors who could be clinical psychologists or line managers rate the person on his potential for managerial success.

Our major focus here will be on the American Telephone and Telegraph Company's Management Progress Study (MPS), directed by Douglas W. Bray. This study, in operation since 1956, is described by Campbell et al. (1970) as "the largest and most comprehensive study of managerial career development ever undertaken" (p. 232). Bray and Grant (1966) describe the three unique features of the MPS as follows:

> 1. There is no contamination of the criterion data by the assessment results. The data are held in strict confidence, not reported to management. The assessment ratings therefore have no effects on the careers of the 442 people studied.
> 2. The subjects have been or will be reassessed; therefore, growth in the assessed characteristics can be taken into account.

115

3. Because the study is longitudinal and includes so many types of data, there are limitless analyses which could be conducted.

The employees in the MPS were drawn from six operating companies of AT&T. About two-thirds were college graduates, assessed soon after being hired for nonmanagement work and then advanced into management careers. Consultation with many experienced members of the Bell system yielded twenty-five qualities important to success in the business. The following techniques were used to generate data upon which to rate people for these qualities: interview; in-basket exercise; manufacturing problem; leadership group discussion; three projective tests (two incomplete sentences and a six-card TAT); ability tests; questionnaire measures of needs, values, and attitudes; personal history questionnaire; autobiographical essay; and a seventy-item self-descriptive Q-sort.

The subjects spent 3½ days at the assessment center, in groups of twelve. At the end of this time, the staff compiled all the data, discussed each assessee in detail, and arrived at ratings of each person on each of the twenty-five dimensions.

The results indicate that the assessment ratings are effective predictors of future middle managerial attainments. As one would expect, such global ratings predict success better than any single measure alone. Combined results show that 51 percent of those who were predicted to make middle management have made it, while only 14 percent of those predicted not to make middle management have reached that level (Bray, Campbell, and Grant, 1974). As one would expect, the two samples having the longest service in management since being assessed show the strongest predictions: of the 55 men achieving middle management, 78 percent were correctly predicted, while of the 73 men who have not advanced beyond the first level, the assessment staffs predicted 95 percent would not reach middle management within ten years (Bray and Grant, 1966). Campbell and Bray (1967) further report that those managers who were assessed as unacceptable but were nevertheless promoted beyond first level tended to be below-average performers. There was also a tendency for participation in the assessment center to produce a modest, but significant improvement in performance at the first level. The AT&T researchers stress that a key factor in the success of the Management Progress Study has been the support and involvement of the line managers in the Bell system.

A number of studies reviewed by Campbell et al. (1970) have similarly shown that clinical assessments resulted in better predictions of later performance than interest, intelligence, or personality tests (correlations ranging in the .40s and .50s). Clinical assessments appear more promising than what Campbell et al. (1970)

term "actuarial methods," in which scores from multiple predictors are combined in some objectively determined, statistical manner, such as multiple regression.

One indicator of the popularity of assessment methods is the growing list of companies that employ assessment centers for the identification of managerial talent. Unfortunately, few companies are conducting the kind of research on these programs which we find in the Bell system.

One further use to which assessment data could be most profitably put would be as *feedback to the assessee*. Precisely because the assessment ratings are so relevant to managerial performance, they are equally powerful as aids to learning and development for the recruit. Some of the qualities may be difficult to change, but many, especially in the attitude and motivational domains, show substantial changes eight years later at reassessment (Campbell, 1968). Therefore, the feedback from these ratings could be extremely useful to a person both for diagnosis of his interests in and suitability for management and for aid in developing his managerial talent more effectively. This feedback would complicate the research problems, and it may mean withholding feedback from a portion of the assessees to continue the validation research, but such practical problems are well worth confronting.

Career Processes versus Performance

We now turn to the career itself as a source of data for career performance—the *process* approach to the study of careers. The assumption here is that the interaction between the person and the work environment produces opportunities, learnings, attitudes, achievements, and other outcomes which affect the future course of a person's work life. Thus, in contrast to the background approach, the personality approach, and the assessment approach, which primarily examine the person for clues about future success, the process approach examines the work environment and the situations encountered therein as heavy influences of later performance. Like most environmental approaches, it assumes that management success can be learned; the three person-oriented approaches carry more of an implicit assumption that managers are "born, not made."

One of the classic studies of career processes is White's *Lives in Progress* (1952). White's intention was to contribute to our knowledge of the growth of human personality in an area largely unexplored by his psychologist colleagues—"the gap at that point where it becomes necessary to consider the continuous development of personality over periods of time and amid natural circumstances" (p. 22). White's book is based upon extensive study **117** of three case studies—people he originally knew as college students and whom he studied again later in their careers.

Although it is not possible to capture the richness of White's insights in a short discussion, his discussions underline four key features of adult development:

1. The person undergoes more or less continuous change,
2. The person is acted upon by a multiplicity of influences to which he necessarily makes a selective response,
3. The person not only receives influence, but he also takes action on the environment. Man is not static, nor is he passive and helpless.
4. It will also be necessary, because our examples of growth include the years of young adulthood, to consider seriously the nature of the reality in which adult development occurs (p. 328).

White concluded with a discussion of four general trends in the process of growth. First, there is a *strengthening of ego identity*. Ego identity refers to the "self or the person one feels oneself to be" (p. 332). Growth here entails developing a clearer concept of what are one's strengths and weaknesses, interests, aspirations, memories, commitments, and other personal characteristics. With growth, the person's ego identity develops clearer definition and continuity. Second, there is a *freeing of personal relationships*, a movement toward relationships that are "less anxious, less defensive, less burdened by inappropriate past reactions, more friendly, more spontaneous, more warm, and more respectful" (p. 343). The person becomes both more autonomous and more capable of concern for others.

The third growth trend is a *deepening of interests*. This does not mean developing more and varied interests, but of becoming deeply absorbed and involved in perhaps just one or two, so that the person carries them through to some end result, with its accompanying sense of fulfillment. The fourth growth trend is a *humanizing of values*. White uses the term "humanizing" to indicate that (1) the person's values become increasingly a reflection of his own experiences and motives, and (2) the person increasingly discovers the human meaning of values and of their relation to the achievement of social purposes. This does not necessarily mean that the person's values change—only that they become better integrated into his own life experiences—i.e., he becomes more integrated as a person.

It is interesting to consider these four growth trends in the light of the mid-career changes, described in Chapter 3, which often involve the re-examination and subsequent re-affirmation of one's identity, with an increased sense of stability as one important outcome. Often the change is precipitated by a deepening of one's interests and an increased tendency to apply one's own values to one's own life experiences. In sum, we might hypothesize that

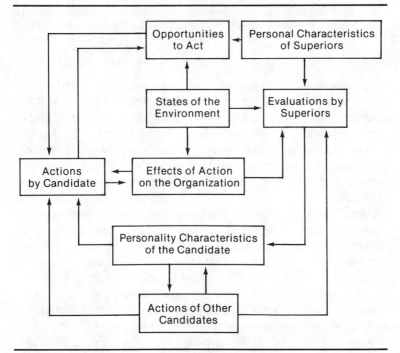

FIGURE 4-6
Relation
Between
Personal
Characteristics
and Performance

From William R. Dill, Thomas L. Hilton, and Walter R. Reitman, *The New Managers: Patterns of Behavior and Development*, p. 6, © 1962. Reprinted by permission of Prentice-Hall, Inc., Englewood Cliffs, N.J.

following a successful mid-career transition, a person would rate higher on White's growth trends than before the changes began, even though that pre-change period may have appeared more stable, successful, and "well-developed" in terms of more popular definitions of career success.

A second important contribution to our understanding of career processes is *The New Managers* by Dill, Hilton, and Reitman (1962), who were strongly influenced by White's book. They consider the attempts that have been made to predict career success from the characteristics of the individual and conclude that they have not been too successful. As an alternative, they present a model of human development in the work career as sequences of interactions between the person and the environment. Their model is shown in Figure 4–6, and is briefly explained as follows:

> Viewed from close range, the impressive thing about the careers of young men in industry is not the consistent long-run relation between "personality" and performance, even within a single job situation. It is, instead, the sequence of short-run interactions between a man, his job surroundings, and others in the organization. Such sequences can exert decisive long-run influences on a man's career, but generally only indirectly, by affecting the interactions which next occur. Thus we observe a continuing pattern of decisions, behaviors, observations of consequences, and learning which results **119**

in modifications of future decisions and behaviors. The managerial aspirant is learning what is expected of him, what opportunities do and do not exist, and how he can influence his chances for advancement. As he learns, he makes decisions that affect both his present and future career possibilities (p. 5).

Several key factors in managerial success are reflected in Dill, Hilton, and Reitman's model. The first element is the individual-as-decision-maker. There is great uncertainty in a managerial career, especially in the early stages, and it is important that the person be able to accept uncertainty while attempting to reduce it as much as possible with rational search and good information. Second, great stress is placed on the *organizational environment* in which the management candidate is to work. The environment is critical for three reasons. First, it provides opportunities to act and learn. Second, the environment also provides feedback on performance—knowledge of results. We know from learning theory and research on goal setting that knowledge of results is important for adaptive learning; it tells the person not only *how well* he is doing but also *how to improve* (i.e., what areas are weak). Third, related to feedback, the environment provides *criteria* (standards and values) by which the person may be judged. In many types of work (e.g., public relations, personnel) there are no objective indicators of success or failure. This is more likely to be even more of a problem in the management of various types of work than in the execution of that work. Effectiveness, then, is often a "social reality" rather than a physical reality, and needs to be defined in terms of the generally accepted standards and values which can be found in the perceptions of other people in the work environment.

The final element in the Dill et al. model is what they call "interpreting the environment." Here the issue is how to deal with the vast amounts of both information and uncertainty that are found in the environment.

> In comparison with the college environment from which he comes the graduate may find the job environment more comprehensive, less static, and less nicely defined by orientation lectures and notebooks. There may be much less guidance in learning what is important or sacred. Official descriptions embodied in organization charts and the like may be meager and (as often as not) misleading.
>
> Masses of data implying many possible causal relations among events must be boiled down to a handful of essentials to be acted upon. The knack for doing this without losing sight of occasional details signaling a change in the environment is a very special skill for managerial candidates in a rapidly evolving world (pp. 13–15).

In essence, then, Dill and his associates describe the career in terms of information processing and person-environment trans-actions. They represent the person, in effect, as an *open system* receiving information inputs from his environment, processing these inputs (thinking, problem solving, etc.), and taking action (i.e., outputs).

These systems concepts are more frequently applied to organizations, groups, and other social systems than they are to individuals, but they can have great value in explaining individual behavior. For example, based on the work of Lawrence and Lorsch (1969), we know that for systems in uncertain and dynamic environments, the more flexible their structures are, the more successfully they will adapt. The same process could be hypothesized for individuals. For example, people in uncertain, rapidly changing fields, such as computer science, may have to be much more flexible (i.e., willing to change locations or employers, willing to learn quickly about new machinery and new customer requirements, etc.) in order to be successful than would an office manager or a production foreman.

Lawrence and Lorsch also found that the most effective systems in uncertain environments showed high degrees of integration (internal communication and coordination) and differentiation (specialization of skills and functions). Translating this idea into individual terms, one could hypothesize that the most successful individuals in career fields with high uncertainty would be those with several well-developed skills and interests (i.e., internally differentiated) who were also able to integrate and utilize these separate interests and skills to solve work problems in novel and creative ways. Indeed, what this means is that the person would have sufficiently complex information-processing and problem-solving capacities to match the complexity of the informational inputs confronting him in his work environment. Undoubtedly, many more analogies could be drawn between the functioning of effective social systems and that of effective individuals. The reader is encouraged to think of individual performance in terms of basic processes of relating to the work environment and then to use his knowledge of organization theory to develop some of his own parallels between organizational and individual performance.

Job characteristics and career development. Undoubtedly, the major source of stimulation and reinforcement for the personal development of the individual (i.e., the major source of inputs, in systems terms) is his or her job. The relationship between the person-job environment interchange and the person's growth is described by Elliot Jacques:

> . . . working for a living is one of the basic activities in a man's life. By forcing him to come to grips with his environment, with his livelihood at stake, it confronts him with the actuality of his personal capacity—to exercise judgment, to achieve concrete and specific results. It gives him a continuous account of his correspondence between outside reality and the inner perception of that reality, as well as an account of the accuracy of his appraisal of himself (1973, p. 6).

121

One of the underlying assumptions of this volume is that careers develop, or that people develop during the course of their careers. Development involves growth and learning over time. The person's stage of development today is very much a product of the stimulation, reinforcement, and learning he experienced yesterday. Therefore, it is not only the person's job which influences his or her career development, but also the job history, the total history of influences in the work environment.

By extending this reasoning to its logical extreme, one can see that the person's initial job experiences can have a long-range effect on his career. Likening the first year of the person's work life with his first year of life, with its "blank-slate" quality, it appears that this is a critical period for learning. The importance of initial job experiences is described by Berlew and Hall (1966) as follows:

> Of particular interest is the early development of performance standards and job attitudes. From the moment he enters the organization, a new manager is given cues about the quality of performance that is expected and rewarded. The probability that these expectations or standards will be internalized is probably higher when the individual has just joined the organization and is searching for some definition of the reality of his new environment.
>
> In terms of Lewin's field theory, when the new manager first enters an organization, that portion of his life-space corresponding to the organization is blank. He will feel a strong need to define this area and develop constructs relating himself to it. As a new member, he is standing at the boundary of the organization, a very stressful location, and he is motivated to reduce this stress by becoming incorporated into the "interior" of the company. Being thus motivated to be accepted by this new social system and to make sense of the ambiguity surrounding him, he is more receptive to cues from his environment than he will ever be again, and what he learns at the beginning will become the core of his organizational identity. In terms of Lewin's model of attitude change, the new manager is *unfrozen* and is searching for information and identification models on the basis of which he can change in the direction he feels the organization expects him to change (p. 210).

Using data from two operating telephone companies in AT&Ts Management Progress Study, Berlew and Hall predicted and found that the level of challenge in the initial jobs of young managers would be related to performance and success six and seven years later. One possible alternative explanation for these results is that the better managers may have been put in the better jobs. However, examination of assessment data indicated little relationship between personal characteristics and initial job assignment, which was consistent with the Bell System's policy of considering all new employees equal until their performance proves otherwise.

A second alternative explanation of the results is that a challenging initial job may give a person high visibility, and that visibility, not performance, may lead to success. However, initial challenge correlated very highly with performance during the first few **122** years of the person's career. Also, when the person's performance over six or seven years was held constant (by partial correlation analysis), the correlation between initial challenge and later success became nonsignificant. This indicates that initial challenge is important because it stimulates a person to perform well in subsequent years. And it is this increased performance, not the initial challenge, or resulting visibility per se, which leads to success.

The positive impact of initial job challenge upon later performance has also been documented in other AT&T companies (Campbell, 1968), as well as in the General Electric Company (Peres, 1966), and the Roman Catholic Church (Hall and Schneider, 1973). At more of a macro-level, Lipsett and Malm (1955) found that the occupational level of the first job, over a number of different occupational groups, was a good predictor of the occupational level the person would attain later in his career.

The author knows of companies that have applied these findings by upgrading initial jobs in an attempt to facilitate the career development of new employees (Hall, 1971b). It appears that improved first jobs reduce the high turnover of the first years. Unfortunately, none of these companies has systematically related improvements in initial job challenge to later performance. This would be a fruitful area for controlled field experiments. There also appear to be two unintended consequences of giving high-quality initial jobs. First, the supervisors of these jobs must be carefully selected and trained, because they are the ones who largely define the job for the employee. Second, when the person advances from his enriched initial job to a "regular" second job, the contrast often results in frustration and dissatisfaction; in fact, the high turnover experienced among second-year employees in one firm suggests that it had succeeded in simply postponing turnover from the first year to the second. Thus, it was necessary to improve second-level jobs in order to retain the new employees. Furthermore, more experienced employees began to resent the attention given to the jobs of new employees. In time, a wide range of jobs in the company were under review. In short, the company found that a program of career development in fact entails a commitment to organization development, a systematic effort to increase the effectiveness of the entire organization through behavioral science methods. It is difficult to change one component of one employee's work environment without affecting another employee's environment; such is the interconnected, interdependent nature of social systems.

Psychological success. In a subsequent report employing data from one of the two companies in the Berlew and Hall paper, Hall and Nougaim (1968) identified a system of interrelated changes in work attitudes and performance which occurs over **123**

the first few years of a young manager's career. This phenomenon, which they termed the *success* syndrome, was hypothesized to occur as follows:

1. For all managers, the need for Achievement and Esteem increases over the years that they are with the company ($p < .001$).
2. Managers who have met high standards of performance will be rewarded with promotions and pay increases, or, in more global terms, with success (Berlew and Hall, 1966).
3. These successful managers have achieved a great deal and have been given additional managerial responsibility. Therefore, their satisfaction with Achievement and Esteem increases and becomes significantly greater than that of their less successful colleagues in the fifth year ($p < .05$).
4. Possibly as a result of their greater satisfaction with Achievement and Esteem, they become more involved in their jobs. By the fifth year their work is significantly more central to their overall need satisfaction than is the work of the less successful group ($p < .05$).
5. With increased job involvement, they are more likely to be successful in future assignments than other managers scoring lower on these dimensions. Thus they are caught in an upward spiral of success.

> The converse of this syndrome does not seem to occur for the less successful managers; although their satisfaction with Achievement and Esteem does decrease, the average Work Centrality score increases slightly. If this score had decreased, we could then say that these people were becoming alienated and withdrawing emotionally from their work. But they seem to remain at about the same level of Work Centrality, with their higher needs increasing at about the same rates as the successful group and with their higher-order satisfactions not increasing (p. 30).

The relationship between challenge, success, and career involvement has been described by this writer in a model of career development. The model is based upon the experimental work of Lewin and his associates on goal setting and levels of aspiration (Lewin, 1936; Lewin et al., 1944). Lewin found that goal-directed behavior was likely to lead to psychological (or self-perceived, intrinsic) success under the following conditions:

1. The goal represents a challenging but attainable level of aspiration
2. The goal is defined by the person
3. The goal is central to the person's self-concept
4. The person works independently to achieve the goal

When these conditions are present, goal attainment should result in a feeling of psychological success. Other people (bosses, peers, parents, etc.) may or may not perceive the attainment as "success," but the person himself should, according to the theory. For example, for a 5-year-old girl who is just learning to swim, being able to swim five yards unaided in the deep end of the pool results in a great flush of psychological success; some other 5-year-olds, old hands at swimming, may tolerate her glee but would not define her feat as an objective success. On the other hand, an Olympic swimmer may set a new record (an objective success to most observers), yet he may not feel psychological success for one of several reasons: (1) he may have aspired for an even faster time, (2) he may not have set any particular goal for himself in that race, (3) he may have seen his feat more as his trainer's and coach's success than his own (an unlikely prospect, to be sure), or (4) setting new records may no longer be important to his self-concept. For many reasons, then, self-defined and externally defined success can often be quite unrelated. However, the research has indicated that self-perceived success has greater impact upon future goal setting and task involvement than externally defined success.

What follows the experience of psychological success? First the person experiences a sense of increased competence and self-esteem relative to that task area. Further, the person is likely to engage in additional goal-directed behavior in that task area, often with an increased level of aspiration (i.e., more difficult goals).

Although Lewin's work dealt with well-defined, specific tasks, his concepts can be logically applied to more complex, inclusive domains of task activity, such as work careers. If a person sets a goal for himself in his work which meets the four theoretical conditions listed above, the attainment of that goal will probably result in feelings of psychological success. Because the goal pushes him to reach some new level of competence, his self-esteem and self-confidence in that area will increase. Furthermore, his increased self-esteem in this area will probably generalize by association to a sense of satisfaction with work in that task area. Thus, his involvement in his job may increase. Because of his increased commitment and confidence, he may now be more likely than before to set additional goals for himself in this area. This cycle of events can be self-reinforcing and continuing. When it occurs, the person shows great enthusiasm for the relevant career area and may describe himself as "really finding himself," or being "really turned on" by his work. In short, this is the process by which "success breeds success." The author's psychological success model of career development is shown in Figure 4–7.

The conditions for psychological success can be translated into requisite conditions in the job environment. In order to be able to work on difficult goals, the job must have a certain degree of objective challenge. What a person experiences as challenge is obviously a function of individual differences in ability and interests, but some jobs, such as stuffing envelopes, would probably be seen as challenging by very few people, while others, like supervising 1000 employees, would have more potential for challenging people. Autonomy is necessary to enable the person to set work goals and to work independently. If he is closely super- **125**

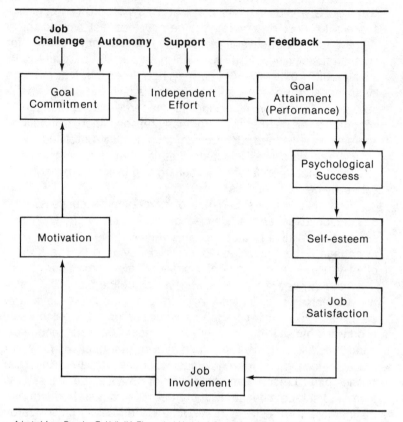

Job
Challenge   Autonomy   Support   ──────── Feedback ────────

| Goal Commitment | → | Independent Effort | → | Goal Attainment (Performance) |

Psychological Success

Motivation

Self-esteem

Job Satisfaction

Job Involvement

FIGURE 4-7
The
Psychological
Success Model
of Career
Development

Adapted from Douglas T. Hall, "A Theoretical Model of Career Subidentity Development in Organizational Settings," *Organizational Behavior and Human Performance,* 6 (1971a), 66.

vised in pursuit of a goal, then he may feel that his goal performance reflects more the success of his supervisor than of himself.
Some degree of support, help, and coaching from the supervisor
is useful in aiding the person to attain his objectives. Feedback
is necessary both to improve performance and to help the person
evaluate his or her performance.

Perhaps an example may help explain this process of career
development. Let us consider a manager about to create a new
management information system. Perhaps his training is in accounting; working with management information systems is a com-
pletely new type of behavior to him. However, he chooses to go
ahead and install the new system. If the system is successful,
the manager may see that he possesses skills in designing and
implementing information systems, skills he never saw as being
part of him before. He may also see that his general managerial
and administrative skills are higher than he realized, since managing such an innovative system affecting the work of so many
people is a good test of these abilities. Thus, his self-esteem as

a manager may grow. His satisfaction with and involvement in his job may also increase. With this success behind him, he may now be more likely to try some other new career behavior at a future date.

Although this model has never been tested in its entirety, data from various studies provide support for particular parts of it. Stedry and Kay (1962) found that employees who were given difficult goals (as opposed to impossible or easy ones) showed the greatest improvements in performance in later months. Other research at General Electric (Kay and Hastman, 1966) indicates that work attitudes improved significantly for men who participated in work-scanning and review sessions as opposed to annual performance-appraisal discussions. Key features of the work-planning sessions were self-appraisal, mutual goal setting, and collaborative problem solving on how to attain future work goals. Further research on work planning by Kay and Hastman (1966) showed that subsequent performance improvement was greater for employees whose work-planning sessions consisted mainly of problem solving on alternative means of work-goal achievement. The least performance improvement occurred following sessions that were conducted like a performance appraisal, with an emphasis on the superior's evaluation of the employee's performance.

Thus, in these GE studies, work performance and attitudes appear to become more positive under two of the conditions necessary for psychological success: one's own setting of goals and independent effort in attaining goals.

In research with Roman Catholic priests, Hall and Schneider (1973) found that the working of the psychological success model was moderated by the job conditions under which the person works, as the model would predict. Under conditions of high autonomy and support, they found the most evidence that work challenge was related to intrinsic work satisfaction, which was in turn related to self-esteem. Under conditions of low autonomy, the model appears to be "short-circuited," and the person's self-esteem is unrelated to his job satisfaction. This is consistent with Hall and Nougaim's conclusion that the success syndrome does not work in reverse; i.e., failure does not lead to decreased involvement. Apparently, a person's psychological reaction to a low-autonomy job is not to become less involved, but to insulate his self-esteem from his low job satisfaction.

In the diocese Hall and Schneider studied, it took a man 22 years to advance from assistant pastor to pastor. Assistant pastors experienced extremely low autonomy and challenge in their work. The researchers found that among older priests, the relationship between use of skills and work satisfaction and between work **127** challenge and use of skills became weaker. They concluded that it appears that when a person is deprived of opportunities for psychological success in an organization over many years, he may lose much of his desire to utilize conditions for psychological success through challenging work when they are finally made available to him.

Supervisory behavior. As we have seen in the discussion of initial job experience, it appears that a person's supervisors may have a strong impact upon the development of his career. The person's boss has a great deal of influence over the objective challenge available in his job. The boss also controls to a great extent the amount of autonomy, feedback, and support the person will receive. All these factors are critical to career development, according to the author's model.

The supervisor can also be important as a sponsor, opening crucial doors to the person, bringing him along with promotions as he (the boss) is promoted (Dalton, 1959; Jennings, 1971). This sponsorship function has been examined more by sociologists than psychologists. Although sponsorship does occur in particular cases, of which the reader is undoubtedly aware of some example, it is not clear that sponsorship is as frequently a factor in aiding a subordinate's career than the less dramatic functions of job autonomy, support, feedback, and challenge.

Work climate. Work climate is often used as an "umbrella" concept, encompassing the array of situational demands and opportunities present in a work assignment. In the organizational behavior literature, climate often covers at least four general features of the work environment: (1) leadership or supervisory style, (2) interpersonal relationships, (3) intrinsic meaning in work, and (4) extrinsic reward characteristics.

Schneider and Hall (1973) view climate as an intervening variable—i.e., one that intervenes in the relationship between independent variables (such as personal or organizational characteristics) and outcome variables (such as performance or satisfaction). In this view the person gradually forms an impression of the climate of the work setting based upon numerous interactions and experiences at work. Thus, climate seems to be more an attitude the person holds toward the job or organization more than an objective characteristic of either.

Work climate is related to the performance of employees (Steiner, 1965; Pelz and Andrews, 1966). Because climate does seem so strongly related to the career development of employees, it would seem to be a useful concept to apply in facilitating careers. However, because it is an intervening variable, climate cannot be manipulated directly. For example, a climate of high trust cannot be achieved directly through a manager's actions; he must take other actions, such as increased openness or new reward practices, which may or may not lead to changes in the trust level of the climate. Therefore, manipulations of the work climate are probably less feasible than more direct manipulation of the factors which create the climate—supervisory practices, job characteristics, interpersonal relationships, the reward system, etc.

Climate may be more easily applied in the case of an individual selecting an organization. There is some evidence that individuals select organizations on the basis of their apparent climate. Furthermore, organizations tend to reward people who do what the climate values (e.g., power-oriented organizations reward people with a high need for power, achievement-oriented organizations reward people who are high achievers) (Andrews, 1967). Therefore, a person interested in strong work performance and achievement should choose an achievement-oriented organization; the climate will help him develop those aspects of himself which he most values.

Organizational characteristics. There is some evidence that the type of organization for which a person works, especially early in his career, can influence later developments in his career. This seems to be a logical analogy to the role of the initial job in career facilitation. In academic careers, it appears that the quality of the university where the person did graduate study and the quality of the organization when he held his first job are both strong correlates of later career performance (Crane, 1965). This result could be due to the challenge of the work, the quality of one's learning, and the contacts one develops, among other factors.

Unfortunately, there is little research on the impact of organization characteristics upon career development, although there is plenty of folklore available. Should a person start with a big firm to learn as much as he can in its training program and then move to a smaller firm? Or should he start with a small firm to acquire early responsibility and more of an overall picture of how the organization operates? Should he go with a company that trains specialists or generalists? Everyone has his own set views on the type of organization that trains people best for later success, but there is little research to distinguish wives tales from wisdom.

Mobility. It is widely believed that a person has to change jobs periodically in order to advance in his career. There is some support for this belief in the literature. Warner and Abegglen (1955), in their classic study, found that top business leaders tended to move from firm to firm. Only one-fourth spent their entire career in one firm, 23 percent were in two firms, 22 percent in three, and 20 percent were in four or more organizations. Similarly, **129**

Jennings (1970) finds that mobility is becoming increasingly important in career development. Jennings describes his findings as follows:

> In my studies of 1,500 managers and executives and 230 presidents from 500 large industrial firms, I have found increasingly close relationships between mobility and success over the 16 years of the study. At growth corporations, for example, it has become common for managers to hold several different positions within a division, and also to move from one division to another. Most men who arrive at the top this year will not have done both. I find that it now takes about 20 years on the average to go from first-level manager to president, during which time there are seven geographical moves, eleven positional ones, and countless numbers of special and project assignments. The mobility pattern is now so reliable that I have been able to write a computer program that predicts, at any point in an executive's career, the approximate level of management he is likely to reach (p. 36).

The Warner and Abegglen (1955) study, data collected in 1952, reported that it took almost twenty-four years to reach the top at that time. Obviously, the Jennings and the Warner and Abegglen samples may not be directly comparable, but the comparative findings do support Jennings' conclusion about the increasing rates of advancement in recent years.

The Warner and Abegglen and the Jennings studies, when considered together, raise an intriguing possibility, however. Jennings reports a decrease in age of corporate top executives from the early 1950s to the late 1960s: 63 years for board chairman, 59 for presidents, and 50 for new officers in the early 50s versus 59, 50, and 41, respectively, in the late 1960s. Warner and Abegglen report an average for chief executives of around 44 in 1952 (which is considerably younger than Jenning's figures); they further report, however, that this represents an *increase* of about five years from a comparable sample studied in 1928 (with an average age of 39). Disregarding the differences in absolute age between the Jennings and the Warner and Abegglen data, the changes in age suggest that American business may go through cycles with varying rates of advancement during different time periods. Young men may have advanced quickly during the "Roaring Twenties"; once they were in power, their relative youth, plus the Depression, may have blocked the advancement of younger men during the 1930s and 40s. Then, faced with a sudden management gap as these older men retired in the 50s, companies may have started moving young men quickly again in the 1950s and 60s. If this cycle theory is true, these rapid advancements of the last two decades, combined with the difficult economy of the 1970s, may forecast another slowdown in the advancement rates of talented young managers.

Person-Organization Fit versus Performance

In addition to characteristics of the organization influencing the development of the person, it might also be argued that the interaction or congruence between the person and his organization could affect his career outcomes. Support for this has already been cited briefly above in a study by Andrews (1967) of two firms in Mexico. One firm was characterized by an extremely high level of achievement motivation in its managers, while the other was characterized by high needs for power. In the former, the people most likely to receive promotions were those who had high needs for achievement; in the latter it was employees with high needs for power. In other words, people whose personal needs best fit the climate of the organization were most likely to succeed.

In a classic study of a bank, Argyris (1954) found that the bank was characterized by what he called a "right type" person. The right-type person was quiet, unaggressive, polite, disliked giving orders, and liked receiving orders. Right types tended to be promoted, while non-right tended to leave. An analogous phenomenon was observed in the United States Forest Service by Hall, Schneider, and Nygren (1970). The Forest Service's primary goal is public service, and the researchers found that the people who identified most strongly with the Forest Service were those who saw themselves as supportive and involved, two characteristics quite relevant to public service. People who saw themselves as intellectual showed no tendency to have either high or low organizational identification. People who identified highly with the Forest Service, in turn, tended to be highly satisfied in their jobs. Thus, the "right types" tend to be rewarded here, too, although the rewards studied were intrinsic rather than extrinsic.

The work of Pervin and of Schneider has focused the most explicitly upon the fit between the person and the organization and his organization. Pervin's (1968) research looked at college students in relation to their university environments. He found that the fit between their self-image and their perceptions of the college was a good predictor of satisfaction with college, but a weaker predictor of academic performance.

Schneider's (1972) research has focused on recently hired life insurance agents. Schneider predicted that the closer the new agent's expectations matched the actual climate of the agency, the higher his production would be. To date it appears that this relationship does not occur for individuals, but it does for agencies. That is, the better the person-agency fit is, averaged for the agency as a whole, the higher the production is in that agency. Unfortunately, though, it does not appear that we can predict individual performance with this fit measure. Pervin's results would **131**

suggest that fit at the individual level might predict individual satisfaction better.

SUMMARY

We have now completed our survey of factors associated with
work performance, which is the first of our four general criteria
of career effectiveness. Let us now consider briefly a question
raised at the beginning of this chapter: What seems to work best?
If you were responsible for personnel development of an organization, what factors would you use in the early identification and
development of management potential?

Unfortunately, we do not have anything so handy as average
predictive validities of the many variables we have considered here.
From the great volume of research on the managerial personality,
we know this variable can give us statistically significant, but not
especially strong, predictions of success. When personality data
are combined with situational exercises, ability tests, and other
measures from an assessment center, predictions of success can
be markedly improved. The assessment center is an extremely
useful, but expensive, means of identifying managerial talent.
However, because it provides information you can't get elsewhere,
the expense is often justified by the benefits.

The other promising area of predicting career success is the
process of the career itself, especially the person's early job experiences in the organization. In addition to its predictive power,
the career process is also attractive to organizations because job
experiences can be controlled and changed in order to aid career
development. Personality characteristics, on the other hand, are
fairly stable and are of little use in career development, except
for selecting work environments that would best fit each individual.

In our discussion of factors related to career effectiveness,
we have been examining the profession of management for illustrative purposes. This completes our analysis of factors that facilitate the task performances of managers in their careers: background factors, assessment data, personal characteristics, career
process data, and person-organization fit. The following chapter
will examine the impact of these five factors on the other three
career outcomes: career attitudes, adaptability, and identity.

Discussion Questions

1. What is career effectiveness? How is career effectiveness related to organizational effectiveness?
2. How does an assessment center operate? Why are assessment centers often
a better means of selection than are other procedures?

3. How can career processes be used to predict career effectiveness?
4. What are the major personality characteristics that correlate with career success?
5. How can success breed success?
6. How can a supervisor affect the career development of his subordinates?

5 PREDICTING CAREER OUTCOMES: Identity, Attitudes, and Adaptability

In the previous chapter we identified four dimensions of career development—performance, attitudes, adaptability, and identity. Because so much of the literature dealt with performance as a criterion, an entire chapter was devoted to that dimension; factors that affect the other three will be considered here. Because the literature on career identity, attitudes, and adaptability is relatively sparse, our discussion will not be organized in terms of the type of predictor data considered (background, career process, assessment, personality characteristics, and person-organization fit). Because attitudes, adaptability, and identity are less occupation-specific than performance, we will return in this chapter to our more general focus on all types of occupations in organizations.

CAREER IDENTITY

Personal Identity via Work Identity

From the point of view of the individual, identity is probably the most important of the four facets of career development. It is the person's sense of identity which, by definition, helps him evaluate himself. It tells him how he fits in to his social environment. And it tells him about his uniqueness as a human being.

In Western society the development of one's personal sense of identity is closely tied to the establishment of one's occupational identity. Often a person "finds himself" through finding work that he loves; conversely, a person's work commitment may grow sharply after he resolves a personal identity problem. We find, therefore, that the age at which people generally work through their personal identity "crises" (late teens, early twenties) is also the age at which individuals in our society are expected to choose occupational identities as well. The question "What do you do?" is often a more acceptable way of asking, "Who are you?"

To give a strong sense of the self-discovery aspect of identity, Erik Erikson quotes William James:

> As a subjective sense of an invigorating *sameness* and *continuity*, what I would call a sense of identity seems to me best described by William James in a letter to his wife. "A man's character," he wrote, "is discernable in the mental or moral attitude in which, when it came upon him, he felt himself most deeply and intensely active and alive. At such moments there is a voice inside which speaks and says, '*This* is the real me.' " (Erikson, 1966, p. 149).

One way to think of career development from the individual's point of view, then, is as a continuing quest for what one truly is and wants to do. As the person develops vocationally, there is a better fit in the integration of his sense of identity and the requirements of his work role. Erikson describes the growth and maturity of identity as follows:

> For a mature psychosocial identity presupposes a community of people whose traditional values become significant to the growing person even as his growth and his gifts assume relevance for them. [We may speak, then, of a *complementarity* of an *inner synthesis* in the individual and of role integration in his group.] (Ibid, p. 150).

And, finally,

> And yet, just when a person, to all appearances, seems to "find himself," he can also be said to be "losing himself" in new tasks and affiliations (Ibid., p. 151).

This idea of career development as increasing the fit between occupational requirements and personal identity shows how career growth is a synthesizing process, integrating the person with his or her work environment.

What Affects Identity Growth?

The important question at this point is, what facilitates the development of the person's sense of identity? This question can be considered in terms of two different time periods in the person's career. The first is when he or she is making an initial career choice, usually in high school or college. We have already examined this literature, which is extensive, separately in the chapter on career choice. The time period to consider is the years following the initial choice—i.e., the duration of the person's occupational or **135** employment career. Unfortunately, we know far less about identity changes during the adult, working years than we know about adolescent changes as related to career choice.

Of the five types of information which predict career outcomes (background, assessment, personality, career processes, and person-organization fit), the one that seems to be the most useful in understanding the person's sense of identity is career process information. It appears that critical events and role transitions may alter a person's identity, or at least trigger personal explorations which later lead to identity alterations.

Before discussing the impact of career processes upon identity, let us briefly touch on one other influence—background factors—which also seems to have a bearing on identity development. Sex, race, national background, and other aspects of social origin all can affect the type of identity a person develops and the way in which it develops. Minority-group members in any setting are often discriminated against, with the result that they often must be "super-people" to attain equal opportunities for good job and advancement. These extra obstacles can lead to identity perceptions that life's rewards are beyond the person's control, leading to feelings of helplessness, dependency, apathy, anger, and self-hate, which have sometimes been reported as part of the identity "baggage" of black people and women in our society.*

In terms of psychological success theory, one would not necessarily expect the self-esteem of disadvantaged groups such as blacks or women to be lower than that of whites or men, respectively. Lewin's research indicates that the person would psychologically withdraw from those arenas in which he or she is experiencing failure and would rather invest himself or herself in success-producing activities. Therefore, what should be different between blacks and whites, between men and women, are the variables to which self-esteem is related. Because of job discrimination, self-esteem should be less related to job factors for women than men, and for blacks than for whites. On the other hand, self-esteem may be tied more heavily instead to family, personal relationships, and community involvements for blacks and women. This idea is often seen in the popular literature, but has not been systematically tested, to this writer's knowledge. And these differences should diminish over time, if career opportunities become equalized for women and other minorities.

Minority-group membership can also add to the difficulty of

---

*See, for example, Thomas Pettegrew, *A Profile of the Negro American* (New York: Van Nostrand, 1964); William H. Grier and Price M. Cobbs, *Black Rage* (New York: Basic Books, 1968); Eldridge Cleaver, *Soul on Ice* (New York: Delta, 1968); Judith M. Bardwick, *Psychology of Women: A Study of Biocultural Conflicts* (New York: Harper & Row, 1971); Virginia O'Leary, "Some Attitudinal Barriers to Occupational Aspirations in Women," *Psychological Bulletin*, 81(1974), 809–26.

resolving identity issues. The paper by Erikson that was quoted from earlier ("The Concept of Identity in Race Relations") is an eloquent statement of the interrelationship between the identity of a person and the communal identity of a people. Similarly, identity development has "two kinds of time: *a developmental stage* in the life of the individual and a *period* in history" (Erikson, 1966, p. 160). Therefore, the member of a minority group must in a sense do double identity work, resolving what it means to be a mature human being and what it means to be a member of a particular group. Often the person feels a strong sense of conflict between these two areas of identity. Examples would be the career woman who feels she has to become less feminine to succeed or the black professional who feels more alienated from his former friends as his successes mount. They both may feel that they run the risk of "selling out" as the price for occupational attainments. In resolving their own personal identities they also must resolve their group identity simultaneously. In actuality, this is an important aspect of the development of equality for the minority group, as a whole, so in a real sense the person is performing double duty.

Identity Changes in the Career

Let us now turn to the changes in identity that are stimulated by events in the process of the person's career. As we have seen in the chapter on career stages, the person's life history may be viewed as a series of passages from one role to another: high school student, college student, company trainee, engineer, manager, etc.

The activities denoting these stages have been termed rites of passage (van Gennep, 1960). It is generally possible to identify three major phases: *separation* of the person from his customary environment, *initiation* from the old role into the new one, and *incorporation or reintegration* into the original or a new environment.

The initiation phase is a highly visible component of institutionalized role transition; in it, personal changes are focused in a fairly short, intense time period. During the initiation the holders of the desired role test the newcomer to determine whether he will measure up to their standards. If he can, he is given public certification that he is now one of them. Because of this certification, he then begins to *feel* more like one of them; i.e. his identity has changed so that he now sees himself as part of the new group. Perhaps the most clear and familiar example of this phase is the fraternity initiation, which we know can cause changes in a person's attitudes.

Although there are obviously few, if any, formal initiation rites **137** in the work career, there are nevertheless many transitions and turning points that serve the function of mini-initiations. For example, the recruitment and interviewing process is an important test of the candidate's abilities; the more difficult he thinks it is to obtain a job offer from a particular organization, the more he might identify with that organization if he is hired. Training programs and probationary periods, especially in firms with "up or out" policies, contain elements of initiation rites. Indeed, some initial job experiences, such as the audit function in accounting firms, are so routine and unsatisfying that they are often experienced as a form of hazing. A newcomer to a particular job may be tested by his boss, peers, or subordinates and may be very much aware of the particular point at which he won their confidence and became one of them. And, of course, induction into career-related organizations such as management clubs or the Million-Dollar Roundtable in life insurance, which denote promotion to a particular level or a certain level of performance, is often treated quite ceremoniously and helps the person accept this advancement or achievement more readily into his sense of identity.

Movement (either transfer, job change, or promotion) from one role to another can also induce considerable identity change, regardless of whether or not a form of initiation is present. When the recent MBA becomes a manager, the expectations which he and other people associate with that role induce new self-perceptions and feelings of responsibility. And the more time he spends in the organization and the higher he moves in the hierarchy, the more strongly he identifies with the organization (Hall, Schneider, and Nygren, 1970).

In their study of Catholic priests making the role transition from assistant pastor to pastor (the manager or administrator of a parish), which was mentioned in the last chapter, Hall and Schneider (1973) found that priests' identity perceptions became more favorable before the advancement. This indicates a process which sociologists call *anticipatory socialization* (wherein the person begins to adopt the attitudes, attributes, and self-perceptions of a particular role before entering it). However, during the three years immediately following the advancement, the new pastors' self-perceptions became less favorable; this was apparently due to the "reality shock" of the hard work and responsibilities of the job, in contrast to the unrealistic expectations which had been developing over the many years of waiting for the promotion (twenty-two years in this particular study). Similarly, research on public school teachers has shown decreases in self-perceptions following the initial teaching experience, which is often reported as disillusioning (Walberg, 1968).

138   On the other hand, studies of medical students (Becker, Geer,

Hughes, and Strauss, 1961) and Ph.D. candidates (Hall, 1968) indicate more favorable self-perceptions and increased identification with the professional role as the person moves closer to the aspired role during graduate training. Relating these studies to those of priests and teachers, the increases during graduate training may again represent anticipatory socialization, to be followed by a decrease in the favorableness of self-perceptions after the graduates assume their professional roles. There tend to be decreases in job satisfaction during the initial career years for employees in general, and this could be quite consistent with decreases in professional self-regard. That is, even though the person may assume the role of manager as more a part of his identity, if he now values that role less or feels less competent in it because of the reality shock of the first job, his evaluations of himself could decrease. Unfortunately, we do not have much data on the identities of managers, as opposed to other professionals, with which to test this hypothesis.*

CAREER ATTITUDES

As is the case with identity, career attitudes are affected strongly by career processes. Naturally, attitudes and values are also affected by personal characteristics, because attitudes are important personal characteristics themselves. Given the tendency toward consistency in the human personality, a person's attitudes are often related to his needs, wants, abilities, and other personal attributes. The general strength of these attitudes and values is related to personality characteristics, while changes in attitudes can be caused by events in the career process.

Role Transitions and Attitude Change

One important influence on work attitudes is formal education and the transition from school or university to the first job. These changes are documented in a longitudinal study of graduate business students at MIT conducted by Edgar Schein (1967). Schein examined the attitudes of business students at three points in time—at the beginning of their two-year graduate program, at the end of the two years of study, and after a year or so of their first jobs. He also measured the attitudes of the management school faculty and those of a group of senior executives, representing the authorities in the educational and work systems, re-

*For more detailed analysis of identity changes during the course of careers in general (i.e., not any particular occupational group), the reader is referred to the work of Strauss and Glaser. See Anselm Strauss, *Mirrors and Masks: The Search for Identity* (San Francisco: The Sociology Press, 1970); Barney Glaser and Anselm Strauss, *Status Passage* (Chicago: Aldine-Atherton, 1971).

spectively. He measured attitudes in areas such as business in society, management theory and attitudes, attitudes toward people, and individual-organization relations.

Schein found, as we have seen in an earlier chapter, that the attitudes of the senior executives and those of the business school faculty were quite different, showing that their environments represent two quite different worlds. (This gap is seen by critics of business schools as evidence that management education is hopelessly irrelevant to the training needs of business firms. Supporters see this discrepancy as a measure of the innovation that business schools create by introducing new attitudes and values into business, through the newly hired MBA.) At the beginning of the master's degree program, the students fell somewhere between the executives and professors on the attitude dimensions. Following the master's program, the students' attitudes moved closer to those of the faculty. Later, however, after some work experience, the students' attitudes moved the other way, closer to those of the senior executives. This indicates that the person's attitudes are affected by the climate and prevailing attitudes of the particular system in which he is working. This does not mean that every person changes or is socialized by his organization, but there is a clear tendency for people as a group to experience some attitude changes. We have similar results from laboratory studies showing the impact of role changes upon attitudes (Janis and King, 1954).

Another important type of attitude is related to the person's satisfaction with his work and his organization. In the satisfaction literature, there is some disagreement, but there seems to be a U-shaped relationship between satisfaction and age. Just after the person starts to work, satisfaction is fairly high. Then over the next few years, it tends to decrease, perhaps out of disillusionment with unchallenging initial jobs and promotion frustrations. Then, later, satisfaction begins to increase and continues to increase for the remainder of the career (Gibson and Klein, 1970). A study described in Chapter 2, focusing on the transition from professional school to the first job, illustrates this process. Initially the person's rating of his chosen organization became more attractive following his decision to accept their offer (but before starting work there). Later, during the first year of employment, the rated attractiveness of the chosen organization decreased (Vroom, 1966; Vroom and Deci, 1971). It is not known whether their ratings increased later, as the people either became adjusted in their jobs or changed companies to more satisfactory employment.

A study (Campbell, 1968) of young AT&T managers in the first eight years of their careers noted a similar decrease in satisfaction over time. However, there was an even greater decrease

140

in career expectations, which may account for the drop in satisfaction. On the other hand, there was an increase in occupational involvement. This latter finding is consistent with several other studies which have found increases in job involvement over time (Lodahl and Kejner, 1965; Hall and Schneider, 1973). The conclusions of Campbell's study seem to generalize rather well, based upon the other research we have reviewed:

> The findings strongly suggest that the young manager goes through a process of adjustment and change during the early years of his career. His attitude toward the company becomes less favorable, and his optimistic expectations are toned down considerably. Examination of case histories and the particular questionnaire items that show the most change indicate that the "negative" changes are realistic ones. For example, it is not uncommon in our samples to find a fairly large percentage of the recently hired college graduates expressing sincerely and with conviction that they expect to become officers of the company. After a year or two of reality testing in the organization, expectations become more realistic. The same point can be made about attitudes toward the company. Some of the new recruits entering the first job of their managerial career have extremely positive views of the company. Their attitudes would be considered naive even granting that the company is very well managed.
>
> It is encouraging to note that despite these "negative" changes, the job involvement of the group is increasing. This suggests that the group has maintained its job and career involvement even though it is going through a difficult period of adjustment and revision of expectations (Campbell, 1968).

Success and Job Attitudes

In this AT&T research all four attitudes studied (company satisfaction, expectations, occupational satisfaction, and occupational involvement) were correlated with managerial success, in both salary progress and management level attained. Expectations and occupational satisfaction were not related to success in year one, but they were correlated with success by the eighth year. These results are similar to Hall and Nougaim's (1968) success syndrome referred to earlier, in which increases in achievement satisfaction and work centrality were strongly related to success in the first five years of the subjects' careers. Further support for these findings comes from the work of Porter and Lawler (1968), who found that good performance can lead to increases in work satisfaction, and it is more likely that performance will lead to satisfaction than that satisfaction will produce good performance.

If the strong performance of the more successful young managers was also perceived by them as psychological success (i.e., if the work goals were challenging, personally meaningful, if they participated in setting them and worked independently to attain them), then the psychological success model of career development (shown in Figure 4–7) would explain their more positive job attitudes. It would also predict that they would experience greater **141** occupational self-esteem and that their self-esteem would be more strongly linked to their job attitudes. Successful subjects are likely to become more involved in a task (by going on to higher performance goals) than are unsuccessful people (Lewin, 1936; Dubin and Champoux, 1974). Further, people who experience task success showed increased liking for the task following their success (Korman, 1968a). Similarly, if a *person is rewarded for performing* a task in a certain way, his or her attitudes toward the rewarded behavior will become more positive (Breer and Locke, 1965). Therefore, career success leads to more career involvement and to more favorable attitudes toward work and company; these outcomes presumably lead the person to work harder and thus to perform better in the future. Thus, success breeds success.

Although the rich get richer, it appears that the poor don't necessarily get poorer. In the AT&T studies, the work involvement of the less successful managers decreased only slightly (Hall and Nougaim, 1968; Bray, 1972). During a twenty-month period of tight budgets and deteriorating job quality, the job involvement of research scientists and engineers remained unchanged (Hall and Mansfield, 1971).

Organizational Commitment

Closely related to the person's satisfaction with the organization is his commitment to or identification with the organization. Satisfaction evaluates the person's attitude to the organization (positive or negative), while identification and commitment tap the psychological involvement the person feels in the organization and the extent to which his company membership is a significant aspect of his personal identity.*

Two distinct orientations a professional person might take toward his career work have been identified (Gouldner, 1957, 1958): loyalty toward the employing organization and loyalty toward the profession. People with mainly organizational loyalties are termed *locals,* and those with mainly professional loyalties are termed *cosmopolitans.* (See pp. 105–106.) At first it was thought that these two orientations were opposite extremes (i.e., mutually exclusive), but subsequent research has shown that they are two separate dimensions. Thus a person can be a cosmopolitan and still identify with a particular organization (a local cosmopolitan).

A key factor influencing the person's identification with his organization is the *extent to which he personally values the goals it is pursuing* (Hall, Schneider, and Nygren, 1970; Hall and

---

*Organizational identification and commitment are not identical, although they are similar and are often used interchangeably, as they will be here. Identification refers to feeling like a "part" of the organization or defining one's self-image in terms of the organization. Commitment is more active, involving a willingness to exert effort on behalf of the organization and a willingness to remain in the organization (Gould, 1975).

Schneider, 1973; March and Simon, 1958). If I work for the U.S. Forest Service, an organization devoted to public service through effective land management, and if I strongly value public service, I will probably identify strongly with the organization. If I couldn't care less about public service, then other conditions would have to be present in order for me to be strongly committed to the organization.

One of these other factors is a *challenging job* (Hall and Schneider, 1973; Patchen, 1970; Lee, 1971; Buchanan, 1974; Gould, 1975). If I see the organization as a setting in which I can do stimulating, success-producing, satisfying work, that association may lead me to become committed to the organization. Two other conditions are position level and length of service in the organization. Generally, the *higher one moves in the hierarchy* and the *longer one has worked for the organization,* the more one identifies with it—indeed the more in reality the person actually *is* a part of the organization (Sheldon, 1971; Lee, 1971; Hrebiniak and Alutto, 1973; Gould, 1975). Naturally, one's position level is a function of length of service, and in two organizations (the U.S. Forest Service and the Roman Catholic Church) the effects of position decreased markedly when length of service was held constant. The effects of length of service were not greatly reduced, however, when position was held constant (Hall and Schneider, 1973). In these two organizations, the effects of length of service were also independent of other variables which might help account for increased identification: job challenge, self-image, need importance, and satisfaction. Turnover and self-selection may have been a factor, with the less committed people leaving early, but turnover was extremely low in both organizations. Hall and Schneider draw the following conclusions about the effects of length of service:

> With length of service a person probably accumulates a complex network of positive and rewarding experiences which become associated with membership in the organization: these eventually may generalize to the organization itself, so that organizational membership eventually becomes functionally autonomous as a motivating factor. Similarly, over time the priest's self-image becomes increasingly correlated with his organizational commitment. When one combines this increasing identity investment with (1) the declining number of outside opportunities as one gets older and (2) the dissonance-reducing process of assuring oneself that he has chosen his commitments wisely, it seems reasonable that time would lead to increasing identification (1973, p. 348).

The *career patterns of employees* and the *promotion policies of the organization* seem to affect the extent to which identification increases with length of service. In an organization with a policy of promotion from within, where people tend to spend their entire career in that organization, identification will probably be more strongly related to length of service than in organizations which hire managers and executives from outside the organization (i.e., **143** where employees have multi-organization careers) (Hall and Schneider, 1973).

Another factor which seems to be related to identification in some organizations, but not all, is the personality of the individual. In a study cited in the last chapter, we saw that people who are the "right type" undoubtedly identified the most with their organizations. In this study, the right type was nonconfronting and unaggressive. In research on two business organizations, the right type in the achievement-oriented firm had strong achievement needs, and in the power-oriented firm he had strong power needs. In the service-oriented Forest Service (a civil service system), high identifiers had strong needs for affiliation and security and saw themselves as supportive and involved with people: where the individual's personality is congruent with the climate of the organization, identification is more likely to occur.

A final factor related to the organizational commitment is the *overcoming of obstacles to obtain organizational rewards.* In a study by Grusky (1966) it was assumed that women would experience more obstacles to promotion than men, and that people with little formal education would encounter more obstacles than those with more education. Holding length of service and mobility constant, Grusky found that within eight of the nine comparisons he made, managers with high school education showed greater commitment to the firm than those with college experience. Similarly, holding mobility constant, he found that women were consistently more strongly committed than men. There is still the possibility that the successful women and those with less formal education were more committed to begin with, and that this initial commitment was responsible for their success. However, the interpretation that overcoming barriers leads to greater commitment is consistent with the theory of initiation and rites of passage. Interestingly, contrary to prediction, the rewards received, independent of the obstacles overcome, did not relate strongly to organizational commitment. This suggests that the person must perceive his attainments as representing a fairly difficult goal (and, therefore, psychological success) before he or she will generate strong identification with the company.

CAREER ADAPTABILITY

Despite the fact that employee obsolescence is a matter of great concern to many organizations, very little research has been conducted on this area of career development.* Perhaps this is

---

*An excellent general reference on obsolescence is H.G. Kaufman, *Obsolescence and Professional Career Development* (New York: AMACOM, 1974). This topic is also treated well in Andrew J. DuBrin, *The Practice of Managerial Psychology* (New York: Pergamon Press, 1972).

because organizations have more pressing short-run needs to facilitate performance and favorable career attitudes, while identity and adaptability have longer-term and less tangible payoffs to the organization. However, the top management of many organizations are now recognizing the need for greater adaptability and technical updating, so that we will probably see more research studies in this area appearing in the future.

Where Obsolescence Occurs

This writer conducted a study of obsolescence in a group of Canadian bank managers who were planning to attend a seminar on the subject. Therefore, the sample is highly biased toward people who are aware of the relevance of possible obsolescence to them; not all reported that they felt obsolete yet, but they wanted to learn about it as "preventive medicine." The areas in which they felt the threat of obsolescence (and hence the need for adaptability) were as follows:

1. The computer and the new skills it entails
2. The company's stress on education and youth (and their relative lack of both)
3. New approaches to banking and the obsolescence of the manager's knowledge and techniques
4. The uncertain role of the manager (more specialists? less independence with computerization? less status?)
5. The changing task activities of the manager over the next 10 to 20 years

Subsequent talks with groups of managers from other industries indicated that these concerns are not unique to banking.

On the other hand, when I asked for areas in which managers felt the least threat of obsolescence, one stood out: interpersonal relationships, the people side of management. If one thinks of work as involving primarily task or technical activities and social interpersonal skills (Bales, 1958), these results indicate that managers probably feel more threat from obsolescence in the technical aspect of their work than in the social aspect. These conclusions are also corroborated by clinical observations (Levinson, 1969).

Maintaining Adaptability

Faced with these areas of strength and threat, the employee (or the organization) has two courses of action available to maintain adaptability. One is to correct the weakness and get updated technically, through continuing education seminars, job rotation into work that demands technical learning, independent study, and so forth. A second alternative is to play to his strength by further improving interpersonal skills. (We assume here that he in fact, is relatively skillful interpersonally; this seems reasonable, since with experience, the person acquires what Levinson calls **145** "wisdom" and certain political skills, which are largely social and which are essential to survival in most complex organizations.)

There is another way to use the interpersonal strategy in a way that accomplishes multiple objectives: developing subordinates and bridging the "generation gap" in the organization. This approach involves working with new, young employees in a coaching capacity. In this way, the older employee can impart to the newcomer his wisdom, political skills, and the ability to "sell himself" while learning the latest technical concepts and methods from the new member, who is relatively current technically. By working as a team this way, the older person combines the complementary strengths of both people, and helps them both overcome their weaknesses. Each person can feel confirmed and successful. A win/lose situation has been converted to win/win.

Another way of tapping the benefits of age is to put the older manager into a job that places a premium on the overall perspective and wisdom he has acquired. Middle age is not a period of hot creativity and insight but of cool reflection and integration, making the person skillful in activities such as long-range planning and adaptation.

> . . . at this point in time the middle-aged manager ideally should be exercising a different kind of leadership and dealing with different organization problems. In middle age, the stage Erik Erikson has called "the period of generativity," if he opts for wisdom, he becomes an organizational resource for the development of others. His wisdom and judgment gives body to the creative efforts to younger men. . . . He shifts from quarterback to coach, from day-to-day operations to long-range planning. He becomes more consciously concerned with what he is going to leave behind (Levinson, 1969, pp. 59, 60).

As a final source of ideas on managerial adaptability, it may be useful to examine the literature on age and professional productivity, most of which is based on studies of scientists and engineers.

In his classic research on age and achievement, Lehman (1953) found that peak creative performance in various scientific fields was most likely to occur in the late thirties or early forties. The peaking seemed to occur earlier in the more abstract disciplines, such as mathematics, and later in more empirical fields, such as biology. Because management seems more empirically based (seat-of-the pants is perhaps more accurate, if less generous) than theory based, perhaps the peak in creative managerial contributions also occurs later, in the forties rather than the thirties. Naturally, a manager may continue to advance after the forties, but there is a general belief among managers that by the time a person reaches this age he knows generally how far up he will move.

146   A study of scientists in organizations found the same peaking in the thirties and forties, but they also found a second peak ten to fifteen years later (Pelz and Andrews, 1966). However, some people remained steadily productive throughout their careers. What distinguished them from the "peak and faders?" For one thing, the adapters, as we might call them, had a greater degree of *intrinsic motivation* or self-reliance. They place a strong emphasis on their own ideas as a source of motivation. They were active rather than passive on the job. The study found strong support for the notion that the mid-career decline occurred "because individuals relax their zeal or motivation after having achieved" (Ibid., p. 197). These findings are corroborated in other research, as well (Kaufman, 1974). Some people might argue that the decline occurs because the peak performers are promoted into management, but this idea received little support from research.

Because personal qualities such as intrinsic motivation seem to distinguish adapters from nonadapters, an effective way for organizations to combat obsolescence is through effective techniques of selection and placement. As one expert puts it:

> Placing newly hired professionals in positions for which they lack the appropriate ability, motivation, and personality practically guarantees the emergence of obsolescence not too long after they begin their organizational careers. The selection process constitutes an input control on the quality of an organization's professional manpower (Kaufman, 1974, p. 69).

Good selection ordinarily consists of a job analysis and identification of the personal attributes necessary for success. In utilizing selection methods for adaptability, the organization would take the additional step of a *future job analysis.* Here the focus would be on future job requirements, especially those that are likely to change the most, and on the personal attributes which will be needed for today's employee to be successful tomorrow (Ibid.). In contrast, however, most organizations select people for today's jobs and then wonder why their employees are not suited for tomorrow's jobs.

Other personnel practices that are helpful in dealing with obsolescence are mid-career assessment centers, career counseling, and more flexible retirement policies (early or late, depending upon the person's ability) (Ibid.). For example, Alcan was forced to terminate (that's "systems talk" for meaning *fire*) many of its managers to help meet a budget crisis (Cuddihy, 1974). After the people who were to be fired were notified of the decision, the company put them through a program of assessment, counseling, and coaching in the skills of job hunting. The reason these managers had to be fired in the first place was that they were not essential in their present jobs and were not adaptive enough to be used in other, necessary jobs. The company obviously was partially responsible for this situation and intended to continue **147** using these selection and development methods for all employees following the firings. In this way, maintaining employee adaptability can become a standard personnel function which should eliminate the need for future "prunings" if done well. (More details on this approach to placement will be found in Chapter 6.)

Factors in the job and organization climate help maintain adaptability (Pelz and Andrews, 1966; Kaufman, 1974). Specifically, the early exposure in depth over a three- or four-year period to all areas of one project (i.e., early job challenge) is important. An experienced, older colleague acting as a coach or mentor is also helpful. It is also critical to reward the person for good performance (with recognition, pay raises, good assignments) in the first ten years. Then in his thirties he should be pushed into a new project in a new area, so he can't "rest on his laurels." And he should be given increased independence from his supervisor or coach. In response to a hypothetical question about the post-forties professional, Pelz and Andrews have an intriguing and perhaps discouraging answer:

> What about the post-40s? Is there anything I can do as a research manager to help my older scientists sustain achievement?
>
> Helpful for all groups after 40 is a well-developed desire to self-confidence about venturing into risky areas. If the man lacks these qualities by 40, it may be too late to build them. Nourishing these attributes is your job in the 30s rather than later (1966, p. 121).

Is Adaptability Valued?

One parting shot before concluding this section on maintaining adaptability in the organizational career: There is some question about how much value top management places on adaptation in the older employee. A study by Siegel and Ghiselli (1971) examined the relationships between measures of managerial talent and organizational rewards (in this case, pay). As expected, the relationships between pay and measures of managerial talent were generally positive for younger managers. However, these relationships generally became weaker with increasing age (twenties to forties and fifties). In fact, the relationship between pay and talent actually became strongly negative in the fifties and sixties. Siegel and Ghiselli conclude the following:

> It would appear that the older managers of high talent who have been passed over for advancement to top management are not only not rewarded with greater pay, but indeed are even negatively rewarded. Quite possibly these people, shelved as they are at the middle managerial levels, "get in the way" when they manifest any of the dynamic qualities of these managerial traits (1971, p. 133).

One possible problem with this study is that the managerial traits **148** were measured by self-description, which may not be a valid assessment of talent. These ratings have been shown to relate to objective performance measures, however, by the second author (Ghiselli, 1971). At the very least we know that the older managers with the most favorable self-perceptions and perhaps those who are in fact most talented, are being penalized by the organization. Much as recently hired employees may complain of age discrimination against young people (often openly practiced under seniority systems), it appears that the organization impartially administers equivalent age discrimination to older people as well. Therefore, how important is employee adaptability to the organization?

SUMMARY

This completes our examination of the factors which influence the development of careers. As the reader can see, the literature is ''top-heavy'' in studies predicting or explaining performance. Less has been done with career-relevant attitudes, career identity, and adaptation. Hopefully, as organizational researchers show more interest in such person-centered issues as quality of work, quantity of life, and personal fulfillment/alienation, there will be more attention given to identity and adaptability.

Now that we have examined some of the factors related to career effectiveness, let us see how these findings can be applied in organizations to improve the development of careers. As a student once lectured to me, the research is nice, but the applications are what it's all about!

Discussion Questions

1. Why has less career literature dealt with identity, attitudes, and adaptability than it has with performance?
2. Identity is an elusive concept. What does it mean to you? How would you describe your own identity?
3. How can success affect career attitudes? Give an example from personal experience.
4. What is career obsolescence? How can organizations act to prevent employees from becoming obsolete?
5. How can effective developmental experiences in early career stages help prevent obsolescence, mid-career stress, and other problems in later career stages?
6. *Should* organizations be concerned about employees' career identity and attitudes? (Are these issues too personal and not the proper concern of one's employer? Are they unrelated to performance or other concerns of the organization?) What do you think? Why?

6

TOWARD MORE EFFECTIVE CAREERS: Redesigning Organizations

To this point we have covered three important areas of careers in organizations: how a person selects an occupation, how he or she develops through general career stages, and career effectiveness factors. Within the preceding chapters we have also considered ways by which organizations might facilitate each of the processes involved in these areas. But how do we take the theory and research we have looked at in earlier chapters, integrate them with the concept of organizations as career systems, and identify ways of developing careers more effectively? This question really involves two issues: (1) What can organizations do to improve the management of their employees' careers, and (2) What can individuals do for better management of their own careers? In this chapter, we will consider the total career, not any single process, and organizational interventions that can enhance overall career effectiveness and organizational performance. At this level we will be talking more about *organizational design* than about actions aimed at individuals. We will discuss actions individuals can take for better management of their own careers in the following chapter.

ORGANIZATIONAL ACTIONS FOR MORE EFFECTIVE CAREERS

The task organizations face in developing better career systems is how to increase the likelihood that the employee will experience *psychological success* (described in Chapter 4) in his or her work experiences. This success, in turn, will lead to greater involvement and the pursuing of more challenging goals.

To see what organizational influences are involved in this process, let us review the model of psychological success presented earlier in Figure 4–7. The factors necessary for psychological success are challenging goals, effort, performance, psychological success, self-esteem, satisfaction, and involvement. To ensure that all of these will be attainable, certain environmental conditions must be present: (1) *challenging jobs* (for challenging work goals), (2) *autonomy and support* (for identifying goals and aiding independent effort), and (3) *feedback* (for guiding effort and evaluating performance). These basic conditions come from several different aspects of the work environment, each of which offers a strategic "leverage point" for career interventions: (1) selection and entry, (2) the job itself, (3) the supervisor, (4) organizational structure and procedures, and (5) personnel policies.

Entry: Changing Employee Inputs

Better links between school and employer personnel functions. There is a pressing need for better integration of the practitioners who specialize in the development of work careers—high school guidance counselors, counseling psychologists in college, personnel specialists in selection and training, and organization development experts who sometimes do career planning as part of their organization development efforts. Furthermore, there is a need to help people achieve greater integration among all the different subidentities or facets of their lives.

Much of the fragmentation of functions could be addressed by increased collaboration between universities and employing organizations. The guidance and counseling departments of some colleges and universities have excellent relations with various businesses, government agencies, and other employers, and this is of tremendous value to students. In these cases, guidance counselors know well what the job markets are like in various occupational fields and geographical areas.

Another form of employer-university cooperation, a less common form, would be for faculty members of various professional schools to meet periodically with practitioners in their respective professions. The agenda could contain questions like, "In what ways are recent graduates poorly prepared or well prepared?" "What are the problems of the newly hired graduate?" "What skills will practitioners need ten years from now?" "In what ways are employers not utilizing the skills and knowledge of the new recruit adequately?" etc.

Because one of the university's functions is to stimulate change, it should be made clear that the college student is not **151** being trained specifically for an entry-level job, but for long-term career growth. Also, his knowledge and skills represent a source of potential innovation to the organization. This innovation may be stressful to the organization, but it should be utilized, not "trained out" of the new recruit.

An illustration of the standard organizational attitude toward new employees recently occurred in a dialogue between a group of business school professors and a group of senior executives. One distinguished-looking executive said, "You know, these students you send us are bright and eager enough, but they are so full of theory and impractical, wild ideas and skills, that it takes us five years to train it all out of them." At this point an equally distinguished senior professor took a long, thoughtful puff on his pipe and replied, "Well, that's interesting to hear. But we are trying to increase it to ten!"

Training students in job-related skills. The other side of this issue is that the student often has little real knowledge of the work world and little training in working with people to better "sell" ideas. As we have discussed in Chapter 3, if the student were given experiences in college dealing with the interpersonal and communications problems to be encountered later in the first job, the "reality shock" of the first job could be greatly diminished.

The importance of communication skills was indicated in a survey of recent graduates who were asked to describe the activities required in entry-level positions. The highest-ranked activity was "selling ideas to others." When asked what classroom activities contribute to effective performance in the first job, the highest-ranked was "writing business letters and reports," followed by "persuasive messages and reports" (Huegli and Tschirgi, 1974–75).

While in school, students tend to underestimate the importance of interpersonal relationships and communication. They take it for granted that technical skills will be the important determinants of success. (Want to know where this assumption comes from? Just take a look at the courses in the curriculum of any professional school!) Therefore, there is a need for more courses, exercises, projects, internships, guest speakers, field trips, etc. aimed at improving communication skills and providing experiences that will demonstrate the importance of these skills.

Realistic job previews in recruiting. As we have also seen before, another way of reducing the first-year reality shock is to provide the job candidate with realistic two-sided information about the job for which he or she is being recruited. What this implies is that the function of recruiting should be shifted from "selling" or "awarding" a job to developing the best possible **152** person-job fit.

The contrasts between traditional and realistic job previews are shown below (Wanous, 1975):

TRADITIONAL JOB PREVIEW	REALISTIC JOB PREVIEW
Sets initial job expectations too high ↓	Set initial job expectations realistically ↓
Job is typically viewed as attractive ↓	Job may or may not be attractive depending upon applicant's own needs ↓
High rate of job offer acceptance ↓	Acceptance rate may be a bit lower but usually is the same as for traditional job previews ↓
Work experience disconfirms expectations ↓	Satisfaction; needs matched to job ↓
Low job survival, dissatisfactions, frequent thoughts of quitting	High job survival, satisfaction, infrequent thoughts of quitting

As an illustration, the following job characteristics were emphasized in a traditional job preview film for operators in a telephone company: "everyone seems happy at work," "exciting work," "important work," and "challenging work." In contrast, the following characteristics were described in the realistic film: "lack of variety," "close supervision," "limited opportunity to make friends," "receive criticism for bad performance, but not praise for good work" (Ibid.).

Better selection methods to identify development candidates. Good development of human talent is dependent upon the prior selection of people who have the potential to be developed. The best career development program in the world will probably fail if low-potential people are put through it. The AT&T Management Progress Study shows the importance of combining good selection methods with good development procedures (Bray, Campbell, and Grant, 1974). More recent career development programs at AT&T continue this integration, and use assessment methods to identify high-potential candidates for development (Joel Moses, personal communication, April 1975).

Good selection methods are relatively easy to develop for particular organizations and jobs—tests, one- or two-day assessment programs, etc. (Schneider, 1976). Research has shown these methods to be effective at identifying high-potential people, as we discussed in Chapter 4. However, such effective selection methods are rarely used. All too often, poor predictors, such as the interview, continue to be used with great frequency. Organizations must learn to apply realistic and proven selection procedures. It makes no sense to waste resources on candidates whose lack of basic skills and aptitudes has not shown up because of the use of poor selection methods.

153

The Job: Development through the Work Environment

One of the most underdeveloped methods of career development in organizations today is the actual *job*. A job places demands and expectations on a person. If a job involves learning new skills, such as international finance or labor law, a person in that job will learn those skills because *that is his job.* There is nothing theoretical or academic about the learning that a job demands. "Management development" or similar off-the-job learning activities are too often seen as unrelated to the improvement of job performance and are not taken seriously enough.

Unfortunately, many managers still think of development as something that happens only in a course or special program, or as something that personnel people take care of. How can the job be utilized more effectively for developing people?

Challenging initial jobs. As we have seen in Chapter 4, the person's initial job assignment is a critical period for learning work attitudes and skills (Berlew and Hall, 1966; Peres, 1966; Bray, Campbell, and Grant, 1974; Buchanan, 1974; Kaufman, 1974). One of the most powerful yet uncomplicated means of aiding the career development of new employees is to assign them to difficult, challenging jobs. However, as one personnel expert said, "In my experience this is somehow very difficult to get through managers' heads, and many new employees still start in a very haphazard fashion" (John Hinrichs, personal communication, 1975). This impression is supported by a survey of research and development organizations (whose professional employees should certainly have the requisite ability), which found that only one out of twenty-two companies had a conscious policy of giving challenging first assignments (Hall and Lawler, 1969). Most companies felt they should bring a person along slowly on easy projects, adding challenge only after the recruit had proven himself. This is more a process for *measuring* competence than *stretching* it.

According to Hinrichs (1974):

> This is glaring mismanagement when you consider the care, attention, and money invested in recruiting and hiring new employees and in designing and conducting training and development programs for long-term employees who should have been properly indoctrinated in the first place (p. 64).

The Bell system, through its Initial Management Development Program (IMDP), has for years had a conscious policy of providing challenging initial assignments. Such a policy does not necessarily involve job enrichment for initial jobs—but it does concentrate on the selection of jobs for new recruits. One way of identifying challenging jobs is to identify competent, demanding supervisors, who will hold high expectations for the new employee.

154   **Periodic job rotation.**   One of the problems with most organizations' personnel policies is that there is a tendency to leave the person in the area in which he or she performs well. This seems logical enough as a way of recovering the organization's investment in the person. In the short and intermediate term, it seems rational, but after several years the field may change and the person may become stale and incapable of adapting to new situations. If employees were moved to new types of work, requiring new learning, every five years or so, they would be forced to remain flexible and to keep learning new skills (Pelz and Andrews, 1966). Kaufman sees this as a future direction organizations should take:

> Provide for changes in job assignments to avoid narrow specialization. Job assignments should require the utilization of different professional knowledge and skills. That would not only help encourage the retention of what the professionals already know but also stimulate the learning of new knowledge and skills and thereby instill confidence that would help the professionals adjust more easily to changing requirements (1974, p. 161).

Colleague stimulation. Colleague interaction can aid a person's performance and development through both emotional support and technical information (Hall, 1971b; Evan, 1963; Pelz and Andrews, 1966). Interaction between younger and older employees can produce a creative blend of experience with enthusiasm, maturity with energy, and ability to sell ideas with creative, fresh thinking. Mixing people from different disciplines or specialties can also lead to creative syntheses and a broader view.

Managers can foster colleague interaction in many ways. The physical arrangements of an office area or a building can bring people together, through coffee areas, library facilities, mailboxes, office arrangements, etc. Managers can heighten interaction within departments by assigning entire departments to one area; interaction between particular departments can be increased if they are placed next to one another.

Work groups, project teams, task forces, and committees can be formed with members drawn from different groups, providing stimulation and exposure to new ideas. New attitudes can develop, too, if young and old, male and female, and black and white employees are on assignments for which they have to work together as equals. A detailed discussion on creating more open communications in organizations is found in Steele (1975).

Frequent feedback and performance review. For people to learn and develop, they need feedback on their performance so they can know how they are doing and where changes should be made. In many organizations, a performance review process exists on paper, but not in practice—the phenomenon of the "vanishing performance appraisal" (Hall and Lawler, 1969). Managers often avoid giving performance appraisals because of the uncom- **155**

fortable face-to-face confrontation involved. They also lack the skills required, even though training can provide these skills fairly easily (Goldstein and Sorcher, 1974). This doesn't even have to be a full-blown, formal performance appraisal. In fact, better learning may come from a periodic general discussion of how the employee's job has been going recently, what the problem areas are, how they can be resolved, what objectives lie ahead for the next few months, and what the boss can do to help.

Feedback is an important way of dealing with the *poor performer*. Through an honest performance review, it may be possible to identify the causes and cures for sub-par work. It is also possible to establish work objectives and timetables for the improvement of deficient work. Then, if the person's work continues to be poor, the manager should take action to terminate or transfer the person.

Rewarding good performance. People tend to repeat behavior that is rewarded (Skinner, 1969). When a person is performing and developing well, one of the best ways to continue that development is through positive reinforcement—perhaps a pat on the back, public recognition, promotion, a complimentary memo, or maybe a pay raise (Hamner, 1974). Failure to reward good performance acts as negative reinforcement for good performers and positive reinforcement for poor performers. Certain organizational personnel policies, such as pay or promotion based upon seniority, actually institutionalize this negative reinforcement of good performance, thus stifling career development.

Changing the Boss' Role

The supervisor has a lot to do with how the job is defined. His role is so crucial in career development that simply changing the boss' expectations of the employee can improve employee performance (Livingston, 1969).

The manager as a career developer. It is possible to move the personnel/career-development job to the line administrator, in a sense. By giving the manager skills that will allow him to help subordinates with career planning and decision making, the personnel or counseling departments would essentially be making the manager into a "career paraprofessional." Most managers are expected to perform employee-development functions as part of their jobs already, but one reason for their failure in this area is that they lack the training and feel uncomfortable in such a role.

In one large Canadian computer company, career planning is built into the manager's role in two ways. First, he is explicitly expected to develop employees and is rewarded for doing so. Second, the manager is required to help each subordinate plan for his or her *next job* in the company. Furthermore, employees are aware that this policy exists and they report that it is being well executed. This effectively counters the "vanishing performance appraisal" (Robert Morrison, personal communication, 1975).

Training managers in job design and career planning. If managers are expected to aid the career development of their subordinates, they must receive training in job analysis and restructuring. They need to know how to identify the most challenging initial job; or how to make one more challenging; how to conduct a good performance review; how to give coaching without controlling; how to listen, counsel, and help plan without directing, etc. With such career-facilitating skills in the manager, the employee will experience career development every day on the job. Goldstein and Sorcher (1974) describe an effective, practical technology for training managers in these helping skills.

Rewarding managers for subordinate development. Another reason administrators do so little career development work with subordinates is that they are generally not rewarded for it. In fact, they are usually punished for it, because (1) training and development (courses, travel to professional meetings, etc.) is considered time off the job and the costs come out of the department's budget; and (2) if the employee does grow on the job, he or she will probably be promoted or transferred to another job, allowing another manager to reap the benefits. This leaves the helpful manager with the task of finding and training a replacement.

Only if a manager is rewarded in some tangible, meaningful way for subordinate development will he or she become more concerned about this process. One idea would be to record the career progress of former subordinates in the manager's file. Another possibility would be for managers to file career development reports each year, documenting the growth of employees under their supervision. Management by objectives (MBO) programs are one means of doing this. If top management clearly tied in employee development with managers' pay increases, this could be a potent form of reinforcement.

The technology of human resource accounting, to be described shortly, is another means of documenting the manager's investments in people. Even though the employee or manager may not be there when the long-term returns are realized, it is possible to reward him for the investments themselves. One interesting twist would be to link his own career development opportunities to those he provides to his subordinates. And of course since the manager could measure any short-term returns on his investments in people, it would also be possible for him to be rewarded for these. **157**

Purcell (1974) describes how GE has used a formal system of managerial rewards and sanctions to aid the career development of female and minority employees. This system entails (1) an equal-employment reporting system that accompanies the manager's annual performance review, and (2) a penalty/reward policy tied to executive compensation. Since the start of this program, the company has increased the number of minority employees in higher-level positions by nearly 250 percent.

Changing Organization Structures and Procedures

The matrix organization structure. One popular form of organization is a matrix or lattice-type structure, for fostering differentiation with integration. In the matrix structure, activities are cross-organized by both function and application (i.e., the product or project which the various functions serve). A given person in the organization would be a member of two groups—a functional department (e.g., personnel) and a product or project group or division (e.g., Oldsmobile). Each product or project group would contain the various functional specialists necessary to produce their output. Each person would have two bosses—a functional manager and a product or project manager. The product or project would be the integrator, while the functional specialty would be the differentiator.

In the career-development field, an organization with a matrix structure could consider people as an explicit ''product'' of the organization. Some functions such as personnel and organization development obviously provide career-relevant services to people. Other functions such as production, sales, finance, and research are involved in activities which directly influence the career opportunities and experiences of their members. These functions are also involved in planning and decisions that have implications for future career opportunities of all the organization's employees.

In practice, in a matrix structure that included people as an output of the system, this new application group might be called the Human Resources Division. Its purpose would be to maximize the utilization and development of human resources, just as a product division is concerned with improving the performance and growth of its product. An example of this at the governmental level is found in the Province of Ontario, Canada, where the Ministry of Human Resources integrates all the people services provided by the province.

Accounting for human resources. If an organization were to develop a human resource division, it would need some way to evaluate the division's performance. (Indeed, perhaps one reason people who provide people services fall between the cracks is that they like the low visibility and lack of performance account-ability!) However, if we are serious about developing integrated career-development efforts in organizations, we will have to dem-onstrate responsibility and accountability to justify the organiza-tion's increased investments in people.

One way to assess the inputs and outputs related to invest-ments in people is the emerging technology of human resource accounting (or human asset accounting). It is not clear whether this field represents an innovation in accounting or just a more precise form of cost accounting, but it does represent an innova-tion in behavioral science measurement. Basically, accounting for human resources involves first identifying as many costs as possi-ble associated with recruiting, evaluating, training, transferring, firing, promoting, and demoting people in a given part of the organization. These costs represent the investment the organiza-tion has in its people. This could be done by measuring either the actual costs that *were* incurred in these personnel actions (historical cost method) or the cost that *would be* incurred in replacing present personnel (replacement cost method). It is also possible to measure in dollar terms the contributions of people to the performance of the organization, although measuring this output side calls for greater ingenuity on the part of the accoun-tant.

These behavioral accounting measures could also be used to assess the impact of organizational attempts to improve per-formance through the development of human resources. This would involve comparing dollar investments in relation to dollar returns over a number of years, to determine the annual rate of return on this human investment. In traditional accounting sys-tems, human resource expenditures such as training and develop-ment are treated as *expenses,* which are deducted from this year's income (and which therefore reduce profit). In behavioral account-ing, these expenditures are treated as investments and are amor-tized over a number of years. With an investment you look for concrete returns (i.e., future payoffs), which should increase prof-its. Thus, behavioral accounting represents a different way of con-ceptualizing people—in terms of expenditures and a cost-account-ing technology for measuring human inputs and outputs more precisely. More details on how human resource accounting can be used to evaluate investments in people can be found in Alex-ander, Goodale, and Hall (1973).

Human resource accounting is also a technology that would enable an organization to measure a manager's performance in developing subordinates. With a measurement method available, it would then be more feasible to reward managers for the career development of subordinates, as advocated earlier in this chapter. **159**

Career-planning services. There is a vital need for organizations to provide career-planning services to employees. These services could be an offshoot of the personnel services which presently are used for selection purposes. Certain personnel staff professions could be designated "career-planning specialists" and given special training in vocational psychology, diagnostic testing, and counseling. They would also need to be quite familiar with the various operations and opportunities available throughout the organization. Career specialists would be available upon request to any employee. The specific types of service provided could vary greatly, but they should contain as a minimum: (1) testing and assessment of occupational interests, education, and competencies; (2) feedback; and (3) a career-planning interview. Career opportunities outside the organization (outplacement), as well as those inside, should be identified. The ultimate purpose of this function would be to increase the fit between person and job, and even if some people left, the improved fit for those who stayed should justify the costs involved. Many companies (e.g., GE, Alcan, IBM, AT&T, 3M) are now providing career-planning and outplacement services such as these through their personnel departments. These activities will be described on pp. 169–170 in more detail.

Changing Personnel Policies

Rotation of managers through "people departments." Another way of involving line managers in employee development is to rotate administrators from other parts of the organization periodically through the personnel department. These would be regular personnel assignments, lasting a year or more, in which the managers would have to learn about personnel and career development as part of the job. Then when the manager is moved back to a line department, he would take these new skills and attitudes with him and integrate them into his work. Thus the individual managers, on the basis of their personnel or counseling experience, would be acting as integrators of the people and production parts of the organization.

Ending job-rotation training; creating lifelong job rotation. Perhaps the two parts of this section heading seem contradictory. However, one problem with the management of careers in most work organizations is that people are moved around too frequently at first, during the so-called training stage of their careers, and too seldom during the later years. In many job-rotation training programs, people are moved from one department to another every few weeks or months, supposedly to be exposed to the functions of other departments. In this way, a person does

not have a real job to do (it can't be a real job if it only lasts a few weeks or months). The result is that the trainees sit around and get bored. They may check out the secretaries and become experts in office gossip, but they learn little about job skills. And their motivation suffers.

In line with our earlier discussions of psychological success, it would be far more valuable to put people in real and demanding jobs when they enter the organization and let the process of success and growth occur through the work itself. There are other ways of helping employees learn about the total organization without sacrificing those critical initial job experiences and successes.

On the other hand, as discussed in Chapter 3, in order to provide varied experiences and prevent obsolescence, it is extremely valuable to rotate people periodically into different departments, where it will be necessary to learn new skills and principles (Kaufman, 1974). Even though it may be tempting for the organization to let a person specialize in an area in which he shows obvious talent, in the long run such specialization can lead to obsolescence if the person attempts to re-live past success by the same methods to which he has become accustomed. This reinforcement of yesterday's successful patterns can also lead to rigidity and resistance to tomorrow's new approaches. There is no logical reason why interdepartmental job transfers would not be just as reasonable for senior executives as for recent college graduates.

An example of later-career job rotation occurred at Union Carbide, where three executive vice-presidents switched jobs (*Business Week,* July 14, 1975). The purpose of the rotation was to give each man a broader view of the overall corporation and to better prepare them for the presidency. One of the men moved. Warren M. Anderson explained how the rotation differed from past policy and why it was necessary:

> We were a holding company until the mid-1950s, and you could count on your fingers the number of people who moved from division to division. You grow up in a division, and you get about four miles tall but not very broad. . . . Everybody had sneered at lateral transfers. Now, they can point to us. I feel this gives me a chance to see the whole business (*Business Week,* July 14, 1975, pp. 82, 84).

Legitimizing downward transfers. This could also be termed "legitimizing demotions," but demotion involves too many negative associations. In our culture, moving up (to a higher job, bigger house, bigger office, higher salary) is considered good, and moving down is considered bad.

However, many basic norms are changing in our culture. It is becoming more acceptable now for women to compete with men. It's not so bad now for men to help care for children, share **161** housework, and be influenced by their wives' career needs. It's not such a terrible thing for a college graduate to be unemployed or to pursue a nontraditional career.

By the same token, if organizations are going to have the internal flexibility to develop people in some of the ways described above, and to move the most competent people into key jobs to help the organization compete in a turbulent environment, it will be necessary to remove barriers to the internal transfer of personnel both upward and downward. One of the strongest barriers to flexibility is the combination of the pyramidal shape of the organization and the norm against downward movement. This is especially problematical in light of the great numbers of competent young people entering organizations and the relatively small number of positions available. It becomes even more of a problem if we accept the importance of early challenge, responsibility, and advancement opportunities. Such conditions are simply not feasible, given the design of many organizations.

Assuming that the top of organizations will probably always be narrower than the bottom, the norm against downward moves seems like the most promising target for change. Two central groundrules would have to be established, however. First, the organization would have to grant a form of career tenure to the employee, say until age 60. Second, there would also have to be a guarantee that the person's pay would never be cut, thus removing the material hardship involved in a demotion. The pay differential is probably inconsequential to the organization, but critical to the person.

With the employee given the guarantee of work and salary, the organization would have more freedom to move people up, down, and across, and in ways that would aid their development and help the organization respond to internal and external needs. Over time, if enough obviously successful and competent people were "demoted," the norm of promotion-as-sign-of-success would be replaced by "movement-as-sign-of-success." The more competent people would be in greater demand in different parts of the organization and the need for one's services could provide the same ego-boost that promotion yields now. Government figures like W. Averill Harriman, Dean Acheson, and Clark Clifford have moved around the U.S. government in a way similar to what is proposed here, although they also have moved in and out of government service as well.

Another benefit of the downward movement of successful, competent people is that the more experienced person could work as a colleague and coach of younger people, helping them develop and benefit from his years of service.

162 One large Canadian oil company that is experimenting with downward transfers for the purposes described here is finding that the anti-demotion norm is very strong, but it seems to be diminishing as more people are moved down. The company attempted to combat the notion that downard movement means failure by moving two of its most obviously successful key executives down first. Although most social changes are hardest on the first people affected, the company has been surprised to find that many older managers confide that they are relieved to be removed from the high pressures and responsibilities of their higher-level jobs. The increasing concern with quality of life may actually help legitimize moves to less-demanding jobs.

An unintended consequence of the downward transfer policy in this organization was improved two-way communication. The people who were moved down acted as good information links, because they knew and trusted the people at the top and yet were now part of the next lower level. Thus, upward communication, especially the flow of bad news, increased greatly.

In time, as the norms regarding downward movement are changed, it should also become easier to move poor performers down to the next lower level, where they presumably had been more effective (thus avoiding the Peter Principle). This particular point is discussed in more detail on p. 164 on fallback positions. (Individuals who continue to perform at very poor levels should be given helpful feedback and coaching from the boss. If no change still occurs, they should be terminated, preferably with a developmental "outplacement" process, such as that at Alcan, to be described on p. 169.)

In sum, then, downward movement offers the following advantages: (1) it increases organizational flexibility in making job assignments; (2) it combats obsolescence for the person transferred; (3) it provides development opportunity for the transferred person's new peers, in that they are given the counsel and role model of a successful, influential colleague; (4) it provides for improved two-way organization communication; and (5) there is some evidence that it promotes individual quality of life—less stress and more satisfaction.

Tenure.   A novel system for insuring early appraisal and feedback for new employees is employed by a medium-sized Pennsylvania manufacturing firm (Seidel, 1974). The president of this firm, Robert Seidel, took a look at how various types of organizations develop personnel and decided that universities, for all their problems, did have one interesting feature, the tenure system. The tenure process forces a university to evaluate academic employees very carefully at least once in their careers, and to give them straight feedback in the form of a "yes" or a "no."

Seidel modified the tenure system as follows. In his company, **163** each employee is carefully appraised by a manager and a personnel expert at the end of his six-month probationary period. If performance has been satisfactory, the two evaluators make a further judgment in terms of the following question: If there is an economic downturn and the workforce must be reduced by 20 percent, would this be a person we would let go? Continued employment is offered regardless of the answer to this question. But the answer is fed back to the employee, giving him a realistic idea of where he stands with the company. People who are not considered part of the lower 20 percent of the workforce are thus granted a form of organizational tenure. The people in the 20 percent group often elect to stay in the organization. In some cases the feedback results in improved performance. The main advantage is that the organization is forced to appraise employees critically on a continuing basis, not on a "crash" basis when a personnel cut is necessary.

Fallback position for promoted employees.   One of the risks involved in promoting a person is that he or she will not be successful in the new position, and because most organizations do not practice downward transfers, the unsuccessful employee may be "stuck" in a level beyond his or her competence—the Peter Principle in action. Without going to a full-blown policy of downward transfers, an organization can reduce the risks of promotion (to both the person and the organization) by assuring each promotee of a fallback position. This guarantees the person a position of status and pay equal to the old job if things don't work out in the new one. This guarantee is especially useful in encouraging a person to move up and into a different department or function for which he has no prior training or experience. (This is the kind of developmental, anti-obsolescence move discussed earlier in this chapter.) In the Heublein organization this method has been used successfully. One management information systems expert was moved to finance and a human resources specialist was put in a manufacturing line management job. Without the fallback position, neither person might have taken the risk. Thus, this is a useful way of helping people who have become highly (and perhaps over-) specialized get into general management. Other companies that have used fallback positions are Procter and Gamble, Continental Can, and Lehman Brothers (see "Heublein Managers Have a Fallback Position," *Business Week*, September 28, 1974).

Incentives for leaving.   Often a person's career development is stifled because he or she stays in the same organization too long. Yet it is difficult for a long-term employee to leave because of dated skills and investments in the organization, such as pensions and other benefits. Indeed, most organizations have rewards for staying and penalties for leaving. If incentives were provided for leaving, however, the options of both organization and individual could be increased.

Early retirement with a full or nearly full pension is one such incentive for leaving an organization. Portable pensions (i.e., pensions in which both the company's and the person's contributions, plus interest, can be taken) would be another incentive for leaving with a minimum of risk to personal security. A third possibility is a system whereby people would be given a certain amount of "retraining" money (based on length of service) when they leave. This method was proposed by Connor and Fielden (1973) as a means of encouraging "shelf sitters" to update themselves or switch fields later in their careers. This idea is already being practiced in some organizations, such as the military (Hughes, 1974).

Involvement of families in career decisions. As organizations make more decisions which affect the personal lives of their members (such as transfers, promotions, and demotions), there are increased conflicts, particularly in relation to the family. Some organizations have found it helpful to involve spouses in employees' career decisions, as well as in problem-solving discussions dealing with the *results* of personnel decisions (such as too-frequent transfers). This is even more critical in the case of dual-career families. Such discussions can effectively demonstrate the need for and value of such actions, thus reducing the pressures on the employee and his or her family. Frequently the discussions can also result in specific actions to help reduce the problems that arise.

HOW IT LOOKS IN PRACTICE:
SOME ILLUSTRATIVE EXAMPLES

To illustrate the application of some of the organizational practices we have just reviewed, let us examine the current career-development practices of a few innovative organizations.

3M Company: Assessment Feedback*

As an outgrowth of a one-day management testing procedure that had been in use for about twenty years, the 3M Company now has a two-day Management Assessment Program (MAP). Instead of relying solely on the traditional assessment methods, the Management Assessment Program puts a greater emphasis on identifying (1) career goals, (2) developmental needs, and (3) placement opportunities—i.e., career planning.

---

*The writer is grateful to Dr. Paul Wernimont for providing this information.

Participation in the program is based upon either volunteering, managers' nominations, or computer identification of "exempt" professional employees in their third year of employment. It is the organization's plan to eventually have every "exempt" employee participate in the program during his third year of employment. Each program contains about fifteen participants, chosen from younger, nonmanagerial employees. During the two days of the MAP, participants complete various tests, exercises, and interviews. They are also evaluated by the professional psychologists in the personnel research staff.

Each participant then has a personal interview feedback session with a personnel research staff member, who gives the general results of the assessment, and suggests specific areas in which the employee could benefit most from further education, training, experience, or development efforts. Field sales people receive feedback reports that have been sent to their individual marketing directors. The assessment information is also used by management for personnel decisions (transfers, promotions, etc.). It is available to the participant's manager at any time for development, vocational guidance, job placement, or review of career objectives. Basically, the purpose of this program is to obtain a better match between the aptitudes and interests of the person and the available career opportunities. The major focus is on *assisting individuals in doing their own planning.*

AT&T: Integrating Assessment and Development*

In an earlier chapter we described the pioneering work of AT&T in the use of assessment centers for the early identification and selection of talented managers. More details on the use of assessment centers in the Bell system is found in Bray, Campbell, and Grant (1974).

AT&T is now using the assessment method for career development as well as for selection. Three career-development programs are in operation now.

The early identification program is for noncollege, nonmanagement people who are being considered for management positions. They first go through a one-day assessment program. Then they are given feedback by a trained person (either in the candidate's own department or in personnel), who then continues to function as that person's *career counselor.* Explicit career plans are made. Then the person and his or her boss jointly set work targets to help achieve the career plan. Although most of the planning is done within the participant's department, the formal process can be monitored by personnel. Because of the high

 *The writer is grateful to Dr. Joel Moses for providing this information.

turnover in superior-subordinate relationships, the third-party career counselor provides more continuity in the career planning process.

A second program exists for high-potential college graduate women who have already gone through the company's regular assessment center. On the basis of the assessment results, the employee, her boss, and a corporate staff person draw up a career plan, containing: a target job, training needed, interim assignments, and a time frame. The three parties review this plan and the progress made every six months.

A third program is a successor to the Initial Management Development Program, but is more "user-oriented" than IMDP. The emphasis is on *boss training,* in the areas of *job restructuring, joint target setting,* and *appraisal skills.* Thus, supervisors are trained in ways of making new employees' initial jobs challenging, in helping set work goals, and in providing performance appraisal and feedback, all essential activities for the operation of the psychological success cycle. At the end of the first year the person goes through a thorough two-day assessment program. Following this is a meeting with the person's boss, a member of the assessment staff, and a personnel coordinator. Then one of three decisions is made: terminate, don't promote, or prepare for middle management. A feedback meeting is held with the employee to discuss the results of the assessment process. Then in the second year, for people with middle-management potential, a formal career plan is drawn up, similar to that for college graduate women.

These career programs in AT&T are based upon the following principles:

1. Emphasize the development of high-potential people only. Don't try to change people who lack management potential.
2. Set specific development objectives. Identify specific job experiences and specific skills the person needs to acquire (e.g., "supervise a central office PBX group").
3. Train the supervisor to provide day-to-day job experiences (e.g., job challenge, performance appraisal) which promote development.
4. Personnel experts should structure and monitor a *process* of career planning and development, but the actual content should be largely the responsibility of the supervisor and the employee. Thus, a personnel staff member often plays a third-party, nondominant role in the process.

Travelers Insurance: Career Planning Conferences*

The Travelers Insurance Company uses a program of *Career Planning Conferences,* coordinated by a company-wide committee representing all major operations of the organization. These eight-

*The author is grateful to Dr. Andrew Souerwine of the University of Connecticut and director of the program for The Travelers for providing this information.

day sessions focus on individual career strategy and are conducted in a university setting, with trained professionals from outside the company as staff members.* Participants are people in their third to seventh year of employment in the company and are judged to have unusual career potential. The company has found that during the three- to seven-year period, employees feel they have reached an initial plateau; it is during this period that the company feels it can help these employees to enhance their careers by having them take a new look at their careers and where they are headed.

Prior to the conference, participants take a battery of tests, which measure interests, values, motivation, personality, and various skills; personal test data are not shared with the company. A key to the conference is the group of outside-company, professional counselors and educators who spend time with participants on a one-to-one basis. In class sessions, participants are encouraged to talk about what they believe goes on in the company, and how to deal with the realities and imperfections of everyday organizational life. Program sessions cover such issues as boss strategies (how to cope with your boss), strategies a person can build into his or her own behavior, on and off the job, and how to identify the key environment variables that affect career plans.

Many of the participants' concerns do not hinge solely on their jobs. Private counseling sessions reveal considerable concern with family issues (a feeling at that stage in the career that the work excludes involvement in other things just as important as the job, that family life may be a bit too shallow, and that not enough is shared with one's spouse); and with professional orientation (confusion about a technical or managerial emphasis to the job).

Another topic of concern to some is the career decision of leaving the company. The company sees its own best interests served when employees re-evaluate the choice of staying or leaving. In an atmosphere where valid information is available, and models for decision making are provided, this choosing process results in a better person-organization fit for the people who stay, at an increased level of commitment.

Each participant develops a six month development plan. Then there is a follow-up contact six months later asking, "Where are you?" and "What were the problems in following through?" These experiences are shared with all participants on an anonymous basis and provide another base for learning from peers. Such anecdotal data indicate considerable impact on behavior, especially in *relationships* with bosses, spouses, and children.

---

*Another program for career development in the insurance industry, focusing on *company* decision making, is reported in LIAMA (1968).

There seems to be more *personal self-direction* on the part of the participants to their careers and an increased sense of personal *achievement,* both on and off the job.

Alcan: Outplacement*

During periods of recession and personnel reductions, many organizations use a process of "outplacement" in an attempt to change firing from a failure to a development experience. In the course of a person's career, he or she can experience psychological failure as well as success. This often leads to a defensive reaction that prevents the person from learning from the experience. However, by stimulating self-appraisal and the exploration of new alternatives, failure can lead to growth, if the conditions are right.

The Alcan Company found itself in a budget squeeze that made it necessary to make a large reduction in personnel. The people cut were those who were in nonessential functions, and those who did not have the skills to warrant reassignment to an essential area. Thus, these were not necessarily ineffective employees, but they were considered nonadaptive.

The first step in the outplacement plan was to inform the employee that he or she was being fired (never at the end of the day, or before a weekend or holiday). The employee was told that company facilities would be provided to help him or her find a new job, and that salary would continue for several months. The emphasis was on getting the person started on the job search immediately, to avoid a long, paralyzing period of grief and anger.

Then the person was put through an assessment program, in which strengths and weaknesses were identified. Feedback of the results was provided, along with counseling and career planning. Specific career skills, such as résumé-writing, interviewing, and salary negotiation were taught. (Many of the people had not written a résumé for twenty years.) An important task here was the rebuilding of shattered confidence and self-esteem. Most people were placed in new jobs, appropriate to their skills, within a few months. The schedule of events in the Alcan outplacement process is shown in Table 6–1.

Similar outplacement activities take place in other organizations such as Exxon, Kennecott, Mutual of New York, General Electric, and Corning Glass Works. In some cases the career counseling and coaching process is aided by outside consultants, such as TH, Inc., of New York, and Man-Marketing Services, Inc., of Chicago (see *Business Week,* July 20, 1974).

*This information is based upon an article by Cuddihy (1974).

Step	Timing
Identification of redundant employee	Informal—usually three to six months before termination
Internal search for alternate job possibilities	One month before termination
Supervisor's initial discussion with special unit, and preparation of termination letter	One to two weeks before termination
Check of employee's medical history	One week before termination
Coaching supervisor on termination interview strategy	One to two days before termination
Termination interview	Should be held from Monday to Thursday *only,* and early in the day—*never* prior to vacation
Meeting of separated employee with line manager of special unit	Immediately after termination interview
Counselling and process of reorientation toward outside world	Same day as termination interview, continuing for one week, with periodic interviews
Initial interviews with outside consultants and with staff psychologist	Within three days of termination
Possible interview with company doctor	Within three days of termination
Beginning of psychological assessment	Within one week of termination
Relocation to new offices	Within one week of termination
Intensive work with consultants to finalize resumés	Within ten days of termination
Consultation with employee benefits staff for advice and clarification of termination policy	Within ten days of termination
Time lag between circulation of resumés and first job interviews	Usually three to four weeks
Counselling with line manager of special unit and with staff phychologist	Continues for two to three weeks and tapers off as the employee gains confidence
Feedback session—results of counselling and assessment	Within two weeks of termination
Time needed for employment interviews	Usually three to four months
New job found	Usually within four months

TABLE 6-1
Steps and
Timing of the
Termination
Process

From B.R. Cuddihy; "How to Give Phased-Out Managers a New Start," *Harvard Business Review*, (July–August 1974), pp. 61–69.

ORGANIZATIONS AS CAREER SYSTEMS: SOME CAVEATS

When planning for change, it is important to consider that organizations can be thought of as *career systems.* That is, one way to understand the workings of an organization is to trace

its effects on the lives of its members, much as we study a biological organism or the physical environment by tracing its effects on the human body. We generally examine an organization from the perspective of the total system or its management; rarely do we look at it through the eyes of its members. We will do this now, to see what implications these ideas have for organizational intervention aimed at employee development.

Career History and Career Plan

To help develop this individual perspective of the organization as a career system, the reader is asked to imagine himself or herself as an inventory clerk in a large factory warehouse. Think of working mostly alone, conducting inventories in a huge building, bringing records up to date, filing orders, replacing stock, dealing with angry foremen when needed items are out of stock, and so forth. What thoughts are you having as you imagine yourself in this job? My first thought is, how can I get out of this job? One idea is to find another job.

But let us assume you have just started this job and other jobs are hard to find. What do you think about now? Assuming you are an educated, upwardly mobile person, you may be thinking about how to get a promotion to a better job in a few months or years. Thus, you may be thinking of ways you can demonstrate excellent job performance and promising future management potential. Or you may be thinking, "This is ridiculous, me an inventory clerk, with my education." In contrast, what would you be thinking if you were a high school dropout, had worked in a factory for twenty years, and had a wife and three teenage kids to support? Is this a different career perspective? How would your work attitudes and performance differ?

What are you saying with thoughts such as these? You are saying, "I am a person with a certain past history—work experience, education, etc.—and some aspirations for the future." In other words, you have a *career history* and a *career plan,* no matter how vaguely thought-out they are. And this career history and career plan will influence your expectations, your attitudes toward work, and your work performance. As you know, there exists a sort of "psychological contract" between the individual and the organization, a set of mutual expectations for anticipated inputs and outputs. And a key factor influencing the individual's side of the contract is the way he feels about his career.

As we have seen earlier, a person's response to a particular job, supervisor, or organization will be affected by his or her *career stage*—where he is psychologically located with respect to his career history and career plan. A young worker in the advancement stage may "hustle" to get promoted out of the inventory clerk's job, while a 55-year-old may have accommodated to it **171** by seeking extrinsic and off-the-job rewards, such as in pay, security, social relationships, and leisure activities.

The *recent experiences* of the individual have a great deal to do with his feelings about his job. Assume two key-punch operators have been promoted into the higher-grade inventory clerk's job. Suppose one has been on an enriched job in which he has worked as part of a team that has been given complete autonomy over particular projects. Suppose the other operator has had a job in which he has been given daily schedules and instructions by a supervisor. The second operator might perceive the inventory clerk's job as containing relatively high levels of autonomy, variety, feedback, and responsibility (i.e., more enrichment than the key-punch job). The first operator, might feel a real let-down. As we will see later, one of the real problems with various attempts at job enrichment concerns *what happens next*.

Influences on Behavior

One way to find out about the career system is to identify some of the key factors in the organization and its environment which influence the behavior and attitudes of employees. These factors are shown in Figure 6-1. They are grouped in terms of the organizational level at which they occur—environment, organization, group, and individual. The farther one gets above the level of the individual employee, the greater the number of people who will be affected by a given intervention, but the harder it is to predict just what those effects will be. For example, environmental stress in the form of an economic recession may result in many jobs being eliminated, or in people being transferred, retrained, going back to school, retiring early, and so forth. We know a recession affects careers profoundly, but in a wide variety of ways. A reduction in one department's budget, on the other hand, will affect mainly people in that department, and the supervisor can work with each separately and have more control over the impact of the budget cut.

We will not discuss each factor in detail; it is assumed that the reader has enough background in organizational psychology to recognize them.

Taking each level of factors in turn, one can begin to think of interventions that would have an impact on particular levels and thus eventually "percolate down" to affect individual careers. For example, at the environmental level, an executive could diagnose the state of the environment and create a selection policy that called for recruitment of only those people who are able to cope with the demands of that environment. You would probably

want flexible, independent, ambiguity-tolerant people in a turbu-

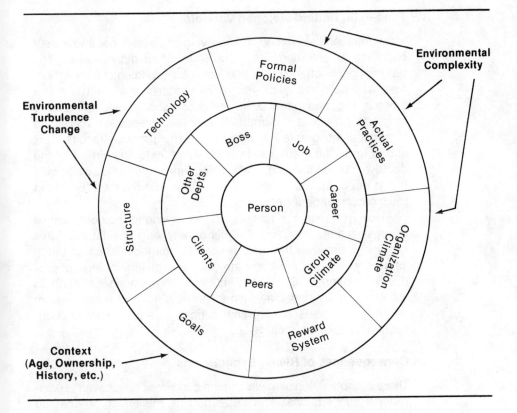

Environmental Complexity

Environmental Turbulence Change

Context (Age, Ownership, History, etc.)

Formal Policies

Technology

Boss

Job

Actual Practices

Other Depts.

Person

Career

Structure

Clients

Peers

Group Climate

Organization Climate

Goals

Reward System

lent environment; but organized, methodical, compliant people for a more stable environment. Abstract, complex thinkers might perform better in a complex environment, while concrete thinkers may do better in a simpler environment. At the organization level, the executive can reorganize the structure (e.g., centralize, decentralize, create a matrix structure, etc.), introduce a new reward system (e.g., the Scanlon plan, Skinnerian reinforcement programs, etc.), introduce new technology, create new practices (e.g., flexitime, four-day week), state new or clarified goals (e.g., long-term planning, MBO), change the top management team, and so forth. At the group or department level, organizations have used interventions such as supervisory training, team building and T-groups, person-job matching, job enrichment, and group incentives. At the level of the individual, common interventions are skill training, career planning, management by objectives (MBO), behavioral reinforcement (Skinnerian), motivation training, etc. In the actual implementation of these interventions, two issues often emerge and reduce their effectiveness—time and system interpendencies, each of which will be considered in the following sections.

FIGURE 6-1 Influences on the Person in the Organization

173

Time—The Underdeveloped Variable

Many interventions aimed at improving organizational and career effectiveness are made as though the future did not exist. The assumption is often made that once management takes action, there will be a response—if not immediately, then within a few months. The manager is evaluated over a short time-span, usually ranging from weeks to months. Only at high executive levels would a manager be granted a year or more to produce results. This shows up in the managerial norms which extol the virtues of the decisive, quick-thinking, fast-acting manager—one who gets things done, makes things happen. Often activity, then, becomes the measure of performance.

However, research has shown that, owing to the complexities of organizational systems, there is a fairly long time lag, perhaps two years, between the occurrence of a managerial action (such as a leadership change) and the eventual equilibrium level of productivity (Likert, 1967). Often an increase in managerial controls will result in an immediate use in productivity and a longer-term decline, as decreased involvement, hostility, and unintended consequences take their toll.

Consequences of Rising Expectations

There is another sense in which time can wreak havoc with organizational interventions. The issue here is the effect of whetting the person's desires for career growth. Consider an organization development (OD) effort—for example, a job-enrichment program—that has eventually resulted in the development of intrinsic motivation, more personal involvement, and better performance after a two-year period. In terms of the research noted above, assume the time lag has run its course, and the long-term effects of the OD effort have been realized. However, where does that leave the employee whose job has been enriched? One of the positive outcomes has been the intrinsic satisfaction of learning a more complex job and achieving a sense of growth and development. We know from psychological success theory and research described earlier that growth experiences are self-sustaining and stimulate desires for further growth, but they require continuing opportunities for growth from the work environment. At this point, the worker for whom the intervention "worked" would be looking for further enrichment—either on his present job or via a promotion to a more rewarding job. The worker who did not respond positively to job enrichment would not hold these expectations for further opportunities.

Unfortunately, in many organizations the OD efforts are aimed at the development of single jobs, not at the worker's career and long-term growth. Therefore, the worker (who by now has been "enriched," too) has no place else to go, little room for further growth. We know from research on rising expectations that the frustration caused by not meeting newly aroused needs for growth can cause greater alienation and hostility than whatever level may have existed before the initial intervention. This brings to mind the old expression, "the operation was a success, but the patient died." Thus, certain steps can be identified in the process by which organizational interventions develop intrinsic motivation:

Step 1: Organizational interventions aimed at enhancing performance often enrich people and develop human resources in the process of enriching the work environment.

Step 2: The person may remain enriched (i.e., possess new skills and aspirations) even if the interventions in the job do not continue.

Step 3: The person may come to expect continuing rewards as a result of his or her development, in the form of opportunities for future growth, advancement, better pay, more leisure, or other extrinsic benefits.

Step 4: If these expectations for the future are not met, the result may be either (1) attempts to influence the organization to provide these rewards, or (2) greater alienation than existed initially, before the intervention. That is, the positive outcomes from one single intervention may not continue indefinitely; unless further growth opportunities are provided, the long-term positive outcomes of an intervention may yield longer-term negative outcomes.

Step 5: This increased frustration and alienation may make the individual resistant to new interventions aimed at intrinsic motivation—"once burned, twice cautious."

Step 6: Therefore, the people who benefit most from an intrinsic motivation intervention may be those who may later suffer the most from it.

These risks are more likely to be present with interventions aimed at higher-order, intrinsic need satisfaction than with those involving extrinsic rewards or controls. This is because the needs satisfied by extrinsic rewards, such as pay, may decrease when satisfied; whereas those needs satisfied by intrinsic rewards, such as greater growth experiences, tend to increase as they become more satisfied (Alderfer, 1972). Although some residual level of mistrust and feelings of manipulation will also exist if a pay incentive program is discontinued, for example, these reactions would probably not be as severe as the discontinuance of a successful job-enrichment program.

System Interdependencies

Closely related to time as an underdeveloped variable is the issue of system interdependencies. As we have discussed in Chapter 3, one company got into job enrichment because of a severe turnover problem among newly-hired college graduates. It had to hire 120 **175** people each year in order to have 20 at the end of the year. So management took a gamble and figured that attrition was caused by unchallenging first-year jobs. The next year the company hired 30 people and worked hard on upgrading their initial jobs. At the end of the year, 25 people were left and were giving far better performance than recruits in previous years. However, because of recruit-supervisor frictions, it soon became clear that the bosses had to be trained as well, so that they could better supervise the new recruit and the enriched job. So then each recruit and his boss went through a training program together.

Then the company realized another problem: as new people were moved into higher-level jobs, turnover increased. Reports indicated that these later jobs were boring and less satisfying than the initial, enriched jobs! In effect, then, the company was simply postponing the turnover problem by enriching only the first assignments. So the company then "enriched" the second-level jobs too. At this point management realized that in improving first-year jobs, they were causing the long-term career expectations of the new recruits to increase (Hall, 1971b). In two other companies it was also found that enriching jobs led to aspirations for further enriched jobs, although less attention was given to training bosses. Responding to the longer-term expectations eventually got the companies into a full-blown program of organization development. Usually the process develops from the other direction (OD efforts often result in career development). In any event, the lesson seems clear: *When pursued organically to their natural levels of activity, the processes of organizational and career development become difficult to separate.*

Therefore, it seems clear that concerns about "quality of life" and "quality of work" basically are concerns about helping employees achieve satisfactory careers. If the employee is intrinsically motivated and job-involved, quality of life to him or her means a high-quality job with good future prospects. If he is not highly job-involved, quality of life may mean the opportunity to expend less time and energy at work and more time in leisure and family pursuits. Here the person is concerned with a good fit between the work career and the family career. In either case, the focus is on the person's total life and career, not just his work behavior at one point in time.

SUMMARY

This completes our discussion of what organizations can do to facilitate the career development of their employees, concluding with the warnings about possible unintended consequences. These **176** recommended steps are summarized in Table 6–2. What seems

I. *Entry: Changing employee inputs*
   1. Better links between school and employer personnel functions
   2. Training students in job-related skills
   3. Realistic job previews in recruiting
   4. Better selection methods to identify development candidates
II. *The Job: Development through the work environment*
   1. Challenging initial jobs
   2. Periodic job rotation
   3. Colleague stimulation
   4. Frequent feedback and performance review
   5. Rewarding good performance
III. *Changing the boss' role*
   1. Making managers career developers
   2. Training managers in job design and career planning
   3. Rewarding managers for subordinate development
IV. *Changing organization structures and procedures*
   1. The matrix organization structure
   2. Accounting for human resources
   3. Career-planning services
V. *Changing personnel policies*
   1. Rotation of managers through "people departments"
   2. Ending job-rotation training; creating lifelong job rotation
   3. Legitimizing downward transfers
   4. "Tenure" and identification of marginal performers
   5. Fallback position for promoted employees
   6. Incentives for leaving
   7. Involvement of families in career decisions

TABLE 6–2
Summary of
Organizational
Methods of
Promoting
Career
Development

clear is that most of these methods do not appear peculiar to the function of career development—*they are basically principles of good, sound human resource management.*

Most of the current organizational practices aimed at developing careers seem to involve the first two areas in Table 6–2—the entry/selection process and the job (plus career-planning services, from the fourth area). Except for the AT&T programs, there has been less emphasis on retraining the boss or changing the boss' role in the career-development process. Various organizations have implemented changes in career-related personnel policies, as we have seen.

It would appear that organizational efforts that attempt to *integrate* several of these different areas of the career experience would be the most effective and the least likely to hit unforseen snags. A good model in this regard is the AT&T approach, which involves (1) selection and entry, (2) the job, (3) the boss, and (4) new organizational functions. The more career development is "built into" the ongoing functions of the existing organization, the more potent and enduring it will be.

What this really gets down to, ultimately, is the development of a role for the personnel function which is both new and at **177** the same time very traditional. The new elements are: (1) *more direct involvement in the superior-subordinate relationship* (for performance appraisal, career planning, and boss training); (2) *more integration of the assessment, selection, and development functions;* (3) *a longer time perspective* (tracking the employee's movement through the organization); and (4) *increased influence with line management* (training bosses, redesigning jobs, changing reward systems, dealing with government agencies and social action groups over EEO [Equal Employment Opportunity] and OSHA [Occupational Safety and Health Act] legislation). The new functions for personnel are traditional in the sense that (1) the focus is still upon the *individual employee;* (2) the basic personnel activities involved in career development still boil down to the traditional *recruitment, selection, placement, training,* and *appraisal;* (3) and ultimate responsibility and power still rests with line management (i.e., personnel will always be a staff function).

So far, most college courses and texts on personnel have not yet caught up with current practices in personnel, but three good guides to this "new world" of personnel can be found in Hamner and Schmidt (1974), Glueck (1974), and DuBrin (1972). It is clear that as legislation and social change give the individual employee more rights and power vis-à-vis the employer, the importance of and pressure on personnel, which has responsibility for employee relations, is increased. This more active role for personnel is not a sudden or recent development, because personnel has been gradually changing to absorb functions such as organization development and job enrichment. It is to be hoped that the new process of career development will not be accepted uncritically or overzealously, since it could easily become just another management fad. Rather, career development, the enhancement of human talent, should be viewed as a function that has always existed in effective organizations, yet one that can benefit from being conceptualized and practiced in new ways.

Discussion Questions

1. Applying either your own past experiences or a site visit, describe what one specific organization is doing to facilitate the career development of its employees. How would you assess these efforts in terms of the criteria of career effectiveness described earlier?
2. How can potential employees get more realistic job information to reduce "reality shock" on entry?
3. How can the job itself be utilized to promote career development?
4. How can bosses aid subordinates' career development? Why do many bosses tend not to engage in career-facilitating activities with their employees?
5. What are the pros and cons of lifelong job rotation? Of downward transfers?
6. How would you assess the probable impact of AT&T's approach to career development? Travelers'? 3M's? Alcan's?
7. What are some of the unintended consequences that may arise as a result of career-development programs in organizations?

TOWARD MORE EFFECTIVE CAREERS: Self-Management

7

Alice: Will you tell me, please, which way I ought to go from here?
Cheshire Cat: That depends a good deal on where you want to get to.
Alice: I don't much care . . .
Cheshire Cat: Then it doesn't matter which way you go.

Lewis Carroll, Alice in Wonderland

THE NEED FOR SELF-MANAGEMENT OF CAREERS

In the management of our own lives and careers, most of us act more like Alice than we would care to admit. Managers and professionals spend most of their work lives planning, organizing, directing, and controlling the fate of people, equipment, and capital, yet it is rare for them to spend as much as one full day per year applying similar systematic planning techniques to their own careers. Indeed, in a study of business executives who had changed jobs, Roe and Baruch (1967) found that these stereotypically "high-powered" people were remarkably passive and reactive in letting the work environment determine the course of their careers. However, a person's goals (Locke, 1968), intentions (Holland, 1973), and expectations (Livingston, 1969) have a strong influence on the direction and success of her activities. In short, people tend to get where they want to go; if you *know* where you want to go, you're more likely to end up there.

On the other hand, if you don't care where you go, the organization you work for will be only too happy to determine your moves for you. Having personal plans and goals is one important way **179** to reduce the control of the organization over the management of your life. In Eugene Jennings' words:

> The larger, more powerful the organization, the more men must manage their careers in terms of their own coordinates and free choices. [Career planning] allows men to intelligently counteract the arbitrary decisions of their corporations, to address themselves as private persons, and to restore the balance between the needs of the individual and those of the organization. In short, the highest good accrues at that point where self and corporation intersect for mutually beneficial purposes (1971, p. 307).

This chapter is a sort of "organizational survival kit," an exploration of ways the individual, through personal goals, planning, and strategy, can achieve greater self-direction in the management of his or her career.

THE PROCESS OF DEVELOPMENT

Before getting into the specifics of managing one's career, let us first review the basic process of career development, which we discussed in Chapter 4. According to the model shown in Figure 4–7, career success occurs in cycles. First, the person selects a particular work goal, chooses a course of action (effort), utilizes whatever support and feedback are available, achieves a particular level of performance, experiences a level of psychological success or failure, experiences increased (or decreased) self-esteem and satisfaction, becomes more (or less) involved in the task, and then recycles, moving on to other tasks and goals.*

As a result of success on a difficult or "stretching" goal, the person develops new skills and abilities, parts of himself that simply did not exist before. Thus, success on challenging goals is one form of self-actualization, bringing into actuality new aspects of the self. The intrinsic reinforcement of increased self-esteem and satisfaction from psychological success can then lead to more goal setting, with more difficult goals. Failure can also lead to growth, if the person searches for information about why the failure occurred and about how to perform better.

The key element in this career development cycle is the pursuit of specific goals. It is possible to work toward goals in different ways. In many cases, people do not initially set goals for themselves, but stumble across them, gradually become aware of them, or have them assigned by someone else (e.g., the boss or a client). Sometimes a person works on a task without being aware that he is working toward a particular goal; then when looking back over his past behavior, he may come to realize the importance

---

*The application of success cycles to employee development is discussed further in Farris (1975).

of that goal. Finally, other people may *perceive* a person as being committed to a certain goal (which he may *not* be, initially); they may communicate their perceptions to the person, create expectations, and in effect commit him to that goal. However, the more conscious the person is of his own goals, the more direct and efficient the pursuit of these goals can be. In the following section we will present some strategies for identifying and implementing career goals.

CAREER-PLANNING STRATEGIES

Our review of ideas for better self-management of careers will be presented in sections below. In the first section we will discuss general career competencies that represent basic building blocks or "meta-tasks" for careers. The following sections will consider more specific strategies for dealing with organizations. The chapter concludes with a more detailed discussion of how to do career planning.

Develop Basic Career Competencies

Based upon the work of Super (Super and Bohn, 1970), Crites (1973b) has identified five career competencies that contribute to a person's career maturity: self-appraisal, occupational information, goal selection, planning, and problem solving.* These are five specific skills that can be developed. Of all the personal guidelines for career growth, these five competencies are the most basic; in a sense the remaining strategies are derivatives of these.

Self-appraisal. A central concept in vocational psychology is self-awareness, or "knowing yourself." As we have seen from the model of career roles and subidentities in Chapter 2 (Figure 2–7), choosing an occupation involves choosing an identity. As Crites says, "To know one's self, then, is considered to be a *sine qua non* of mature career development" (1973b, p. 23).

How do you get to know yourself better? One good way is through the counseling, guidance, career-planning, or personnel office on your campus or in your organization. In the hands of trained professionals, tests such as the Strong and the Kuder can help identify your interests. Other tests can measure your abilities. Counseling interviews can help you come to a clearer understanding of your interests and abilities. If your organization has an assessment center or a career-planning program, sign up for it. The information you will obtain about yourself will not be threaten-

---

*A measure of career choice competencies, as well as measures of career choice attitudes, is found in Crites' (1973b) *Career Maturity Inventory*. This measure is oriented primarily toward adolescents. Little work has been done in this area with employed adults.

ing and it will probably lead to some very specific, concrete action on your part.

There are also various exercises and assignments, done either individually or in small groups, which can aid self-appraisal. Career-planning exercises, such as those in this book and in Hall, Bowen, Lewicki, and Hall (1975), Bolles (1972), and Kolb et al. (1974) are all good ways of learning more about yourself without the help of trained professionals. An excellent self-administered career-planning exercise which attempts to match your interests and abilities with the requirements of specific occupations is Holland's (1973) Self-Directed Search. This instrument is clear, easy to use, and has been validated by a considerable body of research.

There are other, informal ways of learning more about yourself, too. Ask your instructors or your boss for feedback on your performance. Ordinarily, people get very little feedback unless they go out of their way to ask for it. Don't ask just for an evaluation (am I good or poor?), but for areas of strength and weakness. Ask what you might do to develop your weak areas. You could ask your friends or spouse the same questions as well.

You might find yourself getting upset or defensive at some of the feedback you get. (If feedback isn't surprising in some respects, what good is it?) A couple of hints to keep you open: make sure you let the other person do most of the talking (you can ask questions, but try not to make statements), and try repeating what the other person has told you to see if you have heard correctly (i.e., test it out).

Occupational information. Career development is a process of getting a good fit between you (your interests, abilities, experience) and your work (requirements, rewards, opportunities, etc.). Therefore, the other side of knowing yourself is knowing about occupations, organizations, and jobs. Unfortunately, there are fewer standardized ways of obtaining occupational information than there are for obtaining information about yourself. As we saw earlier, Holland's (1973) Self-Directed Search does have a way of linking personal interests and abilities with occupations (through an "Occupations Finder"), as do the Strong and the Kuder measures. The *Dictionary of Occupational Titles* (DOT) gives worker trait requirements for an exhaustive list of occupations.

Another impressive source of occupational information is the U.S. Department of Labor's (1974) *Occupational Outlook Handbook.** The *Handbook* is published every other year and is based upon Bureau of Labor Statistics analyses of data received from

---

*For sale by the Superintendent of Documents, U.S. Government Printing Office, Washington, D.C. 20402. Price: $6.85. (Make checks payable to Superintendent of Documents.)

business firms, trade associations, labor unions, professional societies, educational institutions, government agencies, and other groups. Each occupation is described in terms of the following information: nature of the work; places of employment; training, other qualifications, and advancement; and employment outlook. There is also a useful introductory section called "Tomorrow's Jobs," which describes general growth trends by occupation, industry, and educational level through the next ten years. For example, the 1974–75 edition projects a growth of 38 percent (from 1972 to 1985) in jobs in service-producing industries (transportation and public utilities; finance, insurance, and real estate; services; and government), whereas only 13 percent growth is expected in goods-producing industries (manufacturing, contract construction, mining, and agriculture).

In addition to the *Handbook,* the Bureau of Labor Statistics produces reprints of *Handbook* statements on individual occupations, as well as the *Occupational Outlook Quarterly,* which supplements the *Handbook* with articles on current occupational developments. Getting to know the reference librarian and the reference services in your library is another way of exploring occupational information. Information specifically for women can be found in Rogalin and Pell (1975).

Various interactive computer methods of providing career information have been tried over the years, but one of the most promising is SIGI, developed by Martin Katz (1975) at the Educational Testing Service.

> The ETS has been developing the System of Interactive Guidance and Information since 1968. Students using SIGI engage in a dialog with a computer, asking questions and giving directions through a typewriter-like keyboard. They specify their occupational values, receive specific information about occupations, assess their chances of success in preparing for each occupation, and rehearse the steps necessary to enter a chosen field.
>
> Martin Katz, who directed SIGI's development for ETS, said that the program "does not pretend to give students the one right answer to career uncertainties, but it does help students frame the proper questions and get and use relevant information." Students are encouraged "to modify their plans as they gain new insights, experience, and information" *(Behavior Today,* April 14, 1975, p. 444).

This program is presently being developed at several two-year colleges and one four-year college (Illinois State University) around the United States.*

Goal selection. As we have seen earlier in the model of career development through psychological success, growth occurs through the process of achieving one's goals. The critical aspect of career maturity here is how the person sets his or her goals. According to Argyris (1964), goals that lead to growth are

---

*More information can be obtained from Dr. Katz, ETS, Princeton, N.J., 08540.

those which are (1) challenging or "stretching," (2) relevant to the person's self-image, (3) set by the person (independently or collaboratively), and (4) implemented by the person's independent effort. Therefore, the person must develop enough awareness of self and of work situations to be able to recognize goals with these characteristics. According to Crites:

> In short, the career-mature [person] should be able to select goals for himself which are consistent with his career capabilities. He should be able to "match up" his psychosocial characteristics with those required by the occupations he is considering as possible career options" (1973b, pp. 25, 27).

How does one learn how to select goals competently? This overlaps partly with developing self-awareness and gathering occupational information, which have already been discussed. A good counselor or a sensitive supervisor can help you identify competent career goals. Trial jobs help you recognize, after the fact, which aspects of various work environments are important to you.

Career-planning exercises are becoming a popular way of stimulating goal setting. Three examples are "Life Planning," "Career Problem," and "The Awful Interview" in Hall, Bowen, Lewicki, and Hall (1975).

One important feature of goals is that they change, despite the fact that the word *goal* has a ring of finality to it. One way to get started *identifying* your own career goals is to start working toward some goal, even though you may not be strongly committed to it. Possible goals might be getting all A's next term, getting to know a professor better, finding a more interesting job, or getting into graduate school. In the process of working toward that goal, you will become more involved in an area of work, you will probably experience psychological success, and other goals will probably emerge. The important thing is to *get started* and get into the psychological success cycle. One thing is certain: if you *don't* commit yourself to some goal and make some effort, you won't experience psychological success.

Planning. Once you have identified a goal, the next step is to plan for its achievement. Planning is

> the tendency of the individual to think about the means which are necessary to attain a desired end. Does he simply select a vocational goal and neglect specification of the intermediate steps which lead to it? Or does he "plan out" the entire sequence from its initiation to its completion (Crites, 1973b, p. 27)?

Thus planning is the identification and ordering of action steps necessary to attain a particular goal.

Like goal selection, planning is an active process, not a commodity (like occupational information or self-knowledge). There-

184

fore, it too is best acquired through experience. Career-planning exercises, such as those cited earlier, and counseling can be useful ways of developing one's planning skills.

Problem solving. In the course of pursuing a career, problems often arise. There may be conflicts with parents over your desired occupation, indecision, low ability in your chosen area, and barriers such as a tight economy or minority-group prejudice. The more capable the person is of solving these problems, the more likely he or she is to be effective in the chosen area. Problem-solving skills involve (1) identifying alternative solutions, (2) gathering information to evaluate alternatives, and (3) choosing and implementing a solution. Much of the information gained through attaining self-awareness and occupational information is also useful for general career problem solving. General methods for improving problem-solving skills, such as brainstorming, and group discussion could be easily be applied to career problems.

This completes our discussion of the most basic career competencies. The following ideas represent more specific strategies for dealing with career processes in organizations.

Choose an Organization Carefully

A critical part of the development of your career is the organization you work for. The organization, after all, represents the work environment which provides the conditions necessary for career growth: challenge, support, autonomy, feedback, etc. It is the organization which provides the jobs, the supervisors, the reward system, the promotion sequence, and the personnel policies which will affect the way your career unfolds. In fact, choosing an organization to work for is often one of the most important career choices a person can make. In some cases, choosing an organization even affects one's future occupation, because the organization may transfer a person from one field to another (for example, from engineering to marketing or general management). The organization will be exerting a lot of control over your life and career, so choose it wisely.

Get a Challenging Initial Job

As we have seen, your first job will have a strong impact on your future success. In choosing it, challenge and potential for career growth should be more important than shorter-term considerations such as salary or location. If you are stretched and pushed toward excellence in that first job, you will have an even wider choice of job offers during the next ten or twenty years.

If you are now in school, choosing a job and choosing an **185** organization will represent the same decision. However, if you are in your first year or two with an organization, and if you are not being sufficiently stretched, try to make a change. Let people in personnel know you would like a different assignment. Let your boss know. Let influential managers know. Another possibility is to *redefine your job* and assume more responsibility on your own initiative. *Don't take a passive role regarding your career experiences.* If you can't get a more challenging assignment within the organization, be ready to move.

Be an Outstanding Performer

One of the best ways to generate good career opportunities is to excel in those opportunities you already have. Good performance enhances your own self-esteem (through psychological success) as well as your esteem in the eyes of others. Seek out *feedback* on your work from your boss and colleagues. Don't be afraid to ask for *coaching* from your boss; he will be impressed with your conscientiousness. Ask your boss to work with you in setting and reviewing specific work *goals* to motivate your performance over a six-month period. Chances are, your boss won't initiate these aids to performance but would be delighted to help if you suggest them.

Develop Professional Mobility

One of the keys to success in a career is mobility. The more career options you have, the greater are your chances of being satisfied, and the more influence you have within your organization. Eugene Jennings (1971) has identified a set of rules for developing professional mobility (he calls it "executive chess"). These mobility rules are summarized below.

Maintain the widest set of options. Don't become too technical or overspecialized. It may be tremendously exciting for a few years to become the world's leading expert on vacuum tubes, but what happens when transistors come along? Furthermore, don't be only a staff person if your goal is management; be sure to get line management experience.

Don't be blocked by immobile superiors. An ineffective, immobile superior can block you in two ways: he will not stretch you, and he can block your career path. How do you tell if your superior is immobile? According to Jennings, a mobile superior is one who has moved in the last three years. If you find yourself working for an immobile superior, you have several options, which have just been discussed in the context of the initial job: apply to personnel for a transfer, talk to influential people with "powers of nomination," or ask the superior for a transfer. Whatever you do, don't become a "crucial subordinate" to an immobile boss, or you may have real trouble getting away.

Become a crucial subordinate to a mobile superior.   One of the best ways to challenge yourself is to work for a successful, mobile superior. Not only will this person create job expectations that will stretch your skills, but he will provide a good role model to guide your growth. Furthermore, as this person progresses in his career, this can provide future visibility and exposure for you. You can tell how crucial you are to your boss in three ways: (1) how well you are performing, (2) the number and quality of your special assignments, and (3) how much your behavior produces important consequences.

Always favor increased exposure and visibility.   Not only should you attempt to perform at an outstanding level, but you should not be shy about letting people know you exist (you can become invisible and anonymous all too easily in most large organizations). Know the route to the top in your organization, and be willing to move *down* to move *up* faster elsewhere.

Be prepared to practice self-nomination.   Don't be passive about your career mobility. Don't wait to be "tapped" for key assignments. Let it be known to nominators that you want a particular job and are prepared to work to qualify for it.

Leave an organization at your own convenience.   If problems develop in a job and it looks as if you will be switching jobs, don't wait until the situation deteriorates to the point where someone asks you to leave. Never allow a showdown to occur. Leave on the best of terms; it's better to leave friends in your wake than enemies.

Rehearse before quitting.   If you are going to leave, never do so in a state of high emotion. Tell your family first, take a vacation, see a professional "head hunter," or take some other planning action. Try going through the motions to see how it would feel to quit. But only rehearse once. After that, either quit or forget about the idea.

Plan for a multi-career.   Be a "re-potter," a person with two or three different fields or occupations in his or her career. Never allow success in one field to pre-empt your future by preventing you from moving later to a different field. This is good protection against obsolescence.

Plan Your Own and Your Spouse's Career Collaboratively

In many cases, husband and wife both have careers. This means that both parties will have to work together in career planning. Don't assume that you can just manage your own career and that your spouse will automatically go along. (This is especially **187** important advice for men.) To plan careers jointly requires skills of providing support, mutual decision making, and flexibility. It may also entail living near large urban areas in order to maximize job opportunities for each person.

Get Help in Career Management

Don't assume that your career is such a personal thing that you can't talk to anyone else about it. Learn what career-planning services are available in your school or organization, and take advantage of their services. Sometimes it pays to use professional job counselors or placement specialists. Many universities provide these services to their alumni, as do various professional societies. Informal sources, such as family, friends, and colleagues, can also be of help as well.

Anticipate Chance Events

A critical influence on your career's development, despite all the planning you will do, is still Lady Luck. Chance events often determine what jobs are open at a given time, when the demand for people in your field will pick up or drop off, when a mobile superior may be assigned to your department, etc. However, you can deal with chance events in certain ways. First, you can anticipate what conditions might arise and develop *contingency plans* for them (e.g., "if we have a recession, I'll go back to graduate school"). Ask yourself, "What are all the things that could go wrong?" And "How would I respond to each course of events?" Second, you can prepare yourself to be ready to take advantage of opportunities when they come along. (A colleague recently said, "Luck is the reward of the diligent.") As Allan Cox (1973) remarks in *Confessions of a Corporate Headhunter,*

> Luck, chance, error—all enter into the success of a candidate's job search, and no amount of professionalism will eliminate all these vagaries. If, however, the candidate develops the self-knowledge and the confidence based on his knowledge of [occupational information], he stands a good chance of getting the job he wants and deserves (p. 113).

Continually Reassess Your Career

In addition to the above steps, it is important to review your development from time to time and make "mid-course corrections," much like a space flight. As we have stressed throughout this book, career development is not a one-shot process. You make choices throughout your life, and these choices continue to affect the way you grow and develop (or fail to do so). Be aware of what career stage you are in (early? middle? late?). Know what your developmental needs are in each stage. Be prepared to devel-

I. Develop basic career competencies
   a. self-appraisal
   b. obtaining occupational information
   c. goal selection
   d. planning
   e. problem solving
II. *Choose an organization carefully*
III. *Get a challenging initial job*
IV. *Be an outstanding performer*
V. *Develop professional mobility ("executive chess")*
   1. Maintain the widest set of options
   2. Don't be blocked by an immobile superior
   3. Become a crucial subordinate to a mobile superior
   4. Always favor increased exposure and visibility
   5. Be prepared to practice self-nomination
   6. Leave an organization at your own convenience
   7. Rehearse before quitting
   8. Plan for a multi-career
VI. Plan your own and your spouse's career collaboratively
VII. Get help in career management
VIII. Anticipate chance events
IX. Continually reassess your career

TABLE 7-1
Summary of
Methods of
Improving
Self-Management
of Careers

op in different directions at different points in your career. Periodically drag out those two familiar self-assessment questions: "Where am I headed?" and "Where do I want to be?" The methods for better career self-management are summarized in Table 7-1.

Discussion Questions

1. How much control can an individual have over his own career? Isn't it ultimately in the hands of fate and the organization?
2. What are the basic career competencies? How have you already worked at developing these competencies?
3. Why is effort directed toward specific goals an important aspect of career development? Give an example of a specific career goal toward which you have worked.
4. What can you do to get a challenging initial job?
5. How would you evaluate Jennings' rules for professional mobility?
6. What problems can arise in dual-career families? How can the two parties cope with these problems? What can organizations do to help?

8 CURRENT CAREER ISSUES IN ORGANIZATIONS

Now that we have discussed the basic processes of career development, as well as the steps that can be taken to facilitate this process, let us look ahead and identify some major current issues regarding careers in today's organizations. These issues all point to the need for the organization to become more flexible in regard to employees' lives, providing them more personal choices and opportunities for self-direction.

THE ORGANIZATIONAL GAP: WORKER VERSUS PROFESSIONAL

One of the most glaring problems regarding careers today is that the majority of people employed—lower-level white- and blue-collar workers—do not feel that they have careers. Many nonsupervisory, nonprofessional employees perceive their positions as "dead-end" jobs. Because people often think of a career in terms of climbing the occupational ladder, lack of advancement opportunities is often seen as lack of career.

In addition to lacking advancement opportunities, lower-level jobs also offer little in the way of opportunities for intrinsic motivation or satisfaction. They are often boring, repetitive, unchallenging, overstructured, and confining. In fact, the whole purpose of bureaucratic administration in complex organizations is to design jobs in such a way that they are literally "foolproof." Work is broken down into simple, specialized, well-defined activities requiring little thinking, skill, or intelligence on the part of the worker, so that output and performance will not be affected by individual

190

differences among workers. The great economic efficiency that is the beauty of bureaucracy is also the feature most responsible for the boredom and frustration of the people who perform the work.

For this reason, there is often a conflict between the needs of lower-level workers and the goals of work organizations, which can lead to psychological failure rather than success (Argyris, 1964; Hall and Schneider, 1973). When people are faced with a work situation structured for failure, they attempt to minimize their feelings of failure in the following ways:

1. Withdrawing emotionally from the work situation by lowering their work standards and becoming apathetic and disinterested
2. Placing increased value on material rewards and depreciating the value of human or intrinsic rewards
3. Defending self-concept through the use of defense mechanisms
4. Fighting the organization
5. Attempting to gain promotion to a position with greater prospects for success
6. Leaving the organization (Argyris, 1964)

When alternative 5 (promotion) is effectively blocked by the dead-end nature of lower-level jobs and alternative 6 (leaving) is made difficult by a tight job market, the remaining alternatives seem bleak indeed to the person and the organization. Two widely discussed worker responses are discontent (alternative 4) and alienation (alternative 1), which show up not only on traditional indicators (absenteeism, tardiness, low quality) but also increasingly in more direct forms of worker action: sabotage, work slow-downs, wildcat strikes, in-plant drug and alcohol use, attacks on supervisors, and plant occupations. Indeed, there is evidence of a new force in industrial relations, worker activism—the organized activities of worker groups, outside the traditional union channels, for direct action against management to achieve changes in work conditions and supervision. In one automobile plant in the summer of 1973 two young workers occupied the central control room, locked themselves in, and turned off all electrical power. They told no one else about their plan, for fear that management would find out and frustrate their efforts. However, as soon as they took over the control room, the remaining workers spontaneously surrounded the room, making it impossible for guards and police to get near the two dissidents. The issue centered around a supervisor who was seen as inhumane and had been the object of many grievances. The workers demanded that he be fired. The company agreed after a few hours and fired the supervisor for violating company personnel policies. Similar actions have occurred since then in this company, showing increased worker organization and dealing with specific complaints **191** about the work and working conditions. Similar activities have occurred, with wide publicity, at other automobile production facilities.

Part of the reason for the increase in activism among workers may be the rising expectations of young people entering the workforce. A survey by Daniel Yankelovich indicates a desire for new career rewards among contemporary youth. Four out of five college students believe that a meaningful career is important. The most important factors students report as influencing their career choices are "the opportunity to make a contribution," "job challenge," "the ability to find self-expression," and "free time for outside interests." However, 69 percent of all students no longer feel that "hard work will pay off" (Yankelovich, 1972). More recently, similar changes have been found in the attitudes of non-college youth (Yankelovich, 1974).

A study of college freshman at 300 American colleges and universities showed a similar trend. Compared to freshmen in 1966, 1970 freshmen were more inner-directed about their lifestyles and goals. The 1970 group was more concerned about self-satisfying activities than about those which bring about recognition from the larger society (Astin and Bisconti, 1972). Other longitudinal studies have also shown that students' attitudes toward authority and competition are becoming more negative (Ondrack, 1973; Miner, 1971). What this means is that young people are more likely to value shared authority or at least more approachable, flexible supervision, as well as more individualized, noncompetitive standards of performance.

Two other factors also help explain the rising expectations of young workers today. First, they have grown up accustomed to economic security and perhaps affluence. For their parents, merely having a job and surviving during the Depression was sufficient. Today's young people have passed the security needs, on Maslow's need hierarchy, and have become concerned with "higher-order" needs such as affiliation, esteem, autonomy, achievement, and self-fulfillment.

Another important factor is the educational experiences of today's young people. During the 1960s our educational system was reformed and enriched. More students saw that learning and work can be stimulating, challenging, and satisfying as new teaching methods were developed. The trend in the 1960s and early 1970s was to "turn the student on." The youth culture also stressed stimulation and immediate experience (through social action, interpersonal relationships, drugs, etc.). It is not surprising, then, that the products of this stimuli-rich environment would look for similar stimulation in work.

When rising expectations meet not so quickly rising opportunities, as we know from recent experiences in civil rights and national economic development, the result is high levels of frustration, hostility, and alienation. As education levels and affluence continue to increase, the organization gap between the haves and have-nots (i.e., those who do and don't have career advancement and growth opportunities in their work) will likewise increase.

Yankelovich (1974) argues that the critical factor differentiating the haves from the have-nots will be education. In his 1973 survey he found that college students were increasingly viewing college as preparation for a successful career (66 percent in 1973 versus 55 percent in 1967), in contrast to the anti-career values of the 1960s. At the same time, both college and noncollege youth are placing strong value on self-fulfillment and participation in decision making. However, Yankelovich argues that given the present shortages of fulfilling jobs, only college-educated youth will have a good chance of attaining their work aspirations. The crisis of unmet rising expectations will hit the noncollege majority (70 percent of our young people) the hardest. Yankelovich describes this opportunity gap as follows:

> The split within the young generation is far greater, and more dangerous to society, than the split between generations. While it is comforting to know that educated youth like to work and probably will find fulfilling jobs, those who lack college degrees also want interesting and challenging work, but as work is now organized they will not readily find what they seek. So, because they are less insecure than their parents, these young people take "less crap" on the job. They are not automatically loyal to the organization, and they feel free to express their discontent in myriad ways from fooling around on the job to sabotage. Moreover, if the work itself is not meaningful, they will opt for "30 and out" retirement, shorter work weeks, frequent absenteeism, more leisure, and other methods for cutting back and down on their job commitment. . . .
>
> The stepladder has been removed from the factory floor, and people now gain economic and social mobility through education, not by following the traditional Horatio Alger route. Because young laborers know they are locked into a low caste, the likelihood of renewed class tension increases (1974, pp. 85, 87).

The implication of this opportunity gap is that "unless employers act to humanize the plant and office soon, we are headed for trouble" (Ibid., p. 81).

CAN, OR SHOULD,
WORK ALIENATION BE DECREASED?

Even though work alienation seems to be related to the nature of the work the individual performs, it is not clear how easy it is to reduce alienation. In the first place, it is extremely difficult to redesign work to give it more variety, autonomy, challenge, **193** and wholeness. It often takes a massive job-enrichment intervention to produce small changes in job quality.

Second, we don't know the extent to which the process of becoming alienated is reversible. If people do respond to boring work in supposedly typical ways (with apathy, defense mechanisms, hostility, etc.), will these reactions reverse themselves when they are given challenging jobs? Some organization theorists would argue that it takes time for a person to abandon alienation, since the risks involved in the opportunities for psychological success may seem threatening to a noninvolved worker. If this is true, how long would it take for such a worker to learn to value risk-taking and challenge? What degree of coaching and counseling would the process require? Would such an effort be practical?

Third, we don't know how much alienation is due to individual difference in work values or needs and how much is due to the work itself. Research has shown that not all workers respond equally positively to enlarged jobs. Workers with strong higher-order needs (for achievement, autonomy, self-fulfillment) and workers in rural settings tend to respond more favorably to job enrichment than security-motivated or urban workers, respectively (Hackman and Lawler, 1971; Hulin and Blood, 1968; Lawler, 1973; Wanous, 1974). The urban-rural dimension appears to be related to the worker's commitment to or alienation from the values of the conventional Protestant work ethic, which may be the causal factor here. To what extent are these work values and needs changeable, short of therapy? If they are fairly stable personality characteristics, this means that some workers would never become more involved in their work careers, while others would be capable of developing a more intrinsic career orientation. This would imply that any intervention to increase career commitment would have to be preceded by a diagnosis and selection of the involvement-prone workers.

THE BORN LOSER   by Art Sansom

Reprinted by permission of Newspaper Enterprise Association (NEA).

The other possibility is that work values and higher-order needs can change as a result of psychological success experiences at work. If this is true, it may be possible to "reach" most workers eventually with job-enrichment interventions. One of the prime research needs now in the area of work is the assessment of the changeability of work values and needs in response to changes in the quality of work.

Another consideration is the desirability and ethics of attempting to influence the worker's alienation. Although young people are looking for more achievement and fulfillment in life, many do not see their work careers as the center of their lives. Furthermore, privacy, friendships, family, and freedom also rank high in the value hierarchies of students (Yankelovich, 1972). For the employee who values these non-work concepts, any attempts by the organization to increase his or her involvement may be seen as an invasion of privacy and freedom. This idea has led to another strategy which some organizations have advocated as a means of enhancing the quality of the employee's life: attempting to reduce the time and energy the person invests in work and to increase his or her leisure time, through reduced and flexible work hours. The whole area of alternatives to work—education, hobbies, recreation, community activities—as sources of stimulation and enhancers of quality of life is itself literally a "big business" today.

EQUAL OPPORTUNITY:
FOR A JOB OR FOR A CAREER?

The opposite problem is experienced often by minority groups and women in organizations today: many want to become *more* involved in their careers, but do not have the opportunities to do so. It is true that organizations are hiring many more women and minorities than in the past for jobs that were previously occupied by white males. The pressures of government funding agencies, courts, social action groups, and corporate conscience are creating more open hiring policies, through such changes as affirmative action programs, job postings, quotas, career training, and so forth.

However, many people hired under such programs feel like a new type of employee. Whereas Schein (1970) classified managerial assumptions about people as being rational-economic (i.e., "people work for money"), social, self-actualizing, or complex, the minority recruit might be viewed as *token person*. The psychological contract as defined by the new employee is quite different from what is seen by management. To management, the new female or minority recruit is there to fill a quota and to meet the **195** organization's obligations. Once the person is hired, the organization's responsibilities may be met (in its view).

To the minority employee, on the other hand, the contract reads "career." He or she expects to advance and develop in the new job. Being hired is just the beginning, not the end of the organization's obligations.

The result of this contract mismatch is that the company may have lower expectations of the minority recruit. Because research on career growth has shown that, to paraphrase Flip Wilson, "What you expects is what you gets," if a manager expects low performance, he will probably behave toward the employee in such a way that he will, in fact, create low performance (Livingston, 1969). The organization may invest less in training the minority or female recruit for future development than it would for other recruits. The minority person may be put in a "black job," such as community relations, or a woman put in a "female job," such as a woman's career specialist, with little power and advancement opportunity. And, of course, the recruiting could be focused on lower-level jobs, which by their nature offer little future development. There is evidence that salaries are lower and advancement slower for minorities than for whites with comparable training (Brown and Ford, 1975).

On the other hand, if the organization is truly hiring minorities and women for careers, top management may not realize the long-term effects of the new selection policy. Any time sizable numbers of new types of employees are hired, changes in the functioning of the organization can be expected. Small numbers of "new types" can be assimilated with little organizational accommodation being required, but large numbers will require mutual adaptation by the new recruits and by the organization, as was found in a bank that drastically altered its selection policy (Alderfer, 1971). Ten years after the new policy went into effect, the "new" recruits were in middle management, and there was a constructive intergroup conflict between the old and new types of employees. Furthermore, the organization had adopted early and successfully the great changes which hit the banking industry in the 1960s. Therefore, if an organization plans to hire significant numbers of minority and female employees, it should be prepared to follow through on the long-term effects of the new selection policy.

Dual-Career Families

Related to the issues of women's careers is the problem of how two separate careers can be successfully managed by a husband and wife. There seems to be an interaction effect here that may compound the problems and stresses of each separate career.

YES, HENRY, THIS IS CERTAINLY THE LAND OF OPPORTUNITY.	YOU MIGHT GROW UP TO BE ALMOST ANYTHING-- YOU COULD BE A SCIENTIST,	OR A BIG BUSINESS TYCOON, OR MAYBE AN ASTRONAUT.	YOU MIGHT EVEN GROW UP TO BE PRESIDENT...	THAT'S JUST A CHANCE YOU'LL HAVE TO TAKE.

Reprinted by permission of Newspaper Enterprise Association (NEA).

Pioneering research in this area has been conducted by Fogarty et al. (1971), who identified four key factors that make the dual-career family viable: *commitment* to dual careers by husband and wife, high *energy* levels, *flexibility* in the work and family situation, and *coping* mechanisms. Three types of coping mechanisms for dealing with family-role strains have been identified (Hall, 1972): (1) structural role redefinition (changing other people's expectations for themselves), (2) personal role redefinition (changing one's attitude toward or perception of others' expectations, rather than changing the actual expectations), and (3) reactive role behavior (accepting all expectations and attempting to do all that is expected of oneself). People who use some sort of coping strategy for dealing with family-role strains seem to be more satisfied than those who do not (Hall, 1972).

Many questions regarding dual-career families remain unexplored. What are the differences between successful and unsuccessful two-career families? What are the problems of different types of dual-career marriages: In which both parties are at the same career stage, one spouse is at a later stage, the fields are the same, related, or different; both are equally work-involved or one member is more involved; there are children versus no children, etc. How do organizations view dual-career families? Does a working spouse affect the opportunities provided to the other? How are anti-nepotism rules being dealt with in organizations? Precious little is known about how to manage two careers in the same family.

THE YOUNG EMPLOYEE VERSUS THE ORGANIZATION

Now, let us turn to a particular type of minority, low-power person in organizations: the young employee. This minority group is important because it represents the future of the organization **197**

and a key resource for change. Also, the initial years of employment are a critical period in a person's career, as we have seen
before. How are new employees different from older people, and
what influence could they have in humanizing organizations? What
attitudes toward careers do young people hold today?

The Value/Perception Gap

Much of what is thought to be a generation gap today is more
accurately called a value/perception gap. Part of the difference
between younger and older people is that they tend to value things
differently, and part of the difference is that they perceive things
differently. When a young person thinks about an issue such as
career opportunities for women, she is likely to value equal opportunities more than someone twenty years older. Furthermore, the
young person is likely to stress how far we have to go in this
area (and thus be dissatisfied with developments to date), whereas
the older person is more likely to look with favor on how far we've
come (baby). Dissatisfaction involves a gap between what actually
exists and what should be. There is some evidence, at least among
Catholic priests, that young people tend to expect more and/or
perceive less regarding conditions they value than their older colleagues, feeding into the gap from both sides (Hall and Schneider,
1973).

Some of the value areas in which young people expect more
and perceive less are as follows (Hall, 1971b):

1. There is now more concern about basic goals and values, not just different
   values, but values *per se*.
2. Action is more important. Merely talking about one's values is suspect.
   The cry is "do it!"
3. Personal integrity, honesty, openness, and realness are more important.
4. Many of the "youth" values are humanistic, oriented toward personal
   fulfillment and psychological success. This reflects a shift away from concerns for extrinsic symbols of success and security. The ultimate meaning
   and purpose of living are more important.
5. There is increased concern for the ultimate social value of one's work,
   the *consequences* of that work and not just its content.
6. Authority based on age or position is less highly regarded and the authority
   of one's expertise, personal style, convictions, or competence carries
   much more weight with youth. Shared authority is more important than
   before.

What Recent Graduates Want in Organizations

How do these values translate into specific organizational conditions that a recent graduate might desire? He would probably want
more openness and less secrecy about issues such as pay, promotion, and hiring practices and about how key organizational
decisions are made, why, and by whom. He would want to be
consulted or involved and to have more influence involving deci-

sions affecting his own life—promotions, transfers, pay raises, performance appraisal, and so forth. He would expect to have a colleague relationship with the boss, to be respected, and to share in the important decisions affecting their work group. He would also want his boss and the organization to provide opportunities to learn and grow on the job, to try new activities, to have work assignments reflect his needs as well as the organization's. He would want self-fulfillment on the job. He would want the organization to be aware of its social responsibilities to groups other than shareholders—to customers, to members of the external community, and to members of the internal organizational community (i.e., employees). Implicit in all of the above, perhaps, is a desire for flexibility and openness on the part of the organization, a receptivity to new ideas and possible changes, such as those the young employee represents.

Generation Gap: Something Old, Something New

In many ways there has always been a generation gap. A favorite gimmick of several recent popular articles on the generation gap has been to ask the reader to identify the author of a short passage lamenting the impatience, impertinence, and stubborness of modern youth; the author, perhaps not surprisingly, is Socrates. Rather than debating whether the generation gap is old or new, I will consider very sketchily how it is a bit of each.

First of all, there has always been organizational resistance to change, and young employees have always been important carriers of new ideas, energy, and idealism into organizations. In this sense youth represents a societal change agent. However, in the past two hundred years, most change in organizations has been technological in nature. Now young people are pushing for a new arena of change, social innovation. Almost every profession has its own generation gap—there are "new" doctors, lawyers, psychologists, sociologists, priests, nuns, filmmakers, arts managers, teachers, and businessmen—and the central issue is always, "How can professional knowledge be applied in the form of service, more attuned to the needs of people?" In the past, the issue was more, "How can professional knowledge and competence be extended?"

There has always been a conflict between the needs and aspirations of the individual and the goals and requirements of the organization. In the past, however, the outcome was that the organization socialized the person into accepting its goals. Now, people are likely to innovate or humanize the organization as well. Even though many young people have always seen organizations as threats to their creativity and individuality, now there is a growing sense of youth identity and youth power, which reduces the odds against them. **199**

CHANGING DEFINITION OF SUCCESS:
PSYCHOLOGICAL SUCCESS

One conclusion from research on young people and from surveys of employees of all ages is that the success ethic is changing (Yankelovich, 1974; American Management Association, 1973). In the past, success was most likely to be defined in terms of external factors, such as salary, position level, or status. Now there is more of a tendency for people to use their own personal criteria of success, usually with a focus on self-fulfillment and happiness. Yankelovich expresses this shift as follows:

> Since World War II most Americans have shaped their ideas of success around money, occupational status, possessions, and the social mobility of their children. Now, ideas about success are beginning to revolve around various forms of self-fulfillment. The emphasis is on self and its unrealized potential, a self that cries out for expression and demands satisfaction. If the key motif of the past was "keeping up with the Joneses," today it is "I have my own life to live, let Jones shift for himself" (1974, p. 81).

In terms of the four criteria of career effectiveness, this change means a decrease in emphasis on performance indicators and an increased stress on career *attitudes,* such as satisfaction and psychological success. With this increased stress on individual notions of success, there is a decrease in concern for loyalty to one's employer. This also implies less organizational control over the employee or, put more positively, more freedom for the individual.

AN EMERGING VIEW OF CAREERS:
THE PROTEAN CAREER

When we combine the orientations of young people toward careers (concerns for freedom, mobility, personal fulfillment, shared authority) with the rumblings which are being heard from mid-career executives and professionals (re-examination of career goals, switching fields), there appears to be a new career ethic emerging. In the first chapter we reviewed four different meanings of the term *career:* (1) career as advancement, (2) career as profession, (3) career as lifelong sequence of work experiences, and (4) career as lifelong sequence of role-related experiences. It was pointed out that the most widely held or popular definition is the first one, career as advancement. In contrast, the perspective taken in this book has been the third, career as lifelong sequence of work experiences. As people are becoming less enchanted with advancement via career ladders in bureaucratic organizations and more concerned with the freedom to develop and find challenge

200

in a wider variety of organizations, the popular view of careers seems to be moving toward this same lifelong work-experience perspective and away from the advancement ethic.

To describe this new ethic succinctly, we might think of it as the *protean career.* Here I am borrowing from Robert Jay Lifton, who compared the lifestyle and "self-process" of modern man to the mythological figure, Proteus:

> We know from Greek mythology that Proteus was able to change his shape with relative ease—from wild boar to lion to dragon to fire to flood. But, what he did find difficult, and would not do unless seized and chained, was to commit himself to a single form. . . .
>
> The protean style of self-process, then, is characterized by an interminable series of experiments and explorations—some shallow, some profound—each of which may be readily abandoned in favor of still new psychological quests. The pattern in many ways resembles what Erik Erikson has called "identity diffusion" or "identity confusion," and the impaired psychological functioning which those terms suggest can be very much present. But, I would stress that the protean style is by no means pathological as such, and, in fact, may well be one of the functional patterns of our day. It extends to all areas of human experience—to political as well as sexual behavior, to the holding and promulgating of ideas and to the general organization of lives (1968, p. 17).

This new protean orientation has also been recognized by Jennings, who uses the term mobicentric to describe the phenomenon:

> The mobicentric man values motion and action not because they lead to change, but because they are change, and change is his ultimate value. . . . Freedom to him is a form of movement. . . . His faith, often deep, is not in institutions but in himself and perhaps his wife, in their capacity to grow and become more useful as long as they don't get hung up. . . . For him success is represented less by position, title, salary or performance than by moving and movement (1970, p. 35).

What this all amounts to for organizations is that more employees are coming to see their work lives as protean careers. And what exactly do we mean by "protean career?"

The protean career is a process which the person, not the organization, is managing. It consists of all of the person's varied experiences in education, training, work in several organizations, changes in occupational field, etc. The protean career is *not* what happens to the person in any one organization. The protean person's own personal career choices and search for self-fulfillment are the unifying or integrative elements in his or her life. The criterion of success is internal (psychological success), not external.

In short, the protean career is shaped more by the individual than by the organization and may be redirected from time to time to meet the needs of the person. The protean career pattern can be described further in terms of the four dimensions of career **201** effectiveness: work performance, attitudes, identity, and adaptability. In the protean career, performance is defined by the person's own criteria of good performance (i.e., psychological success), whereas in the traditional career, the person accepts the organization's definition of performance (e.g., salary, position level). In the protean career, one's own attitudes play a greater role in determining career choices than they do in the traditional career; in fact, attitudes such as work satisfaction achievement and job involvement with low organizational commitment are core values in the protean career. On the other hand, in the traditional career, attitudes such as organizational commitment and loyalty are valued more.

In the protean career, furthermore, attitudes, identity, and adaptability are simply more salient than they are in traditional careers. Almost by definition, since the protean person feels responsible for the long-run management of his life, he is more likely to be confronted by self-generated questions involving attitudes ("How do I feel about the work I am doing?"), identity ("Now that I'm 45, what do I want to be when I grow up?"), and adaptability ("How can I maintain my flexibility and freedom in the coming years?").

In the traditional career, once the person commits himself to a career ladder in an organization, he can take a more passive

Issue	Protean Career	Traditional Career
Who's in charge?	Person	Organization
Core values	Freedom; Growth	Advancement; Power
Degree of mobility	High	Lower
Important performance dimensions	Psychological success	Position level; Salary
Important attitude dimensions	Work satisfaction; Professional commitment	Work satisfaction Organizational commitment
Important identity dimensions	Do I respect myself? (self-esteem) What do I want to do? (self-awareness)	Am I respected in this organization? (esteem from others) What should I do? (organizational awareness)
Important adaptability dimensions	Work-related flexibility Current competence (Measure: marketability)	Organization-related flexibility (Measure: organizational survival)

TABLE 8-1
Differences between the Traditional Career and the Protean Career

role in managing his career; thus, as long as one concentrates on the performance dimension and is satisfied with one's rewards, there is little need to think about one's career attitude, identity, or adaptability until the career ladder begins to wobble, as it is in the many economy-minded organizations today. What this demonstrates is that along with the greater personal freedom found in the protean career also goes greater responsibility for one's choices and opportunities. This can entail greater feelings of insecurity and fear of failure than would be found in the traditional career, for the protean person knows that he cannot depend too heavily upon the employing organization for direction and security. These features of protean and traditional careers are summarized in Table 8-1.

NEED FOR INCREASED
PERSONAL AND ORGANIZATIONAL FLEXIBILITY

What implications does the protean career pattern have for the structure of organizations? Because of the need for organizations to mirror to some extent the characteristics of its members, and vice versa, the fluidity of the protean career calls for increased flexibility on the part of the organization and for better self-management of careers by individuals. If individuals are going to feel less commitment to the organization, if they will look for opportunities to further their personal development, and if they want to be more independent of organizational constraints, then organizations must gear themselves to a more mobile, independent work force. In short, they will have to adapt to the changing orientations of employees and they will have to be able to individualize jobs somewhat to accommodate a range of people with quite different concerns and needs. To an extent, then, the organization will have to be "humanized" or "individualized" to better meet the needs of employees. In the years to come, the career will become more of a process through which organizations influence people *and* people influence organizations (Porter, Lawler, and Hackman, 1975).

The need for more flexible organizations has been discussed by numerous theorists. Most writers see the major pressure for flexibility coming from the turbulent, complex *external environment* or the advancing technology of the organization; in order to survive these external threats, the organization must have the flexibility to obtain valid information and to adapt quickly. In this volume we are coming to the same conclusions regarding the need for system flexibility, but we reach it through analysis of the *internal environment* (i.e., people) of the organization. Indeed, the same principles of organization-environment interaction should logically hold, whether we consider the internal or the external environment. What we have seen is that the internal environment (people and their emerging protean careers) of the organization is just as turbulent and complex as the external environment of competitors, suppliers, government, technology, and consumers. The in-   **203** creased complexity and variety of employee values and motivations requires a more complex, individualized approach to the management of people (Lawler, 1973). Fortunately, the organizational characteristics demanded by both the external and internal environments—sensitivity to the environment and flexibility to respond appropriately—do not appear to be in conflict with each other (Porter, Lawler, and Hackman, 1975).

SUMMARY

Many of the issues discussed in this book have dealt with increasing the adaptiveness of people and organizations, as well as with the identity needs of employees. As we have seen throughout this book, identity and adaptability are the two most underdeveloped dimensions of career effectiveness in the organizational literature today. Hopefully, the suggestions in the preceding pages have stimulated the reader's thinking (agreement, disagreement, elaboration, implementation, other suggestions) and will lead to more refined approaches to facilitating career identity and adaptability.

If the author were able to make only one recommendation to the reader about how to enhance these two facets of his or her career effectiveness, he would stress the value of *process training.* By this is meant learning the processes through which one can continue to achieve goals, learn, change, and help others change. These processes involve human relations, communication, managing conflict, overcoming resistance to change, learning independently, and diagnosing or understanding people and situations accurately. All of these processes help a person remain open to changes in his or her work environment (new people, knowledge, technology, and so forth).

On the other hand, material covered in *knowledge or method training,* although certainly necessary, is more likely to become obsolete a few years after college or graduate training. The person needs specific knowledge and competencies in order to perform effectively at work. But if you do not also know how to continue to learn and change in your work, your specialized competence can become a trap which can render you as well as your knowledge obsolete.

A major problem facing organizations today is a severe shortage of energy: electricity, natural gas, and petroleum. We also see shortages of raw materials, such as paper, petroleum-derived products, and food. Because of international competition and inflation, there is also a strain on financial resources. Because of these shortages, many of yesterday's necessities, such as business travel, round-the-clock operations, research and development, are seen as today's luxuries or impossibilities. Whereas in the past organizations could afford some waste and inefficiency in the utilization of energy and resources, today waste is simply not possible in many cases, because of either the high costs or the inavailability of the resources and energy. Therefore, organizations are learning to utilize these inputs more efficiently.

Although most of the concern in the media so far has dealt with physical inputs, the same need for better utilization exists with human resources and energy. One reason for this is that it will be people (employees) who will (or will not) enable organizations to use physical inputs more efficiently. The person on the line knows the tricks for getting the most out of the machine he or she operates, as well as how to jam it "accidentally." It will be the decision of the individual taxi-driver if he will use jack-rabbit starts or if he will drive to conserve fuel. And so forth.

The second reason for concern about people is that they themselves represent resources and energy. Because the largest expense for many organizations is labor (salaries and wages), the more effective utilization of human resources will become more important than ever as our financial resources become more limited and expensive. Furthermore, those organizations that have already planned for the development of creative, flexible, involved employees will probably be better able to cope with the situation than those that haven't.

Perhaps the silver lining to this cloud of scarcity and worldwide competition is that organizations can no longer afford the luxury of squandering the work lives of their human resources. As senior administrators realize the importance of harnessing the creativity, flexibility, and commitment of their employees, one curious side effect of the resource "pinch" may be that almost by accident, the work environment of those employees may become more humane and conducive to career growth.

Discussion Questions

1. What is the coming crisis within the generation of young employees to which Daniel Yankelovich refers?
2. Should efforts be made to reduce employee alienation? Why or why not?
3. How might recent organizational experiences with affirmative action illustrate the unintended consequences of the career-development programs described in the previous chapter?
4. What is a protean career?
5. Why does the protean-career pattern demand greater organizational flexibility?

Case Studies for Careers in Organizations

Case Study: Chapter 1. The Awful Interview*

Purpose
1. To practice interviewing skills, especially in dealing with difficult interview questions frequently asked by interviewers.
2. To sharpen your awareness of your strengths and weaknesses in interviewing for a job.

Advance Preparation
Read the Introduction and think about some questions that might be included in the list in Procedure, Step 1. If you can't think of good, mind-boggling questions, ask friends who have some prior experience in job interviews.

Introduction
Employment interviews are frequently traumatic experiences; interviewers know what they are looking for—and you don't. They are prepared, and you are not. They are relaxed and you are tense. The cards are all stacked in the interviewer's favor it seems.

Interviewers are also notorious for asking some of the most disconcerting questions. "Tell me about your goals in life." "Why do you want to work for International Widgets?" Obviously, if you answered these questions candidly, but right off the top of your head, you might never get a job. It would be easy to blurt out: "My only goal is to get a job so I can begin to find out whether I really like it." Or, "I want to work for International Widgets because I don't have any other likely looking offers right now." If you have been confronted with questions like these, you will understand why we have titled this exercise, "The Awful Interview"!

You don't have to let them catch you by surprise. This exercise is based on the assumption that practice can help you prepare for these situations. We will also assume that honesty really is the best policy. The job-hunter who concentrates on building a facade to convince an employer that he or she is just the person they want is employing a defensive strategy. Maintaining defenses and false impressions absorbs a lot of energy. You may become so preoccupied with protecting your "image" that you have little energy left for the real problem of showing the interviewer what careful thought you have given to planning your career. At best, you stand to get a job that does not suit you; one which only fits the facade you have erected.

Procedure
Step 1. (*15 minutes*)
The entire group will develop a list of the *ten most awful questions* one can be asked in a job interview. An "awful" question is one which you would find threatening or difficult to answer honestly in a job interview. When the list is completed, *write them down*. You will need them in the remainder of the exercise. NOTE: List only questions which have actually been asked in all seriousness in job interviews you or somebody else has experienced.

Step 2. (*5 minutes*)
The instructor will specify whether the group should break into groups of threes or fours. However this is done, choose people to work with whom you will be comfortable with, people who can be most helpful in providing useful feedback on your interviewing style.

When the groups are formed, the instructor will advise you where you are to hold your small group meetings.

Step 3.
Meet with your trio or quartet. Proceed as follows:
a. One member volunteers to answer the first question; another is chosen to ask the question.
b. Choosing a question from the list, the interrogator asks the interviewee the first question.
c. The interviewee must try to *answer the question as truthfully and honestly as he or she can.*
d. After the answer, other members of the group provide feedback to the interviewee on how they experienced the answer just given. Remember the criteria for effective feedback emphasized in the reading as you provide your feedback.
e. Upon completion of the feedback, the interviewee becomes the interrogator, chooses a question and a new interviewee, and a new round begins.
f. Continue taking turns until each person has answered at least three questions, or until you are instructed to stop by the instructor. (The instructor will indicate which rule to follow.)

Step 4. (*10 minutes*)
Take 10 minutes and write a brief note to yourself covering the following (this note is for you—nobody else will see it):

---

*Developed by Donald D. Bowen. From D.T. Hall, D.D. Bowen, R.J. Lewicki, and F.S. Hall, *Experiences in Management and Organizational Behavior*. Chicago: St. Clair Press, 1975, pp. 197–199. Reprinted by permission.

a. What questions did I handle well? What were my strengths?

b. What questions did I handle poorly? Or what questions asked of others would give me problems?

c. What can I do to deal more effectively with the questions that give me problems?

Step 5.
Reconvene with the entire group for discussion of the exercise.

Discussion Questions

1. What did you learn during the exercise about how to answer interviewers' questions more effectively?

2. Do you think employment interviewers obtain valid data in the interview? Why?

3. If you were an interviewer, what kinds of questions would you ask?

Generalizations and Conclusions
Concluding Points

1. What do authorities in the field have to say about the validity of employment interviewing?

2. Why is the interview so widely employed as a selection device?

3. What steps can the interviewee take to assure a more effective interview?

Case Study: Chapter 2. Career Choice: A Counseling Interview

Purpose

1. To help you become more aware of your career orientations and the motivation behind them.

2. To increase your skills in career counseling.

Introduction

Because you are reading this book, you are probably at a point in your career where you have already made some important choices, such as choice of an occupation or general field of work, or choice of a degree program. However, there are always other issues to be resolved and decisions to be made throughout a career.

It sometimes aids the decision process to talk it over with someone else. In this exercise, you will be working in groups of three. Each person will have the opportunity to be

TABLE 1
Career Choice
Interview Schedule

1. How would you describe yourself as a person?
2. What are you best at doing? Worst?
3. What do you really enjoy doing most? Least?
4. What have been one or two of your best successes—times when you felt especially productive and proud of your capabilities and potential?
5. What would you stop doing if you could?
6. What would you like to do more?
7. What would you like to learn more about?
8. What aspects of yourself do you like most? Least?
9. Could you describe your ideal self?
10. Who are your heroes? What do you like about them?
11. If you could have any job at all, what would you do? What would be an ideal job for you?
12. What do you plan to do during the next five years? (If you haven't yet decided, pretend you had to decide *right now*. What would you choose to do?)
13. What are the pros and cons of the different career options you are considering right now?
14. Which way are you leaning?
15. Pretend a person amazingly similar to you (background, interests, plans, etc.) came to you for advice on the same issue you're wrestling with now. What advice would you give this person?

Interview schedule originally developed as a class exercise in collaboration with Clayton P. Alderfer.

interviewed about his or her career choices, to be a career interviewer (or counselor), and to be an observer. Try to learn from each role—how to be a better career decision maker, how to be a better career counselor, and how to be a more sensitive observer of interviewing and helping processes.

Procedure

The class will be formed into groups of three. There will be three rounds to the exercise. In each round, there will be three roles: interviewer, interviewee, and observer. At the end of each round, you will switch roles and assume a role you haven't played yet. Therefore, at the end of the third round, each person in the trio should have had a chance to try every role.

Step 1: Round 1

Pick one person to act as interviewer, one as interviewee, and one as observer. For 15 minutes, the interviewer will conduct a counseling interview with the interviewee on the topic of career choices. The interview questions in Table 1 are provided as a guide; questions may be selected from Table 1, or the interviewer may make up his or her own.

During the interview, the observer should be silent and should take notes on the process of the interview. The observer should

also act as *timekeeper*, stopping the interview after 15 minutes.

For the next 5 minutes, the observer will feed back his or her observations, and all three members will discuss the interview. Focus on the following two issues:

a. What did the interviewee learn?

b. What did the interviewer or interviewee do that helped or hindered the interview?

Step 2: Round 2

Switch roles, (e.g. interviewer becomes interviewee, interviewee becomes observer, observer becomes interviewer). Follow the same procedure as in Round 1.

Step 3: Round 3

Switch roles again, as in Round 2. Be sure that no one plays the same role twice. Follow the same procedure as in Round 1.

Step 4: Class Discussion

Meet again as a total class. Discuss what the interviewees seemed to be learning. What career choice issues were discussed most frequently? What choices or solutions were considered?

Also discuss what people learned about the process of interviewing and helping. What did the interviewer do that helped or hindered the decision-making process? What did the interviewee do to help or hinder his or her own progress?

Case Study: Chapter 3. Career Stages*

Problem: Career Development Experiences Through the Life Cycle

Different people develop different needs as they progress through various stages in the life cycle. It is important that administrators and helping professionals recognize employees' changing developmental needs and learn to respond to them. In this problem you will be given an opportunity to exercise your diagnostic and training skills.

Procedure*

1. Meet in groups of five.
2. Decide in your group on two of the following stages upon which you will focus:
   a. Trial stage
   b. Establishment/advancement stage
   c. Mid-career (maintenance)
   d. Late-career (decline)
3. Each person will individually think of *two specific people* you have known, one for each of the two stages your group has chosen. Write down first the *developmental needs* that each of those two people had. Next write down *one specific training or development experience* for each person that would have improved his career effectiveness.

4. As a group, discuss the developmental needs identified for people in each stage. List these needs on the board or on a sheet of newsprint. Identify those needs which are mentioned most often. These may be fairly general career development needs for people at each of those two stages.
5. Next, as a group, list the training or development experiences which have been identified. Attempt to reach a consensus on the *three* most promising experiences for each stage.
6. Meet again as a total class. Have a representative from each group report to the class on the stages chosen, needs identified, and developmental experiences recommended.

Based upon the inputs of all the groups, conclude with the following questions:

A. What stages were chosen most frequently for analysis?

B. For each stage, on what developmental needs was there most agreement? Which developmental experiences?

C. What would be the obstacles to a work organization's implementing these developmental experiences? How could this resistance be overcome?

---

*The author is indebted to W. Clay Hamner for suggesting the idea for this exercise.

Case Study: Chapter 4.

ROLE PLAYING: PROBLEM SOLVING—THE APPRAISAL INTERVIEW*

Preparation for Role Playing

1. The instructor will read "General Instructions" (D.1) and place the organizational chart shown in figure case 4-1 on the easel.
2. The class should then be divided into groups of three, one member being assigned the role of Stanley (D.2), the other the role of Burke (D.3) and the third the role of observer.
3. When the Burkes have finished reading their parts they should stand and remain standing until further instructions are given.
4. When all of the Burkes are standing, the instructor should be sure that they know who their Stanleys are and that the observer is somewhat on the sidelines. The observer's presence is to be ignored by Stanley and Burke.

The Role-Playing Process

1. When the stage is set, the Burkes will be instructed to knock on Stanley's door (make-believe door) to present themselves for the scheduled interview.
2. Role playing should proceed for about half an hour. Regardless of whether all have finished, they should have reached a point where comparisons in outcome can be made.
3. When the interviews have been terminated by the instructor, he should ask each

Stanley to assign two letter grades (A, B, C, D, or E) to Burke; one, for his estimate of Burke before the interview, the other, for his present estimate. These grades should be written down and not be visible to either the observer or Burke.
4. After Stanley has assigned his grades, the observer and Burke should individually write on slips of paper the two grades they think Stanley wrote on his paper and avoid being guided by what grades they think he should have assigned. The appraisal judgments should be set aside for use in later discussions.

Discussion

1. *Each observer should report on any changes that will result from the interview.* The instructor should *check with the role players* to determine the accuracy of the observers' judgments. The instructor should briefly summarize points on the chalkboard.
2. After each observer has reported the changes expected, they should in turn report on Tom's job interest. These judgments also should be checked with Tom. The findings should be posted on the chalkboard.
3. The observers should report the before and after interview grades they think Stanley assigned. Tom's opinion and Stanley's estimate should then be post-

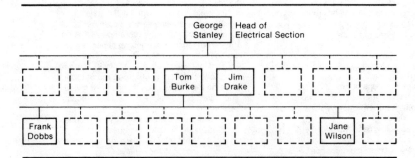

Case 4-1 Organizational Chart of Electrical Section of American Construction Company. The names of the persons that may be mentioned in this case are given, together with their positions in the organization. Only George Stanley and Tom Burke are involved in the role playing.

*Reprinted from Norman R.F. Maier, *Psychology in Industrial Organizations*. Boston, Mass.: Houghton Mifflin, 4th ed., 1973, pp. 604–608. Reprinted by permission of the publisher.

ed to test the observer's sensitivity as well as Tom's.
4. The observers should next be asked to go into a huddle with the Burke and Stanley they observed, and point out opportunities they missed, where things went wrong, and why problem solving was not effectively used. The instructor should terminate these discussions after five minutes.
5. The instructor should summarize the discussion, evaluating the place of appraisal programs in organizations, the differences in job perception of the superiors and subordinates, and the potential use of problem solving in situations of this kind.

Materials for the Case

General Instructions

George Stanley is the electrical section head in the engineering department of the American Construction Company. The work in the department includes design, drafting, cost estimates, keeping maps up to date, checking standards and building codes, field inspection, follow-up, and so on. Eight first-line supervisors report to George Stanley. The duties of the supervisors are partly technical and partly supervisory (see figure case 4-1).

Company policy requires that all section heads interview each of their supervisors once a year, the purposes being: (a) to evaluate the supervisor's performance during the year; (b) to give recognition for jobs well done; and (c) to correct weaknesses. The company believes that employees should know how they stand and that everything should be done to develop management personnel. The appraisal interviews were introduced to serve these purposes.

Tom Burke is one of the supervisors reporting to Stanley, and today we will witness an appraisal interview conducted by Stanley with Tom Burke.

Tom Burke has a college degree in electrical engineering. In addition to his technical duties, which often take him to the field, he supervises the work of one junior designer, six draftsmen, and two women clerks. He is highly paid, as are all the supervisors in this department because of the high requirements in technical knowledge. Burke has been with the company for 12 years and has been a supervisor for two years. He is married and has two children. He owns his home and is active in the civic affairs of the community in which he lives.

Role for George Stanley, Section Head

You have appraised all the supervisors who report to you and during the next two weeks will interview each of them. You hope to use these interviews constructively to develop each man. Today you have arranged to interview Tom Burke, one of the eight first-line supervisors who report to you. Here is the information and his appraisal as given in your files.

Thomas Burke: 12 years with company, two years as supervisor, college degree, married, two children. Evaluation: highly creative and original, and exceptionally competent technically. His unit is very productive, and during the two years he has supervised the group there has been a steady improvement. Within the past six months you have given him extra work and he has had it done on schedule. As far as productivity and dependability are concerned, he is your top man.

His cooperation with the other supervisors in the section leaves much to be desired. Before you made him a supervisor his originality and technical knowledge were available to your whole section. Gradually he has withdrawn and now acts more as a lone wolf. You've asked other supervisors to talk over certain problems with him, but they tell you he offers no suggestions. He tells them he's busy or listens disinterestedly to their problems, kids them or makes sarcastic remarks, depending on his mood. On one occasion he allowed *Jim Drake,* one of the supervisors in another unit, to make a mistake he could have forestalled by letting him know the status of certain design changes which he knew about and had seen. It is to be expected that supervisors will cooperate on matters involving design changes that affect them.

Furthermore, *during the past six months he has been unwilling to take two assignments. He said they were routine,* that he preferred more interesting work, and he advised you to give the assignments to other supervisors. To prevent trouble, you followed his suggestion. However, you feel that you can't give him all the interesting work and that if he persists in this attitude there will be trouble. You cannot play favorites and keep up morale in your unit.

Burke's failure to cooperate has you worried for another reason. Although his group is highly productive, *there is more turnover among his draftsmen than in other groups.* You have heard no complaints as yet, but *you suspect that he may be treating his men in an arbitrary manner.* Certainly if he talks up to you and to other supervisors, he's likely to be even more that way with his men. Apparently the high productivity in his group is not due to high morale, but to his ability to use his men to do the things for which they are best suited. This method won't develop good draftsmen. You hope to discuss these matters with Burke in such a way as to recognize his good points and at the same time correct some of his weaknesses. Feel free to handle the interview in the manner you think best.

Role for Tom Burke, Supervisor

One junior designer, six draftsmen, and two women clerks report to you. You feel that you get along fine with your group. You have always been pretty much of an idea man and apparently have the knack of passing on your enthusiasm to others in your group. There is *a lot of "we" feeling in your unit* because it is obvious that your group is the most productive.

You believe in developing your subordinates and always give them strong recommendations. You feel you have gained the

211

reputation of developing your employees because *they frequently go out and get much better jobs.* Since promotion is necessarily slow in a company such as yours, *you feel that the best way to stimulate morale is to develop new people and demonstrate that a good worker can get somewhere.* The two women in your unit are bright and efficient and there is a lot of good-natured kidding. Recently one of your clerks, *Jane Wilson,* turned down an outside offer that paid $35 a month more, for she preferred to stay in your group. You are going to get her a raise the first chance you have.

The other supervisors in Stanley's section do not have your enthusiasm. Some of them are dull and unimaginative. During your first year as supervisor you used to help them a lot, but *you soon found that they leaned on you* and before long you were doing their work. *There is a lot of pressure to get out production.* You got your promotion by producing and you don't intend to let other supervisors interfere. Since you no longer help the other supervisors your production has gone up, but a couple of them seem a bit sore at you. *Frank,* your junior designer, is better qualified than most of them and you'd like to see him made a supervisor. Since the company has some dead wood in it, Stanley ought to recognize this fact and assign such units the more routine jobs. Then they wouldn't need your help and you could concentrate your efforts on jobs that suit your unit. At present, George Stanley passes out work pretty much as he gets it. Because you are efficient you get more than your share of these jobs, and you see no reason why the extra work shouldn't be in the form of "plums." This would motivate units to turn out work. When you suggested to Stanley that he turn over some of the more routine jobs to other supervisors, he did it, but he was reluctant about it.

You did one thing recently that has bothered you. There was *a design change in a set of plans and you should have told Jim Drake (a fellow supervisor) about it, but it slipped your mind.* Drake was out when you

had it on your mind and then you got involved in a hot idea that Frank, your junior designer, had and forgot all about the matter with Drake. As a result, Drake had to make a lot of unnecessary changes, and he was quite sore about it. You told him you were sorry and offered to make the changes, but he turned down the offer.

Today you have an interview with George Stanley. It's about this management development plan in the company. It shouldn't take very long, but it's nice to have the boss tell you about the job you're turning out. *Maybe there is a raise in it, maybe he'll tell you something about what to expect in the future.*

Instructions for Observers

Read the roles of Stanley and Burke for background, sensitizing you to the problem. Do not participate in the interview or offer suggestions. Your task is to observe and evaluate. Do not discuss observations or conclusions with Burke or Stanley since you will report to the class as a whole.

Although the *tell-and-sell* method is usually followed by supervisors in situations of this type, we are concerned with whether Stanley tries to involve Tom Burke in problem solving. Pay especial attention to the following points.

1. *Does Stanley praise or criticize?* How are these evaluations received by Tom?
2. *Does Stanley raise problems to (a) invite participation in solving them or (b) to let Tom know about them?*
3. Does Tom ask for certain things (e.g., special treatment of any kind)? If so, does Stanley explore with him how to do it without creating new problems, or does he turn Tom down?
4. What skills does Stanley display that have been discussed in the course? List them as they occur.
5. At the end of the interview, indicate how you think Stanley or Burke might behave differently in the future.
6. *Has Tom's job interest gone up, down, or stayed the same?*

Case Study: Chapter 5. Case of the Plateaued Performer*
E. Kirby Warren, Thomas P. Ference, and James A. F. Stoner

"Grow old along with me, the best is yet to be." When Robert Browning expressed this sentiment, he was not writing as a spokesman for business to promising young executives. Yet in the nineteenth century, while such poetry may have been out of place in business, the thought was very fitting.

In fact, until quite recently corporations have been able to reward capable employees with increased responsibilities and opportunities. Based on our recently completed research into nine companies, however, the more prevalent corporate sentiment might be, "Stay young along with me, or gone you well may be."

We found a large number of managers who, in the judgment of their organization, have "plateaued." That is, there is little or no likelihood that they will be promoted or receive substantial increases in duties and responsibilities. These long-service employees are being regarded with growing concern because plateauing is taking place more markedly, and frequently earlier, than in years past. Further, executives feel that plateauing is frequently accompanied by noticeable declines in both motivation and quality of performance.

While plateauing, like aging, is inevitable, in years past it was a more gradual process.

*Reprinted from *Harvard Business Review,* January–February, 1975.

For the most part, those who sought advancement in their managerial careers had ample opportunity to get it, within broad limits of ability, while those who did not desire advancement (including competent individuals content with more modest levels of achievement and success) could be bypassed by colleagues still on the way up.

Today the situation has changed. Declining rates of corporate growth and an ever-increasing number of candidates have heightened the competition for managerial positions. The top of the pyramid is expanding much more slowly than the middle, and the managers who advanced rapidly during the growth boom of the 1960s are now at or just below the top. Their rate of career progress has necessarily slowed, and yet they are still many years from normal retirement and with many productive years to go. As these managers continue in their positions, the queue of younger, aggressive aspirants just below them is likely to grow longer, with spillover effects on opportunities and mobility rates throughout the organization.

This is precisely the dilemma confronting Benjamin Petersen, president and chairman of the board of Petersen Electronics.

Petersen founded the company in 1944, and it grew rapidly during the 1950s and 1960s, reaching sales of $200 million in 1968. Growth since then, though, has been uneven and at an average of less than 5 percent per year. However, 1974 was a good year, with sales and profits showing leaps of 12 percent and 18 percent, respectively.

Despite the good year, Benjamin Petersen, now 61 years old, is concerned about the company as he nears retirement. His major problem involves George Briggs, 53, vice-president of marketing, and Thomas Evans, national sales manager, who is 34 years old and one of Briggs's four subordinates. Nor have the implications of the situation between Briggs and Evans been lost on Victor Perkins, 39, vice-president of personnel.

PETERSEN'S VIEW
OF THE PREDICAMENT

"When we started, a handful of people worked very hard and very closely to build something bigger than any of us. One of these people was George Briggs. George has been with me from the start, as have almost all of my vice-presidents and many of my key department heads.

"For the first five years, I did almost all the inventing and engineering work. Tom Carroll ran the plant and George Briggs knocked on doors and sold dreams as well as products for the company.

"As the company grew, we added people, and Briggs slowly worked his way up the sales organization. Eight years ago, when our vice-president of marketing retired, I put George in the job. He has market research, product management, sales service, and the field sales force (reporting through a national sales manager) under him, and he has really done a first-rate job all around.

"About ten years ago we began bringing in more bright young engineers and MBAs and moved them along as fast as we could. Turnover has been high and we have had some friction between our young Turks and the old guard.

"When business slowed in the early seventies, we also had a lot of competition among the newcomers. Those who stayed have continued to move up, and a few are now in or ready for top jobs. One of the best of this group is Tom Evans. He started with us nine years ago in the sales service area. Later, he spent three years in product management.

"George Briggs got him to move from head of the sales service department to assistant product manager. After one year, George Briggs named him manager of the product management group, and two years later, when the national sales manager retired, George named Evans to this post.

"That move both surprised and pleased me. I felt that Evans would make a good sales manager despite the fact that he had had little direct sales experience. I was afraid, however, that George would not want someone in that job who hadn't had years of field experience.

"I was even more surprised, though, when six months later (a month ago) George told me he was afraid Evans wasn't working out, and asked if I might be able to find a spot for him in the corporate personnel department. While I'm sure our recent upturn in sales is not solely Evans's doing, he certainly seems to be one of the keys. Despite his inexperience, he seems to have the field-sales organization behind him. He spends much of his time traveling with them, and from what I hear he has built a great team spirit.

"Despite this, George Briggs claims that he is in over his head and that it is just a matter of time before his inexperience gets him in trouble. I can't understand why George is so adamant. It's clearly not a personality clash, since they have always gotten along well in the past. In many ways, Briggs has been Evans's greatest booster until recently.

"Since George is going to need a replacement someday, I was hoping it would be Evans. If George doesn't retire before we have to move Evans again or lose him, I'd consider moving Evans to another area.

"When we were growing faster, I didn't worry about a new challenge opening up for our aggressive young managers—there were always new divisions, new lines—something to keep them stimulated and satisfied with their progress. Now I have less flexibility—my top people are several years from retirement. And yet I have some younger ones—like Evans, whom I would hate to lose—always pushing and expecting promotion.

"Evans is a good example of this; I could move him, but there are not that many *real* opportunities. He could go to personnel or engineering or even finance. Evans has the makings of a really fine general manager. But I'd hate to move him now. He really isn't ready for another shift—although he will be in a few years—and despite what George claims, I think he is stimulating teamwork and commitment in the sales organization as a result of his style.

"Finally, while I don't want to appear unduly critical of Briggs, I'm not sure he could get the job done in these competitive times without a bright young person like Evans to help him."

BRIGGS' ACCOUNT OF THE SITUATION

"Before I say anything else, let me assure you there is nothing personal in my criticism of Evans.

"I like him. I have always liked him. I've done more for him than anyone else in the company. I've tried to coach him and bring him along just like a son.

"But the simple truth is that he's in way over his head and showing a side of his personality I've never seen before. I brought him along through sales service and product management and he was always eager to learn. While I couldn't give him a lot of help in those areas (frankly, there are aspects of them I don't yet fully understand), I still tried, and he paid attention and learned from others as well.

"The job of national sales manager, however, is a different story. In the other jobs Evans had—staff jobs—there was always time to consult, to consider, to get more data. In sales, however, all this participative stuff he uses takes too long. The national sales manager has to be able to make quick, intuitive decisions. What's more, like the captain of a ship, he has to inspire confidence in those below him. If the going gets rough, the only thing that keeps the sailors and junior officers from panicking is confidence in the skipper. I've been there and I know.

"Right now, with orders coming in strong, he can get away with all of his meetings and indecisiveness. The people in the field really like him and are trying to keep him out of trouble. In addition, I have been putting in sixty to seventy hours a week trying to do my job and also make sure he doesn't make any serious mistakes.

"I know he is feeling the pressure, too. Despite the fact that he has been his usual cheery self with others, when I call him in to question a decision he has made or is about to make, he gets very defensive. He was never that way with me before.

"I may have lost a little feel for what's going on in the field over the years, but I suspect I still know more about the customers and our sales people than Tom Evans will ever know. I've tried for the past seven months to get him to relax and let the old man help him, but it's no use. I'm convinced he's just not cut out for the job, and before we ruin him I want to transfer him somewhere else. He would probably make a fine personnel director someday. He's a very popular guy who seems genuinely interested in people and in helping them.

"I have talked with Ben Petersen about the move, and he has been stalling me. I

understand his position. We have a lot of young comers like Evans in the company, and Ben has to worry about all of them. He told me that if anyone can bring Evans along I can, and he asked me to give it another try. I have, and things are getting worse.

"I hate to admit I made a mistake with Evans, but I plan on seeing Ben about this again tomorrow. We just can't keep putting it off. I'm sure he'll see it my way, and as soon as he approves the transfer, I'll have a heart-to-heart talk with Tom."

EVANS' SIDE OF THE STORY

"This has been a very hectic but rewarding period for me. I've never worked as hard in my life as I have during the last six months, but it's paying off. I'm learning more about sales each day, and more important, I'm building a first-rate sales team. My people are really enjoying the chance to share ideas and support each other.

"At first, particularly with our markets improving, it was hard to convince them to take time to meet with me and their subordinates. Gradually they have come to accept these sessions as an investment in team building. According to them, we've come up with more good ideas and ways to help each other than ever before.

"Fortunately, I also have experience in product management and sales service. Someday I hope to bring representatives from this department and market research into the meetings with regional and branch people, but that will take time. This kind of direct coordination and interaction doesn't fit with the thinking of some of the old-timers. I ran into objections when I tried this while I was working in the other departments.

"But I'm certain that in a year or so I'll be able to show, by results, that we should have more direct contact across department levels.

"My boss, George Briggs, will be one of the ones I will have to convince. He comes from the old school and is slow to give up what he knows used to work well.

"George likes me, though, and has given me a tremendous amount of help in the past. I was amazed when he told me he was giving me this job. Frankly, I didn't think I was ready yet, but he assured me I could handle it. I've gotten a big promotion every few years and I really like that—being challenged to learn new skills and getting more responsibility. I guess I have a real future here, although George won't be retiring for some years and I've gone as high as I can go until then.

"George is a very demanding person, but extremely fair, and he is always trying to help. I only hope I can justify the confidence he has shown in me. He stuck his neck out by giving me this chance, and I'm going to do all I can to succeed.

"Recently we have had a few run-ins. George Briggs works harder than anyone else around here, and perhaps the pressure of the last few years is getting to him. I wish he'd take a vacation this year and get away for a month or more and just relax. He hasn't taken more than a week off in the nine years

I've been here, and for the last two years he hasn't taken any vacation.

"I can see the strain is taking its toll. Recently he has been on my back for all kinds of little things. He always was a worrier, but lately he has been testing me on numerous small issues. He keeps throwing out suggestions or second-guessing me on things that I've spent weeks working on with the field people.

"I try to assure him I'll be all right, and to please help me where I need it with the finance and production people who've had a tough time keeping up with our sales organization. It has been rough lately, but I'm sure it will work out. Sooner or later George will accept the fact that while I will never be able to run things the way he did, I can still get the job done for him."

PERKINS' OPINIONS

"I feel that George Briggs is threatened by Evans' seeming success with the field-sales people. I don't think he realizes it, but he is probably jealous of the speed with which Tom has taken charge. In all likelihood, he didn't expect Tom to be able to handle the field people as well as he has, as fast as he has.

"When George put Tom in the job, I have a feeling that he was looking forward to having him need much more help and advice from the old skipper. Tom does need help and advice, but he is getting most of what George would offer from his own subordinates and his peers. As a result, he has created a real team spirit below and around him, but he has upset George in the process.

"George not only has trouble seeing Tom depend so much on his subordinates, but I feel that he resents Tom's unwillingness to let him show him how he used to run the sales force.

"I may be wrong about this, of course. I am sure that George honestly believes that Tom's style will get him in trouble sooner or later. George is no doddering old fool who has to relive his past success in lower-level jobs. In the past, I'm told, he has shown real insight and interest in the big-picture aspects of the company.

"The trouble is he knows he was an outstanding sales manager, but I am not sure he has the same confidence in his ability as vice-president. I have seen this time and again, particularly in recent years. When a person begins to doubt his future, he sometimes drops back and begins to protect his past. With more competition from younger subordinates and the new methods that they often bring in, many of our experienced people find that doing their job the way they used to just isn't good enough anymore.

"Some reach out and seek new responsibilities to prove their worth. Others, however, return to the things they used to excel in and try to show that theirs is still the best way to do things. They don't even seem to realize that this puts them in direct competition with their subordinates.

"What do we do about this? I wish I knew! At lower levels, where you have more room to shift people around, you have more options. When the company is growing rapidly, the problem often takes care of itself.

"In this case, I am not sure what I will recommend if Ben Petersen asks my advice. Moving Tom to personnel at this time not only won't help me (I really don't have a spot for him), but it won't help Briggs or Evans either. Moving Evans now would be wasteful of the time and effort we've invested in his development. It may also reverse some important trends Tom has begun in team building within the sales force.

"If Briggs were seven or eight years older, we could wait it out. If the company were growing faster, we might be able to shift people. As things stand, however, I see only one approach as a possibility. And I'm not entirely sure it will work.

"I would recommend that we get busy refocusing Briggs' attention on the vice-president's job and get him to see that there is where he has to put his time and efforts. Perhaps the best thing would be to send him to one of the longer programs for senior executives. Don't forget he is a very bright and experienced person who still has a great deal to offer the company if we can figure out how to help him."

WHAT WOULD YOU SUGGEST?

Petersen has agreed to talk with Briggs about Evans tomorrow afternoon. As he thinks about the situation, he wonders what he can do that would be best for the company and everyone concerned. Should he go along with Briggs's recommendation that Evans be transferred to personnel? Or would it be preferable to do as Perkins has suggested and send Briggs to an executive program? As you consider the various perspectives, why do you think the impasse came to be and what do you think could be done to resolve it?

Case Study: Chapter 6. Al Ruskin

In the late spring of 1955, Al Ruskin dropped in to see one of his professors at the Harvard Business School. Ruskin had graduated from the school three years earlier.

After a few pleasantries about families and friends, Ruskin began to talk about his current job situation. With the professor interjecting an occasional question and expression of interest, Ruskin proceeded to tell the following story:

AL RUSKIN: I guess you know I'm still working for Amalgamated Industries.

PROFESSOR: Well, I wasn't sure.

RUSKIN: I've been in their sales department ever since I left the school. As you know, we have a huge sales organization. I've had two or three different jobs; but right now, I'm working in the market research division, and there are about thirty of us in that outfit. The work of the division is broken down into four different sections, and then there is another group of clerical people who do the actual figure calculations and help get out the analytical reports of the division. I'm working in one of these four sections as an analyst. There are about six of us doing that kind of work in the section I'm in. We report to our section chief, and then the division has a couple of assistant managers and a manager of the division who reports to a vice-president.

PROFESSOR: What kind of work do you do?

RUSKIN: Well, I'm an analyst, and we work on different management problems that are sent down to us. There's always more than enough work to do. Right now, I'm pretty discouraged about the setup. The trouble is with the supervision up the line. Some of them either don't know about the problems or just don't face up to what's going on. As far as I can see, all of them are trying to act like superanalysts instead of like supervisors. For a while on this job, I was able to look at what was going on in a detached way, and it didn't bother me very much. Sometimes, another fellow who graduated from Harvard Business School and myself get together and discuss these problems and enjoy talking about them. But in the last few weeks, it's been getting under my skin.

Let me give you an instance of what is bothering me. Let me tell you about the first big report I worked on. I got really excited about that job. It involved an issue as to whether or not the company should continue with a certain product line. They had about decided to discontinue it when I started digging into some of the figures, and it seemed to me that the figures indicated they might come out with a different answer. I worked very hard on it. I spent a number of nights working on it and got quite excited about the project.

When I had finished my report, I let my section chief know, and he came right over to my desk. He held out his hand for the report, and I gave it to him; he turned around and walked out of the office and went to see the vice-president.

The other two analysts who were in the office with me had been watching this. As soon as the door was closed, they looked over at me, and one of them said: "Well, how does it feel, Al? Do you like the way it feels?" Then they laughed and said: "Don't worry, Al; after that's happened to you about half a dozen times, you'll get sort of used to the way it feels, and it won't be quite so tough."

PROFESSOR: Did you ever hear anything more about the report?

RUSKIN: Well, a couple of days later, the chief mentioned to me that he had taken it upstairs, and the people there weren't too impressed with the potential profits that could be realized with my proposal. Of course, I don't think my chief or the people he was talking with really understood what I was proposing. But that was the end of it. I think he was a little let down that they didn't get more excited about it. I know I certainly was.

You see, part of the problem is that our supervisors have the notion that they have to do their own analysis job on all the reports we turn in to them. They think they have to have all the answers at their fingertips when they go to talk to the people up the line that the reports are being prepared for.

PROFESSOR: Are most of your reports prepared for the top management group?

RUSKIN: Yeah, we work them up for them. For instance, some fellow at the top of the organization will think of a question he would like to get an answer on. He will wonder what the profit picture is or is going to be on some particular product. He will ask the question, and then it filters down to our group, and we have to go out and dig up or develop all the data and prepare the report for him. I don't think the people at the top often realize how much work is going into those reports, and I don't think we analysts always realize just what problem the executive is really concerned with.

These requests affect our district offices, too. You see, for six months before I got into this headquarters group, I was working as a field analyst in one of our district offices. The three analysts there spent their time running around getting data requested by headquarters. None of them had time to be of help to the local sales force. I was sent out on temporary duty, so I did have time to help the local people on a couple of the studies they were interested in. They really appreciated the help. Those field men impressed me as being "on the ball" and very desirous of having the help of good analytical stuff. They knew what they wanted and used the figures in directing their sales efforts when they got them; but they couldn't get much help from their own analysts because they were so busy doing work for headquarters.

The fellow I was working for out there asked me if I would like to go to work for him on a permanent basis and painted a good picture of the job. I told him I would be interested if it could be arranged. I really enjoyed that kind of work. You felt that you had some notion of what you were accomplishing by your efforts. But there's quite a story on why I didn't get that job.

PROFESSOR: I'd be interested to hear something about it.

RUSKIN: Well, apparently that fellow at the district office really went to bat to try to get my services. What it involved was getting a transfer for me. He went to headquarters with the request and got the approval of the fellow who's head of market research. I didn't learn all this until after the request had finally been turned down. The trouble came up when the division head checked with one of the assistant managers who knew me and my work. Apparently, the assistant manager told the manager that he would like to keep me in this organization. That stopped the transfer. No one asked me about it. I don't doubt the assistant manager who did it thought he was doing it not only for the good of our local section but probably also for my good. But it isn't exactly the way I'd go about doing that kind of thing. I don't think it even occurred to him to check with me on it.

PROFESSOR: How do you account for that?

RUSKIN: Well, I'm not sure just how to account for it. The problem seems to go quite a way up. They tell me that even the vice-president we report to sits down and adds up the figures again on any report or study brought to him. I guess when the rest of the supervisors see him doing that, they figure they've got to sit down and recheck everything and add up all the figures before they pass a report on. They've got a lot of people working for them, but they never think of themselves as doing a supervising job.

Every job that comes along in this division is handled as a crisis. I thought that the job that was hot when I first arrived was an unusual thing—that this was a rush job and that things would quiet down shortly. They never have quieted down. Every job is a crisis. You are always working against extremely tight deadlines, and you always have to do a sort of halfway job. You never know exactly what it is you're supposed to be doing, so you just grind it out as best you can. It seems as if you always make a few mistakes when you're doing it that way.

People in this organization seem to delight in finding the mistakes of others. For instance, our group turns out a periodic letter on commercial operations; and apparently, almost everybody else in the department immediately reads this letter to see if he can find any mistakes in it. Within a matter of a few minutes after the letter is released, we start getting phone calls from people who have spotted things that are wrong. I don't mean by this that they find matters of real significance, but rather such things as a misspelling or a figure that is slightly in error.

It seems as if all the supervisors up the line feel they are in direct competition with one another. They are all concentrating on trying to impress their immediate bosses as being particularly keen analysts. They never seem to have time to look at what is going on in their own groups. You can imagine what that does to the state of mind of the fellows who are at the bottom of the organization. It isn't so bad on me and the other fellow from Harvard Business School, because we have the feeling, rightly or wrongly, that we can leave this company and get good jobs in other companies. We don't feel tied to this organization for our career. But that isn't true of most of the fellows in the department. Most of them do not know of any other place they can work. They feel they have to make the best of the situation for their career. After they have worked around here for a while, most of them seem to get pretty bitter.

The senior analyst I work with is still a pretty young man, but he's amazingly cynical and bitter about the organization. I try to be careful not to be too influenced by his views because, pretty clearly, he is seeing the worst side of things. But that's apt to happen to people after they've been around for a while. However, I think most of the people who have no choice but to stay don't really dare to take a close look at what is going on in the organization and face up to whether or not it is worth while. They seem to get used to the constant state of tension and crisis around the place and sort of resign themselves to it.

Let me see if I can give you some examples of the kind of problems that keep coming up. Just a few weeks ago, I got caught in a bind on a situation typical of the sort of thing that is apt to happen. In order to get a report out in time to meet a deadline, I needed the help and cooperation of a group of the clerical people who were handling the figures. Several people in that group were involved. I had the feeling that there was some confusion about what was needed and when it was needed.

On several occasions, I went to my boss and asked him if he would call a meeting for me with the supervisors concerned with helping me on the job. I thought we needed it in order to get a clear understanding of who was to do what, and when. Each time, he said that I was making too much of a fuss about it and that he didn't see any reason why we needed to get together to get the job done. He said it was perfectly evident that the other people had the responsibility for doing their part of it, and it was up to them to do it.

You see, I didn't think it was a matter of their being willing to do it; I thought it was a matter of some confusion about just what was needed. But as I feared, the jobs I needed them to do for me did not get done as they should have been done and at the right time. I talked to them about it personally, but they still were not getting done on time. So at the last minute, I felt I had to go to my boss and tell him that the work of the other group was not being done properly and on time. He went over to the boss of these people and told the story, and then they were called on the carpet by their boss for not keeping up with our schedule. Of course, they think now that I'm a real s.o.b. for having done this to them.

I guess it's not quite that bad. I think we understand each other pretty well; but it was a messy situation, and I could see it coming and could see no way of avoiding it. I couldn't seem to get the point across to my boss that we needed to get together to make sure that everybody understood what was being done.

I could give you a couple of other instances of the way my particular boss works with me. For example, a while back, he passed me in the hall and, just as a passing remark, said that I'd be getting a raise in my next check. Nothing more was said. I suppose that's the way a lot of people handle an announcement of that kind, but it's not my idea of how to let a fellow know he's got a raise. I muttered, "Thank you," and that was the extent of the conversation. If I were giving a person a raise, I'd use the occasion to sit down and tell him about the things he's doing well and maybe point out some things he's not doing too well.

On another occasion, my boss asked me to get out a fairly simple little statement about some distribution figures. He and the senior analyst and I were sitting around the desk with the reports in front of us, and he asked me simply to draw out and restate in summary form certain figures that were on a piece of paper. He took his pencil and pointed to the items on the list he wanted me to make a summary of. I didn't know anything about what the job was for and simply did as he told me. I took out the particular items and sent in the report.

Well, it turned out to be wrong. We forgot to include some item that should have been included; and because the mistake wasn't caught until some time later, a good deal of work had to be redone in another part of the office. When the mistake was found, my boss called me in and said he was taking responsibility for the error. Then he proceeded for the next fifteen minutes to tell me, in effect, that I'd better be careful not to make mistakes of that kind again.

Well, what can you do when something like that happens to you? I don't blame him too much. It's just that he and a bunch of other fellows are caught in this system of trying to be perfect and not admit any mistakes. It's funny, too; but in that kind of organization, I think all of us make more mistakes than we normally would. Everything is done at such a hectic pace, and there are so many changes being made at the last minute when you're trying to get out a report. You always seem to be making very simple little mistakes. These turn up later on, to everybody's embarrassment. As I said before, they say that the vice-president still gets out his pencil and checks questionable figures; and the awful part of it is, he finds mistakes that weren't caught coming all the way up the line.

You know, I really like the analytical work I'm doing, but I'm getting terribly discouraged with the job. Part of the trouble is that you never know just what's being done with the reports and studies you turn out. Sometimes, I wonder if I have a tendency to exaggerate these problems; but then, some new incident comes along and convinces me that this is the way things are, the way they're probably going to stay.

Lately, I've been doing a little outside job for a small company on some of my week-end time. I'm helping the owner to use available market information in planning his operations and distribution setup. It's a funny thing, but I've been getting more fun out of doing that in my spare time than I ever get out of my regular job. You really feel you're accomplishing something when you do a job for an outfit like that.

I just don't know whether or not it's worthwhile to stay with Amalgamated Industries. I really believe I have a fairly decent chance to move up in the organization. I think if I stuck around another five or ten years, I would be getting up the line. Maybe I'm kidding myself; but I think, without any false modesty, that my prospects are pretty good. But I'm not at all sure it's worth the effort. I'm not at all sure I'd be able to do anything that would really help the situation very much.

PROFESSOR: You don't see any way you can contribute and change this pattern.

RUSKIN: Well, I really don't, from my level of the organization. I think you could if you were higher up the line. I don't know if it would be too easy even then. You see, it takes a lot of courage to say what should be said in order to get these things straightened out. I guess by the time they get up that way, most of the fellows are so worried about their jobs that they don't dare say some of the things they think ought to be said, even if they know what needs to be done. At my level, right now, I don't know just what you could do. I try to talk to my boss about some of these things, but it doesn't seem to make much difference. My senior analyst tells me he's written a number of reports and recommendations suggesting some changes he thinks would begin to get at some of these problems. He has always submitted them to his boss, and nothing more has ever happened to them. At least as far as he knows, nothing has happened at all, and his boss hasn't really explained to him why he hasn't done anything with them. I suppose over a lifetime in this organization, you could really make a little headway; but I don't know, I'm beginning to think life's too short to spend all your time bucking that kind of situation.

Case Study: Chapter 7. Career Planning Exercise

Purpose
To develop or reassess your career and life plans.

Introduction
This exercise will give you an opportunity to examine your own values and priorities for your life and to set career goals for yourself. It is helpful in an exercise like this to share the ideas you generate with other people in a small group setting because the feedback, support, and questions of others are helpful in clarifying your own values and goals. However, you should always feel free to withhold any personal data from others if you would be uncomfortable in sharing it.

PART I: INDIVIDUAL PLANNING
Procedure
Step 1.

On a piece of notebook paper, write WHO AM I at the top. Then make 3 columns on the sheet. Label the first column CAREER, the second AFFILIATIONS, and the third PERSONAL FULFILLMENT. Write the numerals 1 to 20 in the left margin.

In the first column, list 20 adjectives that describe you most accurately in regard to your career.

In the second column, list 20 adjectives that describe you most accurately in regard to your *personal affiliations*.

In the third column, list 20 adjectives that describe you most accurately in regard to your *personal fulfillment*.

Step 2.
This may sound a bit gruesome, but hang in there! Assume you were hit by a car tomorrow and you were killed. Write down what you would like to have for an *epitaph*. (An epitaph is a few well-selected words, a phrase or a sentence, that capture the essence of you.)

Step 3.
Write a one-paragraph *obituary* for yourself as it would appear in tomorrow's paper.

Step 4.
Write a one-paragraph *obituary* as you would like it to be *ten years from now* (assuming you live your life as you would ideally like to over the next ten years).

Step 5.
Take three more sheets of paper. Head them up as follows:
WHERE DO I WANT TO BE?—CAREER
WHERE DO I WANT TO BE?—AFFILIA-TIONS
WHERE DO I WANT TO BE?—PERSON-AL FULFILLMENT
On each sheet, write the numbers 1 to 10, leaving a blank in front of the numbers like this:

```
_____1.
_____2.
_____3.
```
etc.
Fill in the first sheet as follows:
List 10 goals that describe your conception of ideal attainments in your *career*. Be as free as possible in selecting these goals. Summarize your career fantasies on this page. Example: I want to become president of my company.

Then fill in the second sheet:
What would be your conception of 10 ideal attainments in your *personal affiliations*? Be as free as possible in selecting these goals. Summarize your affiliation fantasies on this page. Example: I want to behave in such a way that my mother-in-law will be more accepting of me.

And then the third sheet:
What would be your conception of 10 ideal attainments with regard to your *personal fulfillment*? Be as free as possible in selecting these goals. Summarize your personal fulfillment fantasies on this page. Example: I want to learn to fly an airplane.

Go back to the first sheet and, in the blank in front of the numbers, assign a priority value to each of your *career* goals.
a. Using the following four-point scale, write the appropriate value in the space provided in front of each goal.
1 — of little importance
2 — of moderate importance
3 — of great importance
4 — of very great importance
b. Assign a priority value to each of your

personal affiliation goals (the second sheet). Using the four-point scale above, write the appropriate value in the space provided in front of each goal.
c. Assign a priority value to each of your *personal fulfillment* goals (the third sheet). Using the four-point scale above, write the appropriate value in the space provided in front of each goal.
d. Which of the three sheets (career, affiliations, personal fulfillment) has the most 4s? The most 1s? What does this tell you about the relative importance of these three aspects of your life?

Step 6.
Take another clean sheet of paper, label it *COMBINED LIST*, and list in order of importance all thirty of your goals as generated on the previous three lists. Merge the lists so that this combined list reflects the *relative importance* of the specific goals from the three lists. (You may find it convenient to abbreviate the goal summaries in this listing.) Examine the 4s. What can you learn from them? All the 1s? Single out all the 4s for future examination.

Step 7.
Take 1 more sheet of paper; head it up with *MY THREE GOALS*. From your combined list of goals on the previous page, select three that you want most to attain. Discuss these three in terms of the following questions:
a. What are *my strengths and weaknesses* affecting my ability to achieve these goals?
b. What *obstacles* are to prevent me from achieving these goals?
c. Are these *goals realistic*? What will happen if I do not achieve these goals?

Step 8.
This is an *optional* part of the exercise that you will find very helpful.
You will have to do this part entirely on your own, outside class. If you are really serious about achieving your goals, your chances of success will be much greater if you proceed as follows:
a. From your combined list of goals, select a few for detailed planning. Establish a program, with component steps and deadlines, for attaining each objective.
b. Prepare a written contract with members of your family or close friends in which you commit yourself to achieving the goals in your plan. Identify in advance all the possible *excuses for inaction* that may come up as you work toward these goals. How can you avoid these causes of inaction?

PART II: GROUP DISCUSSION
(In the next two steps, you will have an opportunity to share some of the data generated in Part I with others. Meet in groups of three or four people, preferably people with whom you have worked before, people who know you.)

219

Step 9. (*1 hour*)
Turn to your lists of WHO AM I adjectives, epitaphs, and obituaries. Share these with the group.

    a. Do others agree with your classifications?
    b. Do the other group members agree with your description of yourself?
    c. What are the similarities and differences in the self-descriptions of the various group members?

Step 10. (*1 hour, 20 minutes*)
Using the data from your *COMBINED LIST* of goals, and your discussion of *MY THREE GOALS.*

    a. Share the important goals with others in your group.
    b. Talk about why these goals are important to you.
    c. Discuss the answers you developed for *MY THREE GOALS* in respect to your goals.

Discussion Questions

1. Psychologists often argue that most people have rather fuzzy career plans because their sense of identity (their sense of

who they are) is hazy. From your experience with this exercise, would you agree or disagree? Did the exercise enhance your sense of identity? Did this help you to clarify your career plans?

2. Suggest further steps for continuing your career plans.

3. What parts of the exercise did you find most difficult? Why?

Generalizations and Conclusions

1. Develop a career-strategy statement for yourself that you can use to plan and manage your career. Make your objectives *specific* and *concrete*, develop *action* plans for achieving these objectives, develop a *timetable* for accomplishment of the major steps, and identify a *support group* of people (friends or family) who will encourage you and counsel you on achieving your goals.

2. For many people career planning means a process by which they merely collect information on available jobs and employers. In this exercise, you have been collecting information about yourself. What might be the relationship between these two strategies?

Adapted from J. William Pfeiffer and John E. Jones, eds. *A Handbook of Structured Experiences for Human Relations Training,* Vol. II, rev. La Jolla, Calif.: University Associates, 1974. Used by permission.

Case Study: Chapter 8. Managing Organizational Careers: Some Problems

Purpose
To practice your skills in making organizational decisions and planning programs to facilitate employees' career development.

Introduction
Many of the conditions necessary for better career development seem disarmingly straightforward—e.g., provide more initial job challenge, more realistic job previews, more opportunities for women and minorities. However, when put into practice, some of the unintentioned consequences and system effects (such as uncooperative supervisors or coworkers) come into play, indicating that we are dealing with organization development as well as career development. In the following problems you will be given a chance to try your hand at finding organizational solutions to some thorny career issues.

Procedure
Step 1. Formation. (*5 minutes*)
The class is first divided into groups of four to six people. Each group is assigned one of the problems at the end of the exercise, except for one group, which is designated the *judging group.*

Step 2. Preparation. (*20 minutes*)
Each group will meet separately to develop

a solution to its problem and to prepare a five minute presentation to the rest of the class. In this presentation, the group will identify the problem and develop a persuasive case for the group's solution, while the rest of the class acts as a "board of directors."

During the preparation, the judges will meet to determine what *criteria* they will use to evaluate the presentation.

Step 3. Presentations. (*5 minutes per group*)
Each group will have five minutes to present their solutions. The judging group will act as moderators and timekeepers. If there is time, there will be a question and discussion period following the presentations. The judges may also ask questions.

Step 4. Judging. (*5 minutes*)
After the presentations, the judges will meet briefly and determine the winner. In announcing the winner, the judges should also state the criteria they used and show why the winner won.

Step 5. Discussion. (*varying time*)
During the free discussion, the various solutions might be compared. What are the costs and benefits of each? What resistance would each encounter? How could this resistance be reduced?

CAREER PROBLEMS

Career Program

Design a career planning and counseling program to help employees increase their basic career competencies (in Crites' terms): self-appraisal, gathering occupational information, goal selection, planning, and problem-solving. This program should achieve these career objectives and meet two constraints: (1) moderate cost, and (2) compatibility with most existing personnel management systems.

EEO Versus Seniority

Assume you are personnel manager of a one-thousand-employee technology-based company with no union (and a management who wishes to keep it that way) and a history of good labor-management relations. Although there is no contract and no written agreement on layoffs, the company has honored the tradition of layoffs based upon seniority.

About 75 percent of your revenue is from government contracts from three separate agencies. These agencies have been exerting pressure on you lately to increase the number of women and minority employees in your organization, although there has been no talk of legal action or threats to any contracts yet.

Because of financial problems, you will have to lay off 10 percent of your work force. Through some fine work on affirmative action, the number of women and minorities in the organization has been increasing, but most of these people have been hired in the last two years. Most of your employees have been with the organization five years or more, with a mean seniority of twelve years.

The employees know the layoff is coming. There has been a lot of talk that if it is not based on seniority, a walkout or some other action may occur. Several union organizers have been seen outside the gates recently. For the past month, there have been two or three after-hours meetings of employees per week. Also, you have just received a letter from a compliance officer with one of your contracting agencies, reminding you that a large contract is up for review and that she has been hoping for more progress on affirmative action.

How should the layoff be handled?

The "Dead-End" Employee

Jim Duncan is a 52-year-old department manager in your large manufacturing organization. He has been in this job for eight years. His performance has been very good, but lately has dropped off. He has had more sick days this year than ever before in his career.

Jim is not seen by top management or by personnel experts as having the ability to progress to a higher management position. He seems ideally placed in his present job.

You are Jim's boss, the plant manager. What action would you take to improve his performance and morale?

The "Deadwood" Employee

Ralph Hamner is seen by most employees as "deadwood." He was hired when the organization was much smaller, when you only had a few engineers, who had to be generalists. Now you have an engineering department of fifty people, most with advanced degrees and specialized backgrounds to deal with the increased complexity of your products—calculators and photographic equipment.

Ralph is now a senior engineer and just does not have the new knowledge necessary for most of your products. It has been hard to find projects on which he can use his present knowledge. At the same time, he is blocking the advancement of several promising junior engineers. Ralph is a well-liked guy, but he seems a bit defensive about his technical competence.

You are the personnel manager. What action would you recommend regarding Ralph Hamner?

Loss of Talented Young Employees

Your organization has traditionally been very attractive to college graduates as a place to work. The turnover among new employees has been about average for your industry. However, a recent study has just revealed a critical piece of information: the turnover is now occurring among your highest performing new employees. The people you'd like to lose are staying, and those you want to keep are leaving.

Exit interviews indicate that young people are frustrated by low challenge and low advancement opportunities. You have a lot of people in their fifties in middle management who are blocking promotions now and who are threatened by sharp young employees. But you won't have any good middle managers in ten years (when the present managers retire) if all your best young people leave now. Business has been rather slow lately, and no new positions through growth seem likely for several years.

What should be done to retain more of your promising young employees?

REFERENCES

Alderfer, Clayton P., "Effect of Individual, Group, and Intergroup Relations on Attitudes toward a Management Development Program," *Journal of Applied Psychology*, 55(1971), 302–11.

———, *Existence, Relatedness, and Growth: Human Needs in Organizational Settings.* New York: Free Press, 1972.

Alexander, Michael O., James G. Goodale, and Douglas T. Hall, "Improve your Employees' Quality of Life for Fun and Profit," *The Canadian Manager* (January–February 1973).

Andrews, John D.W., "The Achievement Motive and Advancement in Two Types of Organizations," *Journal of Personality and Social Psychology*, 6(1967), 163–69.

Argyris, Chris, "Human Relations in a Bank," *Harvard Business Review*, 32(1954), 63–72.

———, *Personality and Organization.* New York: Harper, 1957.

———, *Integrating the Individual and the Organization.* New York: Wiley, 1964.

Astin, Helen S., and Ann S. Bisconti, *Trends in Academic and Career Plans of College Freshmen.* Bethlehem, Pa.: College Placement Council, 1972.

Atkinson, John W., "Thematic Apperception Measurement of Motives Within the Context of a Theory of Motivation," in J.W. Atkinson, ed. *Motives in Fantasy, Action, and Society.* New York: Van Nostrand, 1958.

Bales, Robert F., "Task Roles and Social Roles in Problem-Solving Groups," in E. Maccoby, T.M. Newcomb, and E.L. Hartley, eds., *Readings in Social Psychology*, 3rd ed. New York: Holt, Rinehart and Winston, 1958.

Baltes, Paul B., and K. Warner Schaie, "The Myth of the Twilight Years," *Psychology Today*, (March 1975), 35–40.

Bardwick, Judith M., *Psychology of Women: A Study of Biocultural Conflicts.* New York: Harper & Row, 1971.

REFERENCES

Bavelas, A., and G. Strauss, "Group Dynamics and Intergroup Relations," in W.F. Whyte, et al., eds., *Money and Motivation.* New York: Harper, 1955.

Becker, Howard, "Becoming a Marihuana User," in H. Becker, ed., *Outsiders.* Glencoe, Ill.: Free Press, 1963.

Becker, Howard, Blanche Geer, Everett Hughes, and Anselm Strauss, *Boys In White.* Chicago: University of Chicago Press, 1961.

Becker, Howard, Blanche Geer, and Anselm Strauss, *Making the Grade.* Chicago: University of Chicago Press, 1969.

Berlew, David E., and Douglas T. Hall, "Some Determinants of Early Managerial Success." Working Paper #81-64, Sloan School of Management, MIT, Cambridge, Mass., 1964.

————, "The Socialization of Managers: Effects of Expectations on Performance," *Administrative Science Quarterly,* 11(1966), 207–23.

Blau, Peter M., and Otis Dudley Duncan, *The American Occupational Structure.* New York: Wiley, 1967.

Blau, Peter M., John W. Gustad, Richard Jesson, Herbert S. Parnes, and Richard C. Wilcox, "Occupational Choices: A Conceptual Framework," *Industrial and Labor Relations Review,* 9(1956), 531, 536, 537, 543.

Blauner, Robert, *Alienation and Freedom.* Chicago: University of Chicago Press, 1964.

Bolles, Richard N., *What Color Is Your Parachute? A Practical Manual for Job-Hunters and Career Changers.* Berkeley, Calif.: Ten Speed Press, 1975, rev. ed.

Bray, Douglas W., "The Management Recruit: Early Career and Development." Paper read at American Psychological Association meeting, Honolulu, 1972.

Bray, Douglas W., Richard J. Campbell, and Donald L. Grant, *Formative Years in Business.* New York: Wiley, 1974.

Bray, Douglas W., and Donald L. Grant, "The Assessment Center in the Measurement of Potential for Business Management," *Psychological Monographs,* 80(1966), no. 17 (Whole No. 625), 2.

Breer, P., and Edwin Locke, *Task Experience as a Source of Attitudes.* Homewood, Ill.: Dorsey, 1965.

Brown, Harold A., and David L. Ford, Jr., "Employment Progress and Job Satisfaction of Minority Candidates." Presented at the Association of Social and Behavioral Scientists meeting, Charlotte, N.C., 1975.

Buchanan, Bruce, II, "Building Organizational Commitment: The Socialization of Managers in Work Organizations," *Administrative Science Quarterly,* 19(1974), 533–46.

Burke, Ronald J., James G. Goodale, Douglas T. Hall, and Robert C. Joyner, "An Examination of Important Contexts and Components of Individual Quality of Life." ABRP Working Paper #21, Faculty of Administrative Studies, York University, Toronto, 1972.

Burnstein, E., "Fear of Failure, Achievement Motivation, and Aspiring to Prestigeful Occupations," *Journal of Abnormal and Social Psychology,* 67(1963), 189–93.

Cain, L.D., Jr., "Life Course and Social Structure," in R. Faris, ed., *Handbook of Modern Sociology.* Chicago: Rand McNally, 1964.

Campbell, John P., Marvin D. Dunnette, Edward E. Lawler, III, and Karl E. Weick, Jr., *Managerial Behavior, Performance, and Effectiveness.* New York: McGraw-Hill, 1970.

Campbell, Richard J., "Career Development: The Young Business Manager," in J. Richard Hackman, Chmn., *Longitudinal Approaches to Career Development,* symposium presented at American Psychological Association annual convention, San Francisco, 1968.

Campbell, Richard J., and Douglas W. Bray, "Assessment Centers: An Aid in Management Selection," *Personnel Administration,* 30 (March–April 1967), pp. 6–13.

Cleaver, Eldridge, *Soul on Ice.* New York: Delta, 1968.

A Comparison of a Work Planning Program with the Annual Performance Appraisal Interview Approach. Crotonville, N.Y.: Behavioral Research Service, General Electric Company, undated.

Conner, Samuel, and Fielden, John S., "Rx for Managerial Fence-Sitters," *Harvard Business Review,* 51(1973), 113–120.

Cox, Alan J., *Confessions of a Corporate Headhunter.* New York: Trident, 1973.

Cox, R.D., *Youth into Maturity.* New York: Materials for Mental Health Center, 1970.

Crane, Diana, "Scientists at Major and Minor Universities: A Study of Productivity and Recognition," *American Sociological Review,* 30(1965), 699–714.

Crites, John O., *Career Maturity Inventory.* Monterey, Calif.: McGraw-Hill, 1973a.

_____, *Theory and Research Handbook, Career Maturity Inventory.* Monterey, Calif.: McGraw-Hill, 1973b.

Cronbach, Lee J., *Essentials of Psychological Testing,* 2nd ed. New York: Harper, 1960.

Cuddihy, B.R., "How to Give Phased-Out Managers a New Start," *Harvard Business Review* (1974), 61–69.

Dalton, Melville, *Men Who Manage.* New York: Wiley, 1959.

Dill, William R., Thomas L. Hilton, and Walter R. Reitman, *The New Managers.* Englewood Cliffs, N.J.: Prentice-Hall, 1962.

Douvan, Elizabeth, and Joseph Adelson, *The Adolescent Experience.* New York: Wiley, 1966.

Downey, H. Kirk, Don Hellriegel, and John W. Slocum, Jr., "Congruence Between Individual Needs, Organizational Climate, Job Satisfaction, and Performance," *Academy of Management Journal,* 18(1975), 149–54.

Drucker, Peter, "How to Be an Employee," *Psychology Today,* 10(March 1968), 63–69.

Dubin, Robert, and Joseph E. Champoux, "Workers' Central Life Interest and Job Performance," *Sociology of Work and Occupations,* 1(1974), 313–26.

Dubin, Samuel S., "Updating and Mid-Career Development and Change," in Peter Moon, Chmn., *Mid-Career Development and Change,* presented at American Psychological Association Annual Meeting, 1973.

DuBrin, Andrew, J., *The Practice of Managerial Psychology.* New York: Pergamon, 1972.

Epstein, Gilda F., and Arline L. Bronzaft, "Female Modesty in Aspiration Level," *Journal of Counseling Psychology,* 21(1974), 57–60.

Erikson, Erik H., *Childhood and Society,* 2nd ed. New York: Norton, 1963.

_____, "The Concept of Identity in Race Relations: Notes and Queries," *Daedalus,* 95(1966), 145–71.

Evan, William M., "Peer Group Interaction and Organizational Socialization: A Study of Employee Turnover," *American Sociological Review,* 28(1963), 436–40.

Evans, M.G., "The Effects of Supervising Behavior on the Path-Goal Relationship," *Organizational Behavior and Human Performance,* 5(1970), 277–98.

Farris, George F., "Chickens, Eggs, and Productivity in Organizations," *Organizational Dynamics,* 3(1975), 2–15.

Fiedler, Fred E., *A Theory of Leader Effectiveness.* New York: McGraw-Hill, 1967.

Fogarty, Michael P., Rhona Rapoport, and Robert N. Rapoport, *Sex, Career, and Family.* Beverly Hills, Calif.: Sage, 1971.

Fordyce, J., and R. Weil, *Managing With People.* Reading, Mass.: Addison-Wesley, 1971.

Ghiselli, Edwin E., *The Validity of Occupational Ability Tests.* New York: Wiley, 1966.

_____, *Explorations in Managerial Talent.* Pacific Palisades, Calif.: Goodyear, 1971.

224

Gibson, J.L., and S.M. Klein, "Employee Attitudes as a Function of Age and Length of Service: A Reconceptualization," *Academy of Management Journal,* 13(1970), 411–25.

Ginzberg, E., J.W. Ginsburg, S. Axelrad, and J.L. Herma, *Occupational Choice.* New York: Columbia University Press, 1951.

Glaser, Barney G., *Organizational Scientists: Their Professional Careers.* New York: Bobbs-Merrill, 1964.

————, *Organizational Careers: A Sourcebook for Theory.* Chicago: Aldine, 1968.

Glaser, Barney G., and Anselm L. Strauss, *Time for Dying.* Chicago: Aldine, 1968.

————, *Status Passage.* Chicago, Aldine-Atherton, 1971.

Glueck, William F., *Personnel: A Diagnostic Approach.* Dallas: Business Publications, 1974.

Goffman, Erving, ed., *Asylums.* New York: Anchor Books, 1961.

Goldstein, Arnold P., and Melvin Sorcher, *Changing Supervisor Behavior.* New York: Pergamon, 1974.

Golembiewski, Robert T., *Renewing Organizations.* Itasca, Ill.: Peacock, 1972.

Goodale, James G., and Douglas T. Hall, "Inheriting a Career: The Effects of Sex, Values, and Parents," *Journal of Vocational Behavior,* (1976). Forthcoming.

Gottfredson, Gary D., and John L. Holland, "Vocational Choices of Men and Women: A Comparison of Predictors from the Self-Directed Search," *Journal of Counseling Psychology,* 22(1975), 28–34.

Gould, Sammy B., *"Organizational Identification and Commitment in Two Environments."* Unpublished Ph.D. Dissertation, Michigan State University, 1975.

Gouldner, Alvin W., "Cosmopolitans and Socials: Towards An Analysis of Latent Social Roles," *Administrative Science Quarterly,* 2(December 1957 and March 1958), 446–50, 465–67.

Grant, D.L., Walter Katkovsky, and Douglas W. Bray, "Contributions of Projective Techniques to Assessment of Management Potential," *Journal of Applied Psychology,* 51(1967), 226–32.

Grier, William H., and Price M. Cobbs, *Black Rage.* New York: Basic Books, 1968.

Grusky, Oscar, "Career Mobility and Organizational Commitment," *Administrative Science Quarterly,* 10(1966), 488–503.

Guion, R.M., and R.F. Gottier, "Validity of Personality Measures in Personnel Selection," *Personnel Psychology,* 18(1965), 135–64.

Hackman, J. Richard, and Edward E. Lawler, III, "Employee Reactions to Job Characteristics," *Journal of Applied Psychology,* 55(1971), 259–86.

Hall, Douglas T., "Identity Changes During the Transition from Student to Professor," *School Review,* 76(1968), 445–69.

————, "The Impact of Peer Interaction During an Academic Role Transition," *Sociology of Education,* 42(1969), 118–40.

————, "A Theoretical Model of Career Subidentity Development in Organizational Settings," *Organizational Behavior and Human Performance,* 6(1971a), 50–76.

————, "Potential for Career Growth," *Personnel Administration,* 34(1971b), 18–30.

————, "A Model of Coping with Role Conflict: The Role Behavior of College Educated Women," *Administrative Science Quarterly,* 17(1972), 471–86.

————, "Pressures from Work, Self, and Home in the Life Stages of Married Women," *Journal of Vocational Behavior,* 6(1975), 121–32.

Hall, Douglas T., Donald D. Bowen, Roy J. Lewicki, and Francine S. Hall, *Experiences in Management and Organizational Behavior.* Chicago: St. Clair Press, 1975.

225

Hall, Douglas T., and Francine E. Gordon,"Career Choices of Married Women: Effects on Conflict, Role Behavior, and Satisfaction," *Journal of Applied Psychology,* 58(1973), 42–48.

Hall, Douglas T., and Edward E. Lawler, III, "Unused Potential in Research and Development Organizations," *Research Management,* 12(1969), 339–54.

Hall, Douglas T., and Roger Mansfield, "Organizations and Individual Response to External Stress," *Administrative Science Quarterly,* 16(1971), 533–47.

————, "Relationship of Age and Seniority with Career Variables of Engineers and Scientists," *Journal of Applied Psychology,* 60(1975), 201–10.

Hall, Douglas T., and Khalil Nougaim, "An Examination of Maslow's Need Hierarchy in an Organizational Setting," *Organizational Behavior and Human Performance,* 3(1968), 12–35.

————, "Correlates of Organizational Identification as a Function of Career Pattern and Organization Type," *Administrative Science Quarterly,* 17(1972), 340–50.

Hall, Douglas T., Benjamin Schneider, and Harold T. Nygren, "Personal Factors in Organizational Identification," *Administrative Science Quarterly,* 15(1970), 176–90.

Haller, A.O., and A. Portes, "Status Attainment Processes," *Sociology of Education,* 46(1973), 51–91.

Hamner, W. Clay, "Reinforcement Theory and Contingency Management in Organizational Settings," in Henry L. Tosi and W. Clay Hamner, eds. *Organizational Behavior and Management: A Contingency Approach.* Chicago: St. Clair Press, 1974, pp. 86–112.

Hamner, W. Clay, and Frank L. Schmidt, *Contemporary Problems in Personnel.* Chicago: St. Clair Press, 1974.

Hedlund, D.E., "A Review of the MMPI in Industry," *Psychological Reports,* 17(1965), 874–89.

"Heublein Managers Have a Fallback Position," *Business Week* (September 28, 1974), p. 100.

Hinrichs, John, *The Motivation Crisis.* New York: AMACOM, 1974.

Hirschman, Albert D., *Exit, Voice, and Loyalty.* Cambridge Mass.: Harvard University Press, 1970.

Holland, John L., *Making Vocational Choices: A Theory of Careers.* Englewood Cliffs, N.J.: Prentice-Hall, 1973.

————, *The Psychology of Vocational Choice.* Waltham, Mass.: Blaisdell, 1966.

Horner, Matina, "Toward Understanding of Achievement-Related Conflicts in Women," *Journal of Social Issues,* 28(1972), 159.

House, R.J., "A Path-Goal Theory of Leader Effectiveness," *Administrative Science Quarterly,* 16(1971), 321–39.

Hrebiniak, L.C., and J.A. Alutto, "Personal and Role-Related Factors in the Development of Organizational Commitment," *Administrative Science Quarterly,* 18(1973), 555–72.

Huegli, Jon, and Harvey D. Tschirgi, "The Entry-Level Job—A Neglected Target for Our Business Schools?" *Collegiate News and Views* (Winter 1974–75), pp. 21–23.

Hughes, Ellen C., "Shelf-Sitters Reexamined" (Special Report), *Harvard Business Review,* 52(1974), 38–40, 44, 46, 160, 163, 164.

Hulin, Charles, and Milton Blood, "Job Enlargement, Individual Differences, and Worker Responses, "*Psychological Bulletin,* 69(1968), 41–55.

Ingraham, M.H., *My Purpose Holds: Reactions and Experiences in Retirement of TIAA-CREF Annuitants.* New York: TIAA-CREF, 1974.

Jacques, Elliott, "Death and the Mid-Life Crises," *International Journal of Psychoanalysis,* 46(1965), 502–14.

————, "Equitable Payment, 1961," in Task Force for the Secretary of HEW, *Work in America.* Cambridge, Mass.: MIT Press, 1973, p. 6.

Janis, Irving L., and Bert T. King, "The Influence of Role-Playing in Opinion Change," *Journal of Abnormal Psychology*, 49(1954), 211–18.

Jennings, Eugene E., "Mobicentric Man," *Psychology Today* (July 1970), pp. 35–40.

————, *Routes to the Executive Suite*. New York: McGraw-Hill, 1971.

Johansson, C., "Stability of the Strong Vocational Interest Blank," unpublished manuscript, University of Minnesota, 1966. Study quoted in J.P. Campbell, M.D. Dunnette, E.E. Lawler, III, and K.E. Wieck, *Managerial Behavior, Performance and Effectiveness*. New York: McGraw-Hill, 1970.

Johnson, J.C., and M.D. Dunnette, "Validity and Test-Retest Stability of the Nash Managerial Effectiveness Scale on the Revised Form of the Strong Vocational Interest Blank," *Personnel Psychology*, 21(1968), 283–93.

Katz, Martin, Educational Testing Service, Princeton, N.J., personal communication, 1973.

————, *Behavior Today* (April 14, 1975), 444.

Kaufman, H.G., *Obsolescence and Professional Career Development*. New York: AMACOM, 1974.

Kay, Emmanuel, and R. Hastman, *An Evaluation of Work Planning and Goal-Setting Discussions*. Crotonville, N.Y.: Behavioral Research Service, General Electric Company, 1966.

Kinslinger, H.S., "Applications of Projective Techniques in Personnel Psychology Since 1949," *Psychology Bulletin*, 66(1966), 134–49.

Kolb, David, Irwin Rubin, and James McIntyre, *Organizational Psychology: A Book of Readings*, 2nd ed. Englewood Cliffs, N.J.: Prentice-Hall, 1974.

Korman, Abraham, "Self-Esteem as a Moderator of the Relationship between Self-Perceived Abilities and Vocational Choice," *Journal of Applied Psychology*, 51(1967), 65–67.

————, "Task Success, Task Popularity, and Self-Esteem as Influences on Task Liking," *Journal of Applied Psychology*. 52(1968a), 484–90.

————, "The Prediction of Managerial Performance: A Review," *Personnel Psychology*, 21(1968b), 295–322.

Kroll, A.M., L.B. Dinklage, J. Lee, E.D. Morley, and E.H. Wilson, *Career Development: Growth and Crisis*. New York: Wiley, 1970.

Kutner, David H., "Crisis and Decision at Mid-Life." Unpublished paper, Yale University, New Haven, Conn., 1971.

Lansing, J.B., and L. Kish, "Family Life Cycle as an Independent Variable," *American Sociological Review*, 22(1957), 512–19.

Lawler, Edward E., III, "For a More Effective Organization—Match the Job to the Man," *Organizational Dynamics*, 3(1947), 19–29.

————, *Motivation in Work Organizations*. Monterey, Ca.: Brooks/Cole, 1973.

Lawrence, Paul R., and Jay W. Lorsch, *Organization and Environment*. Homewood, Ill.: Irwin, 1969.

Lee, Sang M., "An Empirical Analysis of Organizational Identification," *Academy of Management Journal*, 14(1971), 213–26.

Lehman, H.C., *Age and Achievement*. Princeton, N.J.: Princeton University Press, 1953.

Levinson, Daniel J., C. Darrow, E. Klein, M. Levinson, and B. McKee, "The Psychological Development of Men in Early Adulthood and the Mid-Life Transition," in D.F. Hicks, A. Thomas, and M. Roff, eds., *Life History Research in Psychopathology*, vol. 3. Minneapolis, Minn.: University of Minneapolis Press, 1974.

Levinson, Harry, "On Being a Middle-Aged Manager," *Harvard Business Review*, 47(1969), 51–60.

Lewin, Kurt, "The Psychology of Success and Failure," *Occupations*, 14(1936), 926–30.

Lewin, Kurt, Tamara Dembo, Leon Festinger, and Pauline Sears, "Level of Aspiration," in J. McV. Hunt, ed., *Personality and Behavior Disorders.* New York: Ronald Press, 1944.

LIAMA, *Recruitment, Selection, Training, and Supervision in LIfe Insurance.* Hartford, Conn.: Life Insurance Agency Management Association, 1966.

————, "Career Guidance in the LIfe Insurance Industry," *Personnel Psychology,* 21(1968), 1–21.

Lifton, Robert Jay, "Protean Man," *Partisan Review,* 35(Winter 1968), 17.

Likert, Rensis, *The Human Organization.* New York: McGraw-Hill, 1967.

Lipsett, Seymour M., and F. Theodore Malm, "First Jobs and Career Patterns," *The American Journal of Economics and Sociology,* 14(1955), 247–61.

Livingston, J. Sterling, "Pygmalion in Management," *Harvard Business Review,* 47(1969), 81–89.

Locke, Edwin A., "Toward a Theory of Task Motivation and Incentives," *Organizational Behavior and Human Performance,* 3(1968), 157—89.

Lodahl, Thomas, and Mathilde Kejner, "The Definition and Measurement of Job Involvement," *Journal of Applied Psychology,* 49(1965), 24–33.

Lopata, Helene Z., "The Life Cycle of the Housewife," *Sociology and Social Research,* 51(1966), 5–22.

Lorsch, J.W., and Louis B. Barnes, *Managers and Their Careers: Cases and Readings.* Homewood, Ill.: Irwin-Dorsey, 1972.

March, James, and Herbert Simon, *Organizations.* New York: Wiley, 1958.

Maslow, Abraham A., "A Theory of Metamotivation: The Biological Rooting of the Value-Life," *Psychology Today,* 2(July 1968), 38, 39, 58–61.

————, *Motivation and Personality.* New York: Harper, 1954.

McClelland, D.C., "Achievement Motivation Can Be Developed," *Harvard Business Review,* 43(1965), 6–24, 178.

————, *The Achieving Society.* New York: Free Press, 1967.

McGregor, Douglas, *The Human Side of Enterprise.* New York: McGraw-Hill, 1960.

Miller, D.C., and William H. Form, *Industrial Sociology.* New York: Harper, 1951.

Mills, Edgar W., "Career Development in Middle Life," in W. Bartlett, ed., *Evolving Religious Careers.* Washington, D.C.: Center for Applied Research in the Apostolate, 1970.

Morrison, Robert F., "A Study of Adaptive and Non-Adaptive Mid-Career Managers," Mimeograph, Faculty of Management Studies, Toronto, 1975.

Morse, Nancy C., and R.S. Weiss, "The Function and Meaning of Work," *American Sociological Review,* 20(1955), 191–98.

Munley, Patrick H.,"Erik Erikson's Theory of Psychosocial Development and Vocational Development," *Journal of Counseling Psychology,* 22(1975), 314–19.

Nash, A.N., "Vocational Interests of Effective Managers: A Review of the Literature," *Personnel Psychology,* 18(1965), 21–37.

————, "Development of an SVIB Key for Selecting Managers," *Journal of Applied Psychology,* 50(1966), 250–54.

Occupational Outlook Handbook, U. S. Government Printing Office, Washington, D.C. 20402.

O'Leary, Virginia E., "Some Attitudinal Barriers to Occupational Aspirations in Women," *Psychology Bulletin,* 81(1974), 809–26.

Ondrack, Daniel A., "Emerging Occupational Values: A Review and Some Findings," *Academy of Management Journal,* 16(1973), 423–32.

Osipow, Samuel, *Theories of Career Development.* New York: Appleton-Century-Crofts, 1968.

OSS Assessment Staff, *Assessment of Men.* New York: Rinehart, 1948.

Parsons, Talcott, *Structure and Process in Modern Societies.* New York: Free Press, 1960.

Patchen, Martin, *Participation, Achievement and Involvement on the Job.* Englewood Cliffs, N.J.: Prentice-Hall, 1970.

Pelz, Donald C., and Frank M. Andrews, *Scientists in Organizations.* New York: Wiley, 1966.

Peres, Sherwood H., *Factors Which Influence Careers in General Electric.* Crotonville, N.Y.: Management Development and Employee Relations Service, General Electric Company, 1966.

Pervin, Lawrence A., "Performance and Satisfaction as a Function of Individual-Environment Fit," *Psychological Bulletin,* 69(1968), 56–68.

Pettegrew, Thomas, *A Profile of the Negro American.* New York: Van Nostrand, 1964.

Porter, Lyman W., and Edward E. Lawler, III, *Managerial Attitude and Performance.* New York: Wiley, 1968.

Porter, Lyman W., Edward E. Lawler, III, and J. Richard Hackman, eds., *Behavior in Organizations.* New York: McGraw-Hill, 1975.

Purcell, Theodore V., "How GE Measures Managers in Fair Employment," *Harvard Business Review,* (1974), 99–104.

Roe, Anne, "Early Determinants of Vocational Choice," *Journal of Counseling Psychology,* 4(1957), 212–17.

Roe, Anne, and Rhoda Baruch, "Occupational Changes in the Adult Years," *Personnel Administration,* 30(July–August 1967), 26–32.

Rogalin, Wilma C., and Arthur R. Pell, *Women's Guide to Management Positions.* New York: Simon & Schuster, 1975.

Rosow, Jerome M., *The Worker and the Job.* Englewood Cliffs, N.J.: Prentice-Hall, 1974.

"Rotating Top Jobs at Union Carbide," *Business Week* (July 14, 1975), pp. 82, 84.

Schein, Edgar H., "How to Break the College Graduate," *Harvard Business Review,* 42(1964), 68–76.

———, "Attitude Change During Management Education: A Study of Organizational Influences on Student Attitudes," *Administrative Science Quarterly,* 11(1967), 601–28.

———, "The First Job Dilemma," *Psychology Today,* 1 (March 1968a), 27–37.

———, "Organizational Socialization and the Profession of Management," *Industrial Management Review,* 9(1968b), 1–16.

———, *Organizational Psychology,* 2nd ed. Englewood Cliffs, N.J.: Prentice-Hall, 1970.

———, "The Individual, the Organization, and the Career: A Conceptual Scheme," *Journal of Applied Behavioral Science,* 7(1971), 401–26.

Schneider, Benjamin, "Organization Climate: Individual Preferences and Organizational Realities," *Journal of Applied Psychology,* 56(1972), 211–17.

———, *Staffing Organizations.* Pacific Palisades, Calif.: Goodyear, 1976.

Schneider, Benjamin, and Douglas T. Hall, "Toward Specifying the Concept of Work Climate: A Study of Roman Catholic Diocesan Priests," *Journal of Applied Psychology,* 56(1972), 447–55.

Schrage, Harry, "The R&D Entrepreneur: Profile of Success, *Harvard Business Review,* 43(1965), 56–69.

Seidel, Robert B., "New Approaches to Organizational Design." Address to Young Presidents Organization meeting, Pompano Beach, Florida, February 20, 1974.

Sewell, W.H., A.O. Haller, and G.W. Ohlendorf, "The Early Educational and Early Occupational Attainment Process: Replication and Revisions," *American Sociological Review,* 35(1970), 1014–27.

Shearer, Richard L., and Joseph A. Steger, "Manpower Obsolescence: A New

Definition and Empirical Investigation of Personal Variables," *Academy of Management Journal,* 18(1975), 263–75.

Sheldon, Mary E., "Investments and Involvements as Mechanisms Producing Commitment to the Organization," *Administrative Science Quarterly,* 16(1971), 143–50.

Sheppard, D.I., "The Measurement of Vocational Maturity in Adults," *Journal of Vocational Behavior,* 1(1971), 399–406.

Siegel, Jacob P., and Edwin E. Ghiselli, "Managerial Talent, Pay and Age," *Journal of Vocational Psychology,* 1(1971), 133.

Skinner, B.F., *Contingencies for Reinforcement.* New York: Appleton-Century-Crofts, 1969.

Slocum, Walter L., *Occupational Careers: A Sociological Perspective.* Chicago: Aldine, 1966.

Soelberg, Peer O., "Unprogrammed Decision Making," *Papers and Proceedings,* 26th Annual Meeting, Academy of Management, San Francisco, 1966.

Sofer, Cyril, *Men in Mid-Career.* London: Cambridge University Press, 1970.

Stedry, Andrew, and Emmanuel Kay, *The Effects of Goal Difficulty on Performance.* Lynn, Mass.: Behavioral Research Service, General Electric Company, 1962.

Steele, Fritz, *The Open Organization: The Impact of Secrecy and Disclosure on People and Organizations.* Reading, Mass.: Addison-Wesley, 1975.

Steiner, George A., ed., *The Creative Organization.* Chicago: University of Chicago Press, 1965.

Stoner, J.A.F., T.P. Ference, E.K. Warren, and H.K. Christensen, "Patterns and Plateaus in Managerial Careers—An Exploratory Study." Research paper no. 66, Graduate School of Business, Columbia University, August 1974.

Stouffer, Samuel A., Edward A. Suchman, Leland C. DeVinney, Shirley A. Star, and Robin M. Williams, *The American Soldier: Adjustments During Army Life.* Princeton, N.J.: Princeton University Press, 1949.

Strauss, Anselm, *Mirrors and Masks: The Search for Identity.* San Francisco: The Sociology Press, 1970.

Strong, Edward K., Jr., *Vocational Interests of Men and Women.* Stanford, Calif.: Stanford University Press, 1943.

Super, Donald E., *The Psychology of Careers.* New York: Harper & Row, 1957.

Super, Donald E., and Martin J. Bohn, Jr., *Occupational Psychology.* Belmont, Calif.: Wadsworth, 1970.

Super, D., Crites, J., Hummel, R., Moser, H., Overstreet, P., and C. Warnath, *Vocational Development: A Framework For Research.* New York: Teachers College Press, 1957, pp. 40, 41.

Super, Donald E., and Jean Pierre Jordaan, "Career Development Theory." Teachers College, Columbia University, undated.

Super, Donald E., and Phoebe L. Overstreet, *The Vocational Maturity of Ninth Grade Boys.* New York: Teachers College Press, 1960.

Taft, R., "Multiple Methods of Personality Assessment," *Psychological Bulletin,* 56(1959), 333–52.

Taussig, F.W., and C.S. Joselyn, *American Business Leaders.* New York: Macmillan, 1932.

Tiedeman, David V., and Robert P. O'Hara, *Career Development: Choice and Adjustment.* New York: College Entrance Examination Board, 1963.

Tom, Victor R., "The Role of Personality and Organizational Images in the Recruiting Process," *Organizational Behavior and Human Performance,* 6(1971), 573–92.

Tomlinson-Keasey, C., "Role Variables: Their Influence on Female Motivational Constructs," *Journal of Counseling Psychology,* 21(1974), 232–37.

Tresmer, David, "Fear of Success: Popular but Unproven," *Psychology Today,* (March 1974), 82–85.

van Gennep, Arnold, *The Rites of Passage.* University of Chicago Press, 1960.

Vroom, Victor, "Organizational Choice: A Study of Pre- and Post-Decision Processes," *Organizational Behavior and Human Performance,* 1(1966), 212–25.

Vroom, V., and E. Deci, "The Stability of Post-Decision Dissonance: A Follow-Up Study of Job Attitudes of Business School Graduates," *Organizational Behavior and Human Performance,* 6(1971), 36–49.

Wainer, Herbert A., and Irwin M. Rubin, "Motivation of Research and Development Entrepreneurs: Determinants of Company Success," *Journal of Applied Psychology,* 53(1969), 178–84.

Walberg, H., "Professional Role Discontinuities in Educational Careers," in J.R. Hackman, Chmn., *Longitudinal Approaches to Career Development,* symposium presented at American Psychological Association Annual Convention, San Francisco, 1968.

Wanous, John P., "Effects of Realistic Job Preview on Job Acceptance, Job Attitudes, and Job Survival," *Journal of Applied Psychology,* 58(1973), 327–32.

————, "Individual Differences and Reactions to Job Characteristics," *Journal of Applied Psychology,* 59(1974), 616–22.

————, "Realistic Job Previews for Organizational Recruitment," *Personnel,* 52(April 1, 1975), 50–60.

Warner, W. Lloyd, and James Abegglen, *Occupational Mobility in American Business and Industry.* Minneapolis, Minn.: University of Minnesota Press, 1955.

White, Robert W., *Lives in Progress.* New York: Dryden, 1952.

————, "Motivation Reconsidered: The Concept of Competence," *Psychological Review,* 66(1959), 297–323.

Yankelovich, Daniel, "Turbulence in the Working World—Angry Workers, Happy Grads," *Psychology Today,* (December 1974), pp. 81–87.

Zalesnik, Abraham, Gene W. Dalton, Louis B. Barnes, and Pierre Laurin, *Orientation and Conflict in Career.* Division of Research, Harvard Business School, Boston, 1970.

Zener, T.B., and L. Schnuelle, "An Evaluation of the Self-Directed Search," Baltimore: Center for Social Organization of Schools, Report No. 124, (February 1972).

NAME INDEX

233

SUBJECT INDEX

235